THE CHALLENGE OF THINGS

100

An Introduction to Philosophical Logic
The Refutation of Scepticism
Berkeley: The Central Arguments
Wittgenstein
The Long March to the Fourth of June (with Xu You Yu)
China: A Literary Companion (with Susan Whitfield)
Philosophy 1: A Guide Through the Subject (editor)
Russell
The Future of Moral Values
Philosophy 2: Further Through the Subject (editor)
The Quarrel of the Age: The Life and Times of William Hazlitt
Herrick: Lyrics of Love and Desire (editor)
What is Good?
Descartes
The Meaning of Things
The Reason of Things
The Mystery of Things
The Heart of Things
The Form of Things
The Continuum Encyclopaedia of British Philosophy (editor)
*Among the Dead Cities: Was the Allied Bombing of Civilians in WWII
a Necessity or a Crime?*
Against All Gods
*Towards the Light: The Story of the Struggles for Liberty and Rights that
Made the Modern West*

THE CHALLENGE
OF THINGS

Thinking Through Troubled Times

A. C. Grayling

BLOOMSBURY
LONDON • NEW DELHI • NEW YORK • SYDNEY

First published in Great Britain 2015

Copyright © A. C. Grayling, 2015

The moral right of the author has been asserted

No part of this book may be used or reproduced in any manner
whatsoever without written permission from the publisher except in the
case of brief quotations embedded in critical articles or reviews

Every reasonable effort has been made to trace copyright holders of
material reproduced in this book, but if any have been inadvertently
overlooked the publishers would be glad to hear from them

Bloomsbury Publishing Plc
50 Bedford Square
London WC1B 3DP

www.bloomsbury.com

Bloomsbury is a trademark of Bloomsbury Publishing Plc

Bloomsbury Publishing, London, New Delhi, New York and Sydney
A CIP catalogue record for this book is available from the British Library

ISBN 978 1 4088 6461 6 (hardback edition)
ISBN 978 1 4088 6464 7 (trade paperback edition)

10 9 8 7 6 5 4 3 2 1

Typeset by Newgen Knowledge Works (P) Ltd, Chennai, India
Printed and bound in Great Britain by CPI Group (UK) Ltd, Croydon CR0 4YY

For Maddie with love

verbis accipe: aequitas causa sapienta

occasio tempus

CONTENTS

CONSTRUCTIONS

and

CREATIONS

Introduction

Did we come here to laugh or cry?
Are we dying or being born?

Carlos Fuentes, *Terra Nostra*

When a war begins, most people hope that it will be brief. Very few people realise that it will almost certainly outlast the actual shooting. It takes centuries to build a town, a society, a culture; it can take mere seconds of bombing to destroy them. Rebuilding is part of a war – indeed all of a war's consequences are part of the war. This includes legacies of resentment, changed orders of things, displacements of populations. What, therefore, of the non-material – the civilisational – scars left by war and conflict? As Christian Friedrich Hebbel said, 'What a vast difference there is between the barbarism that precedes culture and the barbarism that follows it.'

It is a commonplace that every age, or almost every age, thinks that its own time is one of special difficulty. The barbarians seem always to be at the gate. Alas, in our present day this is rather too literally so. But what many fail to realise is that the barbarians are a more various and numerous group than just those unspeakable villains who behead hostages in the desert. Barbarians might also wear ties and travel business class, they might occupy seats of power in government. They might be us, ourselves, when we give up certain civil liberties and betray our own values in the spurious belief that this will protect us from terrorism, organised crime, unwelcome immigration. Forms of dismantling civilisation might differ, but the result is the same.

It is food for thought to recall that the Pyramid of Cheops at Giza was the tallest building in the world for 5,000 years. We are used to tall buildings now; everywhere aspires to be Manhattan. In their rush to mimic that architecture, the cities of the Middle East and Far East, from Abu Dhabi to Shanghai's Pudong district, show how much peoples can desire what they also resent, and what flattery and anger, what rivalry and ambition there is in emulation. Two Middle Eastern cities built enormous twin-tower skyscrapers in the years immediately after New York's twin towers were destroyed in a murderous spectacular. China has torn down its *hutong*s and replaced them with forests of tall buildings separated by multi-lane highways, in its headlong rush to seem more modern than the times. The world has become one self-similar place to outer view, but it remains various and unpredictable within, moving in directions that our eyes are not always looking in. Do we see things as they are, or do we see the illusions we create out of our worst fears and simplest hopes?

At time of writing we are fixated on the difficulties of one part of the world – the Middle East – while the world's centre of gravity is shifting with increasing rapidity to the Far East, where the dynamics of change, across everything from energy hunger, population explosion, the rush for wealth, and militarisation, pose a new pattern of questions for the future.

Every generation needs to attempt an interpretation of the time it lives in. The essays that follow are a miscellany unified by the effort to do that: to explore, and to suggest perspectives upon, different facets of this time in our world. The first part addresses some of the negatives of our circumstances, the second some of the positives. They are offered as contributions to the conversation we have with ourselves about these matters, from the small and relatively unimportant to the great and significant: war, weapons, China and the future, Russia, human rights, the Middle East, the meaning today of the history of the West, oil, religion, education, thinkers and ideas. Our many and various concerns have one thing in common: they are *our* concerns, unignorable and pressing.

These reflections are, in the broadest sense of this term – the sense that belongs to everyone – philosophical reflections, because they touch on the general that lies in every particular, and on the matters of principle that run beneath every matter of the moment.

For if there is one thing we can know with certainty it is that we must keep thinking and discussing, presenting each other with ideas and listening to each other's proposals for how we can move from our dilemmas towards a better world, relying on our best hopes. We have to have the courage to keep thinking in the face of all that confuses and disconcerts us. As C. P. Snow said, despair is a sin: we have to keep searching for a way through the hedge of thorns to the hidden garden beyond, believing in ourselves enough to think that if that garden does not exist, we can create it from those very thorns if need be.

Many of the essays originated in places as various as *Prospect* magazine, the *Guardian*, *Observer*, *Times*, *New Statesman*, *New York Review of Books*, talks on the BBC, chapters in edited collections, and elsewhere. I am grateful to editors and commissioners for the initial stimulus and opportunity provided, and to readers and audiences for their responses. It is a privilege to be part of the conversation, from which one always learns more than one can hope to contribute.

New College of the Humanities
London, 2014

DESTRUCTIONS
and
DECONSTRUCTIONS

The First World War

It is an unwelcome reflection that history tends to be a thin list of names and dates for most people, its sweated and bloody realities and their meanings lost among labels. Take the label 'the First World War'. Even as it happened people called it 'the Great War', because not since the seventeenth century had conflict been so general across Europe, though this time with the benefit of industrial means of slaughter in the form of new military technologies. But the appropriation of a label is the first step to limiting the perception of those who were not there, and therefore only grasp at third hand the true significances of the event.

Consider what these are in relation to the First World War, which occasioned a shocking change to history of such deep seriousness that we are trying to deal with it still.

Everyone knows about the massacre of the trenches – the result of a hideous encounter between modern weaponry and outdated tactics, which saw men walking line abreast into hailstorms of machine-gun and artillery fire. But it is a surprise to remember that it was a short war, only four years in duration against the Second World War's six years and the ten years and counting of the conflict in Afghanistan.

But we need to remember too the collapse of Russia into revolution, and the Soviet era that followed; and of the Spartacist uprising in Germany at the war's end, along with the redrawing of Europe's boundaries and the reshuffling of colonial holdings in Africa and elsewhere.

We need to remember that in the shock and depletion of the war's immediate aftermath, a global influenza pandemic killed more people than died in the war: the war's four years of military and civilian deaths totalled 37 million, the one year of the pandemic killed over 50 million.

We need to remember that women moved in large numbers from the home to the munitions factories and farmlands, inducing a major change in social attitudes and women's status. In Britain women replaced 2 million men in the workforce, producing 80 per cent of the munitions. Their 'reward' in 1918 was to be given the vote for the first time – though only for those of thirty years of age and over; it took another ten years for the voting age to be equalised for both sexes. Millions of women experienced widowhood and spinsterhood as a result of the war, or found themselves caring for disabled and traumatised husbands and male relatives for the rest of their lives.

We need to remember that in the decade following the war, the 'Roaring Twenties', there was a subliminal note of hysteria reflected variously in the paintings of George Grosz, the crime epidemic of America's 'Prohibition' madness, the jazz scene, the economic collapse of 1929 and subsequent Depression, the rise of Fascism, and much besides. This frenetic time is captured in *The Long Weekend* by Robert Graves and Alan Hodge, depicting an era of vivid abandon and trauma.

But above all we need to recognise that 1914 saw not just the beginning of the First World War, but the beginning of an epoch of hot and cold conflicts in various guises that still continue today. There is no disagreement that the mistakes and unfinished business of the First World War's 'ending' led to the Second World War, which itself 'ended' only with the impasse of the Cold War, which in turn sparked many hot proxy wars around the globe from South America to Vietnam and beyond.

We certainly need reminding of the First World War's responsibility for what is currently happening in the Middle East. The British Empire had more than a million soldiers in that region by 1918, fighting Germany's Ottoman allies in order to protect the land and sea routes to India and to control the Persian oilfields. Winston Churchill, as First Lord of the Admiralty, had in 1911 ordered the Royal Navy (then the world's largest by far, and the Empire's – indeed the world's – police force) to switch from coal-fired to oil-fired engines to prevent it being held hostage by striking coal miners in Wales and Yorkshire. That meant Britain had to take on a new responsibility: controlling the Persian oilfields.

Then, as Colonial Secretary in the years after the war, Churchill presided over the division of the Ottoman Empire, creating Iraq, Saudi Arabia and Syria out of nothing and giving the latter to France. Before the 1921 Cairo Conference at which this happened, John Maynard Keynes said to Churchill, 'If you cut up the map of the Middle East with a pair of scissors you will still be fighting wars there in a hundred years' time.' He has been proved right.

In many ways, therefore, the First World War is still with us. My paternal grandfather fought and was wounded in that struggle, and then until 1920 worked for the War Graves Commission in Flanders, laying out the cemeteries where the bones of huge armies of boys and young men lie buried. Many of us from around the world have relatives memorialised on those serried ranks of gravestones and on the Menin Gate at Ypres – from Britain, France, Canada, India, South Africa, the United States, Australia and New Zealand, while in Russia,

Turkey, Austria and Germany equal and often greater losses are recorded in the rolls of what must surely be one of the least pointful and most humanly destructive conflicts ever to occur in history.

Even though we have too much justification for thinking that the memory of past wars will not make us wise enough to avoid wars in future, it is still right to recall the experience of them, if only to keep alive the hope that wisdom will one day come; and to remember the vast fields of young promise that were so wantonly mown flat – in the hope, the vain hope, that the 'sacrifice' would bring peace. By one of those dreadful ironies that the label version of history obscures, it was not the living who found peace, but only the dead who died for them.

The Ethics of Drones

Almost every technological advance in the means of warfare brings new ethical problems. In the mid-nineteenth century a Hague Conference outlawed newly invented bullets that split apart inside a victim's body to increase the incapacitating effect; in the 1890s – before heavier-than-air flight had become possible – another Hague convention outlawed aerial bombardment (it had in mind the throwing of grenades from balloons). After the 1914–18 war chemical weapons were outlawed. And after the 1939–45 war much of the focus has been on limiting the spread of nuclear weapons.

Thus the vain attempt to minimise the extent of harm that technologies of warfare threaten. Throughout history it has been technology that has made the chief difference in warfare – the spear, the metallurgy of swords and shields, armour, the crossbow, the arquebus, artillery, rapid-fire small arms, aircraft, missiles, the logistical equipment used in moving forces and supplies, all represent the inventiveness of urgency in times of danger, and whoever had the superior technology has had the better chance of prevailing.

Asymmetric warfare, in which small groups of insurgents can encumber huge military resources of an orthodox kind, bucks this trend. But the technologists are not wholly without answers. One such is the unmanned drone aircraft, used for surveillance and offensive engagement in circumstances and terrains where conventional forces are at a huge disadvantage. The badlands of the Afghanistan–Pakistan border provide a classic example of where drones best do their work.

Able to stay aloft for long periods, hard to detect and defend against, formidably armed, drones are chillingly effective weapons: and to top it all, they put no operating personnel at risk. This is an important point for the home team using them. Insurgency-type conflicts apart, the world might be moving towards a situation where war mainly consists of robot forces doing the attacking and much of the defending, with civilian populations as the main front-line targets, and destruction of the morale of the enemy – meaning its willingness to continue the conflict – the main aim.

What ethical considerations are raised by drones as currently deployed in theatres of conflict? The fact that they are unmanned, controlled from thousands of miles away by operators sitting safely before a screen, and that these operators are chosen for their X-Box gaming skills, somehow seems to make them more sinister, somehow less 'fair' and right. In particular, the move from violent video games to the dreadful reality of killing actual human beings seems to cast a deeper moral shadow over the latter activity.

One is reminded of the world press's reaction in 1911 when the very first aerial bombing took place. An Italian airman threw grenades out of his monoplane onto Ottoman troops in North Africa. The world's press were outraged at the 'unsporting' nature of the venture, on the grounds that the victims suffering on the ground were unable to retaliate. This quickly proved wrong; Ottoman troops shot down an Italian aeroplane the following week, with rifle fire. Less than forty years later the British and Americans were indiscriminatingly dropping millions of tons of high explosives on German and later Japanese civilian populations night after night for years.

If anything is moral in war – and precious little is – drone activity is at the friendlier end. It is supposed to be more selective, more targeted, less likely to produce 'collateral damage' (the nasty euphemism which mainly means 'killing bystanders' and which drone activity regularly does: but to a much lesser extent than indiscriminate high-level carpet bombing), and it does not put one's own in harm's way.

For these reasons drones are an improvement in the matter of blowing human beings to pieces, if this has to be done. The seemingly inhuman nature of their operation – the deadly machine without a person in it, faceless, remote, weighed down with missiles, remorselessly homing in on its target – is a prompt for extra dislike of it; and yet it reprises a form of killing that anciently recommended itself: like long-range missiles, or high-level carpet bombing, it embodies the same principle as stoning to death, distancing the killer from the victim to a sanitary remove.

Only consider: no RAF bomber pilot in the Second World War would ever have dreamt of putting a pistol to the heads of a woman and her child and pulling the trigger, but on repeated occasions he released huge tonnages of bombs on many faceless women and children in the dark cities below him. Not touching the victim, not being in the same corner of space, is a sop to the conscience. The screen-gazers in Texas who steer their drones to targets in Afghanistan have the advantage over bomber pilots of guaranteed safety as well as the stone-thrower's remove.

In the first line I said 'almost every technological ...' The drone is a technological advance, but if anything it marginally diminishes the all-too-familiar ethical problem of using explosives against one's enemies, given that explosives are too apt to include unintended along with intended targets and that drones can somewhat diminish that problem. It suggests another and better future for warfare, if there has to be warfare at all: like medieval knight champions, opposing forces could represent their side of the argument but, unlike them, be fully robotic, meeting on a jousting field in space, and harming only our national budgets.

If there has to be warfare at all, that is.

Irredentism and Associated Evils

Most borders between states are drawn in the blood of wars. Most states, even small ones, are aggregates of territories once separate and – in many cases even now – desirous of being so. A state is a highly artificial thing, a fiction of history, an uneven line on a map turned into a fetish and a *casus belli* and a licence for all the arrant nonsense we call nationalism, patriotism, jingoism, and other dangerous absurdities.

Everywhere one looks around the planet there are claims by one country to ownership of part or even the whole of another country. One of the more comical is Spain's claim to Gibraltar – comical because Spain possesses about a dozen Gibraltars on and around the North African coast and even inside France. What difference is there between Spain's 'island' of Peñón de Vélez de la Gomera, attached to the Moroccan coast, and Gibraltar, in respect of being one country's appendage on another country's shore? Yet Spain wants Gibraltar 'back'. It has about as much right to it as Turkey has to Spain itself, through the historical link of the Caliphate.

The world's most irredentist state today is China. It claims ownership of everywhere that was once part of the greatest extent of its imperial past, and more – including the Spratly Islands in the South China Sea and the continental shelf under the East China Sea practically all the way to the Japanese coast. These latter claims have more to do with oil and gas than history, but it is history that makes Tibet a beaten, oppressed, pummelled victim of Chinese territorial terrorism, and Taiwan an aircraft carrier pointed nervously at the giant claiming suzerainty over it. China's 'Constitution' says: 'Taiwan is part of the sacred territory of the People's Republic of China. It is the lofty duty of the entire Chinese people, including our compatriots in Taiwan, to accomplish the great task of reunifying the motherland.' Nauseating pietism like this is the very stuff of irredentism; and it is, as history abundantly shows, too often the prelude to much murder.

By the lights of Spain and China, or of Argentina and 'Las Malvinas' and any of the scores of other countries claiming bits of other countries, Mexico is entitled to a big slice of the US, England is entitled to claim ownership of France (and vice versa), and Israel is entitled to Palestine. But wait: this last raises the question of how long claims of ownership legitimately last. Is there no historical statute of limitations? If the Jewish peoples have a 2,000-year-old title to Jerusalem, then Calais is definitely English, and all other like claims become justiciable.

One reason for the messy situation over state boundaries is demographic fluidity. People and peoples move in tidal fashion, pushed by conflicts or climate change, pulled by the attractions of greener pastures. As a result, ethnic and political boundaries scarcely ever coincide. Pieties over nationality, language and culture keep the sense of old ties alive, with the potential for trouble.

Irredentism is, obviously enough, dangerous. It keeps frictions and tensions alive, and therefore drains money and energy into defence budgets and diplomatic endeavours. Europe after the Second World War offers a model for a solution. In 1945 the continent was a chaos of major population displacements and uncertain boundaries; but the arrangements that followed have on the whole been accepted (except in parts of the Balkans: but that is par for the course there). Among the reasons for that acceptance is realisation of the interdependence of neighbours, if peace and its possibilities for prosperity are made the chief consideration. In its turn, that realisation weakens the sentimental power of local feeling, the root of nationalisms and patriotisms; and out of that come the enlarged unions which offer so much more than local sentiment ever can. One example is the US, another is the EU.

There are Israelis and Palestinians who together believe in a one-state solution – an Israel-Palestine – and there are both ultra-orthodox Jews and anti-Israeli Palestinians who also believe in versions of a one-state solution, but an exclusive one, without the other half of the equation in it. Getting over history and accepting present realities is the transparently obvious necessity for a peaceful two-state solution. What would it take to get it? If there were a Nelson Mandela-like figure on each side of the divide, each big enough of heart and mind to envisage a good future instead of being enslaved to a bad past, things might change. (Tolstoy was wrong: individuals can indeed make history.)

Humanity's track record is very poor on the irredentism question, though, so there is no point in holding one's breath over any of the major problems it causes. But if there were just one place where a solution would really help the world as a whole, it is in that vexed fragment of unpropitious earth between the Mediterranean Sea and the too suggestively named Dead Sea.

Guns

In discussion of the atrocity that, to the world's horror, occurred in the peaceful and mature state of Norway on 22 July 2011 – when the repulsive maniac called Anders Behring Breivik killed seventy-seven people, most of them teenagers attending a Youth League camp on the island of Utøya – there was one subject which was notable by the almost total silence about it: *guns*. In response to recurring massacres in American high schools and British villages, in response to footage from Africa and Afghanistan showing ragged, untrained young men brandishing automatic small arms, in response to a man coolly murdering dozens of youngsters in an hour and a half funfair-like shooting spree on a Norwegian island, where is the outrage at the fact that the world is awash with small arms, that people are making money legally and without blemish to their reputations out of the manufacture and sale of instruments purposely designed to kill?

It is said that you can get a Kalashnikov in the Horn of Africa in exchange for three small children. But before the sale of children for weapons, and before the mayhem and death that results from those weapons' use, there is the arms trade in a wide range of handguns and high-powered automatic rifles. Every one of these instruments is designed and created for the express purpose of killing things. The irresponsible argument of the American gun lobby, that it is not guns that kill but the people who handle them, is the first point to contest: if Anders Behring Breivik had carried only a knife or a wooden club, he would have been severely restricted in the harm he could do. The same would have been true at Hungerford in England and Dunblane in Scotland, at Columbine High School and Kent State University in the United States; the agonies of Darfur in Sudan and Helmand in Afghanistan would be vastly less; in fact the world would be a different and happier place if guns were few and their possession a matter of strict official control.

Our world stands on its head in most things, but in nothing more so than the fact that a crazy person can buy a gun, an extremely dangerous device, in an American or Norwegian shop, yet 'drugs' are prohibited and policed at vast expense to society. Indeed the ironies are still greater: because drugs (excluding some of the most dangerous and harmful, such as alcohol and nicotine) are criminalised but the gun trade is not, the gangs who smuggle the drugs shoot each other with the guns, and not infrequently shoot the policemen who chase them also. This is a stark example of the irrationality of our arrangements. Instead of banning heroin and allowing the sale of guns, do the reverse. Ban guns and put heroin under the same licensing regulations as alcohol – fools will continue to abuse heroin and alcohol, harming mainly themselves: but the abuse of guns harms others, and too often many others – and at a stroke billions of dollars and thousands of lives would be saved. Think Mexico and its savage drug wars: legal drugs and no guns would end those wars, and restore lost tracts of that country to a semblance of civilisation.

Guns should be the subject of worldwide outrage. Their manufacture and sale should be a human rights abuse, on which we pour vilification and horror. They should be illegal for all but properly constituted, trained and controlled agencies of governments, provided of course that the governments in question are themselves properly constituted and controlled by democratic means in a society where the rule of law obtains.

Human rights agencies with representation at the UN in Geneva should campaign for the manufacture and sale of small arms to be universally outlawed, and governments with responsible attitudes to gun control should be urged to join the campaign. The United Kingdom has a more rather than less sensible attitude to guns: but alas, the United Kingdom is one of the world's major arms manufacturers and exporters.

There are easy ways to deal with the need of farmers to control rabbits and game park keepers to cull overpopulated herds: if there are genuinely no alternatives to the use of guns in such cases, a small range of suitable guns could be borrowed from the authorities, under strict licence and for short periods, for the express purpose in hand, but not allowed to remain in the community otherwise. If we can legislate for car-seats for children, we can legislate to keep highly dangerous killing instruments out of public hands.

'Highly dangerous killing instruments': language matters: let us no longer use the word 'gun' but that phrase 'highly dangerous killing instrument', and perhaps perceptions will change. No doubt weapons manufacturers and lobbyists everywhere would regard with equal outrage the idea of severely limiting the number of *highly dangerous killing instruments* in public circulation, their existence being permitted only under official lock and key. What would these lobbyists argue in opposition? That *highly dangerous killing instruments* are for sport, for hunting (this last will not wash: killing things for sport? that is itself disgusting), for the fun of loud noises?

Americans with views not too far removed from those of Anders Behring Breivik say that they 'need' their *highly dangerous killing instruments* to 'defend their freedoms', meaning against the tyranny of government and Federal taxes. They should be reminded that it is the ballot, not the bullet, that is meant to do that job for them.

In fact there are no good arguments in favour of the existence of *highly dangerous killing instruments*, and millions of excellent arguments against them, these being each human being, and indeed each elephant and tiger, shot to death by them. The Norwegian tragedy and others like it should be absolutely the last straw for civilised humanity on this subject, no further excuses allowed.

The Berlin–Baghdad Railway

Here are two facts which, when one first learns them, have a jolting effect on one's perceptions of today's tensions flowing from the environs of the Middle East. One is that the empire which at its height had more Muslim subjects than any other empire ever – counting as subjects over one in three of the world's Muslims – was the British Empire.

The second fact is that at the end of the First World War the British Empire had more than a million soldiers in the Middle East, and in the years immediately following it cut up the map of the region into the shape it bears today, creating entirely new countries in the process and putting British nominees and clients into power in them.

A third fact fits with these: in 1911 Winston Churchill was First Lord of the Admiralty, in charge of Britain's mighty Royal Navy. Years of strikes by well-organised militant miners in the coal-fields of Britain had made Churchill worried that the far-flung fleets and therefore the empire itself could be held to ransom by – name of malediction! – socialists. He therefore ordered the navy to switch from coal-fired to oil-fired engines. That obliged Britain to help itself to parts of the world with oil wells: Persia was the first port of call, soon to be followed by British-created Iraq.

And how about a fourth fact: that imperial Britain never allowed any hostile power to threaten the approaches to its huge milch-cow of India. That explained the struggles with Russia in Central Asia and Afghanistan in the nineteenth century; in the early twentieth century Germany's friendship with the Ottoman Empire made Britain wary of any threat to its sea route through Suez and the overland route through Persia and

Afghanistan. Britain therefore took Egypt and Persia under its control, and when war began it poured troops into the region and fought very hard – and after stiff resistance, successfully – to destroy the Ottoman Empire and dispose of its remains as it wished.

This tale has been well told a number of times, though because of the intricate complexity of the alliances, double-crosses and diplomatic and military shenanigans that infected the build-up to war and its conduct in the region, it has generated much controversy among historians. Who said what to whom, who did what when and why, who is to blame, what might have happened – the usual jungle of opinion finds lavishly fertile soil here.

One of the too little recognised causes of the scale of the First World War struggle in the Middle East was the building of a railway from Berlin to Baghdad in the years before the First World War, a railway conceived by Kaiser Wilhelm of Germany as an artery along which the lifeblood of a new and mighty German empire would flow. Instead, one of its immediate consequences was that human blood copiously flowed.

Along the faltering line of that railway can be strung a tale of intrigue, callous calculation, human misery, skulduggery, cheating, revolution, murder and war. The history of the railway illuminates much about the history of the Eastern Question, the Young Turk revolution, and Britain's demolition of the Ottoman Empire – one of four empires to implode in that struggle: German, Austro-Hungarian, Russian and Ottoman, with a fifth (the British) beginning to bleed to death. With a shock of recognition that story reminds us also of the German aim of promoting an Islam-wide jihad against Britain, and prompts the question that has exercised historians: was that a hasty 1914 improvisation, or a more circumstantial plan resting on the already decades-long relationship between Berlin and Constantinople, which had begun in the enthusiasm for all things Islamic and Ottoman acquired by Kaiser Wilhelm ('Hajji Wilhelm') on his state visits to the Sublime Porte and its territories?

It happens, though, that in the summer of 1914, as a result of the Young Turk revolution of several years before, German–Ottoman relations were at a low ebb, and the Wilhelmstrasse – Germany's foreign ministry – had sent a not especially competent ambassador to Constantinople. In line with its own longstanding policy of playing the Great Powers off against each other, Constantinople was keeping everyone guessing about its intentions in the coming conflict, and in fact was secretly exploring the possibility of alliances with all parties, not just Berlin. But when the crunch came the Young Turk government sided with Germany, in the process extracting hugely advantageous terms for itself from Berlin, some of it by trickery, more of it by very astute use of the state of emergency then prevailing.

The importance of the story is enormous. As Sean McMeekin says in *The Berlin–Baghdad Express* (2010), 'Few decisions in world history have been as fraught with consequences as Turkey's entry into the First World War. From the closing of the Straits [the Bosphorous] for years to Russian commerce – a major cause of the economic upheaval which led to the Russian Revolution – to the creation of the modern Middle East out of the wreckage of the defeated Ottoman Empire, the Turks' decision to fight in 1914 lies at the root of the most intractable geopolitical problems of the twentieth century, many of which are still with us today.'

Under the influence of the irrepressible Middle Eastern scholar and enthusiast Baron Max von Oppenheim, the Germans devised the stratagem of having jihad, Holy War, pronounced in fatwahs (in Turkish, fatvehs) against all infidels except Germans, Austrians, Americans, and any other ally of the Porte or any significant neutral. Some thought this message was likely to prove confusing to fanatics bent on murdering anyone who did not look Turkish or Arab, and the thought proved prescient. Its main aim was to get the huge number of Muslim subjects of the British Empire to rise against their masters, thus saving Germany and its allies the trouble of defeating Britain themselves.

In the words of the American ambassador to the Porte, Henry Morgenthau, 'the Kaiser's desire' was 'to let loose 300,000,000 Mohammedans in a gigantic St Bartholomew's Day massacre of Christians'. One of the pamphlets distributed by the Germans blamed what it called 'the state of degradation to which the World of Islam has arrived' on the European Christians who in India, Egypt and the Sudan had subjugated hundreds of millions of Muslims. And the worst of these 'enemies of God', said the pamphlet, were 'the infidel English'. The pamphlet told Muslims everywhere 'that from today Holy War has become a sacred duty and that the blood of the infidels in the Islamic lands may be shed with impunity (except those who enjoy the protection of the Muslim power and those to whom it has given security and those who confederate with it)'. And in a phrase that remains chillingly resonant today, the pamphlet concluded, 'The killing of the infidels who rule over the Islamic lands has become a sacred duty, whether it be secretly or openly; as the great Koran declares in its word: "Take them and kill them wherever you come across them".'

As it turned out, the call for universal jihad was very patchily received. Some atrocities occurred, but hopes for a rising of Muslims against their British masters in India and Egypt did not materialise. Indeed when an abortive German-Turkish attack was made on the Suez Canal in 1915 the British troops repulsing it included Muslim soldiers from India.

Of interest also is the battle waged by the German-Ottoman alliance against the British for the loyalty of the Arabs. It was almost exclusively a battle fought with gold – and won by the British – because the Arab tribes, mainly devoted to inter-tribal feuding and looting, were an independent and largely irreligious group (except for the ferocious Saud clan, who were, as they remain, fundamentalist Wahhabis of an uncompromising kind; but no less keen on gold for all that) who did not take to the discipline of organised military endeavour, and responded only to bribes of gold and weapons – which nevertheless never guaranteed their loyalty or aid.

An example was the chieftain Mumtas Bey, 'who went so far as to promise the Ottoman army command that "he and his Bedouins would either die or raise the Ottoman flag on the Citadel in Cairo." Mumtas was then given enormous sums in gold, whereupon he disappeared into the desert.' He had in fact been scared off by a reconnaissance party of British troops; one of the German agents in Damascus wrote that this 'squalid fiasco' was further proof that the Arabs were 'cowardly and insubordinate'.

The Arabs accordingly earned the opprobrium of one of the more thoughtful Central Powers agents sent to induce them to fight for the Ottoman cause, the Austrian scholar Alois Musil, one of the few clear-thinking European observers of the Arabs in that period. Besides decrying their incessant feuding,

Musil objected to their taking twelve-year-old girls as wives and concubines. The German commander of the Ottoman troops in Damascus, Friedrich Kress von Kressenstein, agreed with him about this, and further noted with distaste how the Bedouins 'regularly bought and sold women as chattels, with fathers often selling "pristine young daughters" for proper riding camels or a mature date tree. Widows or divorcees, by contrast, would usually only fetch a pack animal in barter.'

Students of the era will know that T. E. Lawrence, doing with some panache and showmanship on the British side what Musil and Kress were attempting on the German-Ottoman side, cultivated the Hashemite Prince Feisal of the Hejaz as leader of the largely cosmetic 'Arab revolt' that British gold purchased, eventually making him King of the newly invented Iraq (a Sunni put in place over a Shia people: the problems thus begun continue today). But before he became a client of the British, Feisal negotiated on the matter of his loyalty with the Germans, saying to Max von Oppenheim in Constantinople, 'I thank God that the interests of Islam are entirely identical with those of Germany ... It is true that there is a difference in religion between Muslim countries and Germany. But in material interests relative to this world, differences over religion should never stand in the way of these reciprocal interests.' As this shows, almost everyone betrayed almost everyone else in that dirty war over the rotting Ottoman carcass.

Another complicating factor in this very tangled tale is Zionism. Germany encouraged the Zionists in the hope of promoting an uprising in the Pale against Russia, which meant that it was prepared to make sympathetic noises about Jewish settlement in Palestine. But because this was inconsistent with their pro-Ottoman policy and their desire to recruit the

Arab tribes for war against British Egypt, the German Foreign Ministry dragged its feet over a public announcement to that effect – and was pre-empted by the Balfour Declaration. But this latter was also the outcome of a calculation that the British came to regret, another twist in a very convoluted tale.

Among much else that might be said about this tragically tangled and mighty affair, there is this one final note to add: there can now be no place to hide for Turkish deniers of the Armenian massacres of 1915 – the 'Medz Yeghern' or *Great Crime* as the Armenians themselves call it – or indeed for deniers of earlier Armenian massacres by the Ottomans, of which there were a number in the preceding decades. The atrocity of 1915 has been exhaustively documented: it really happened – and the explanation (not excuse) for it lies in the precarious military and supply situation for Turkey in eastern Anatolia when the Armenian uprising occurred. The events were appalling, even for a generally appalling war: up to a million and a half Armenians died in massacres and through forced labour and starvation, while on the death marches to the Syrian desert rape and murder were commonplace.

To understand our situation now, more needs to be known of everything that happened in the decades before and after the Middle East's involvement in the First World War, because it was in that period that what – from the point of view of its suppuration of religions millennia before – had been a closed ulcer on the face of the planet, was torn open again with the gangrenous effects we see today.

The Killing of Osama Bin Laden

The killing of Osama Bin Laden rejoiced many, but even among those who despised him and his cause it troubled some. The rejoicers, especially perhaps in the United States, were those who recognised the symbolic status of a man committed to terrorist atrocity as a political and religious weapon, and the equally symbolic status of the process by which he was relentlessly hunted down and punished. It is satisfying to think that people who sponsor indiscriminate mass murder will not be allowed to get away with it.

But those who are concerned have a serious point to make. The United States is a democracy which says that it is committed to human rights and the rule of law. This commitment should be indivisible and exceptionless. Serious commitment to human rights and the rule of law is an onerous, time-consuming and often messy business, but it is a matter of principle, and principle cannot be overridden by convenience – if one is serious about the principle.

The killing of Osama Bin Laden had much to recommend it from a pragmatic point of view. Shooting him like a mad dog, which is what in functional terms he was, probably saved lives in the long run, because if he had remained alive and been taken to Guantanamo or some such place for a lengthy trial, there would have been riots and demonstrations and increased terrorist activity in his name. His iconic status would have been enhanced, and wherever he was and whatever punishment was meted out, he would have been a running focus of attention for years more, keeping alive the political inflammation he caused.

All this is easy to predict, because so much Islamist political and religious sentiment is infantile and simplistic, violent in language and emotion and too often in action. Only look at reaction to the Danish newspaper cartoons: most people in the West were deeply offended by the attack on free speech mounted by intemperate crowds of shrieking intolerant people offering murder and mayhem: but those offended Westerners did not riot or issue threats of beheadings in response. Instead they iterated their view: that it is wrong to offend those who cannot choose their sex, sexuality, age, disability or ethnicity, but as regards matters of choice – your politics, religion, fashion sense – it is open season: you have no right to be protected from the criticism or disagreement of others, and must rely on having a good case to make in response, and if you do not have a good case, that is your own problem.

So the pragmatic case for killing Bin Laden is that it would undoubtedly save lives and huge amounts of trouble. This is true. But it is not the point: in the perspective of history the trouble would have been relatively short-lived, but the long-term outcome would have been immensely good: Western civilisation with its commitment to rights and due process would have maintained its demanding commitment in this respect, and would have kept alight that beacon. How can we urge rights and the rule of law on others, and yet, acting as despots and thugs do, assassinate people because it is more convenient? How can the leaders of a major democracy behave like a Syrian or Libyan dictator? This is a simple but devastating question, and the United States gave it the wrong answer when it shot an unarmed man to death because putting him on trial would have been very inconvenient and costly.

One is reminded of that question about RAF area bombing in the Second World War: 'We are fighting barbarians; why are we behaving like them?'

Principles are indeed costly in the medium term. In the long-term interests of civilisation, these costs are the ones most worth paying.

The Future of the World

I once had a problem with the headlights of my car, a problem which illuminated the truth that the 'smarter' our technologies get, the more things can go wrong. The car's headlights are adjustable, allowing their beam to be cast closer or further away. Because of a bump in the road they became stuck in the most downward position, so that night I could only see a short way ahead.

This is an allegory of thinking in the EU and the US about the world's future. Out there in the dark beyond our habitual short-termist vision we can see a couple of large shapes, in the form of China's fast-approaching economic dominance and superpower status, and the shift from West to East of the global centre of gravity. Today the EU produces nearly 25 per cent of world GDP, so does the US, and until recently the West altogether accounted for over 60 per cent of world GDP. But in a decade it will be less than 50 per cent, and the downward trend will accelerate. Economic power means influence; it is a simple fact of life that the values, practices and assumptions of the rich carry more weight than those of the poor.

At the time of writing, in the middle of the twenty-first century's second decade, China had already overtaken Japan as the world's second biggest economy in dollar terms, and was continuing to move fast towards eventual pre-eminence. Has anyone looked closely at the values, practices and assumptions of a country with one of the world's worst human rights records, which is extremely irredentist and imperialistic, which devotes massive resources to military build-up, which backs every dictatorship and delinquent regime in the world that has natural resources and/or geographically strategic usefulness to China's interests? Has anyone noticed that the successor to the colonial powers in Africa is China's Exim Bank, bankrolling the dictatorships there for such delicacies as oil, copper, bauxite and other minerals?

Those dipped headlights certainly do not shine on Arunachal Pradesh, where a microcosm of the future is being played out between China and another of the future's big powers, India. Arunachal Pradesh is India's far north-eastern state, remotely and tenuously attached to the rest of the country, squeezed between Nepal and Bangladesh. Its border town of Tawang is just 400 miles south of Lhasa in Tibet. A large slice of the north of the state is claimed by China on the grounds that it used to belong to Tibet.

The suspect credentials of this claim are immediately obvious: Tibet only belongs to China at present because of a violent military occupation and forced immigration of Han Chinese to swamp the local population by numbers. The problem is that Tibet and Britain agreed the Tibet–Arunachal Pradesh border (the McMahon Line, fixed by the Simla Convention of 1914) before the First World War, so that if China recognised the terms of that treaty it would ipso facto recognise Tibet's right to have entered into it, which ipso facto again would amount to recognition of Tibet's status as a sovereign state prior to China's invasion of it in 1950. But China refuses to recognise the Simla Convention of 1914, as a function of its aggressive irredentism: because China had invaded and conquered Tibet for a while in the remote past, it now claims it as an inalienable part of itself. (A treaty of 821 ending two centuries of war between Tibet and China registered the mutual acceptance of the sovereignty of each; the stone pillars on which the treaty is engraved still stand in Lhasa and on the Sino-Tibetan border. This, of course, China ignores.) And if a single inch of territory was ever thought to have belonged to any territory to which China now or once had a claim, it claims it too.

The result? A chilly stand-off between heavy Indian and Chinese military forces along the disputed Tibet–Arunachal Pradesh border. The Chinese constantly mount aggressive 'patrols' into Indian territory every year (over 2,000 instances in 2008 alone), directed from its regional HQ in Bumla, and in recent years the Indian army has moved extra forces into the area, heightening tensions.

The stand-off does not only take place along the physical border. In 2013 China tried to block a $3 billion loan to India from the Asian Development Bank, part of which was earmarked for flood control measures in Arunachal Pradesh. This was simply and solely an attempted spoiler by China to inconvenience India as part of the border cat-and-mouse game. For India the issue is as serious as its tensions with Pakistan, and the fact that it has dangerous borders to both west and north-east is a consideration not lost on China, which is only waiting its time – it has great patience, and thinks in the long term, unlike the West with its electoral-cycle mentality – to help itself to bits of India just as it will help itself to Taiwan, the Spratly Islands, and anything else it can find even the most spurious historical reason to claim as its own, by military force if necessary.

Prediction might be a mug's game, but if any one prediction is sure, China will one day assert its regional claims militarily if it has not yet got them by the current means of manipulation, bribery, economic muscle and sheer diplomatic attrition. The US has been doing the same thing ever since it has had the capability, and the UK did it when it had the capability (and still pretends to it now), but China's current political arrangement exhibits even fewer scruples, and experiences far less constraint from internal dissent and criticism, than is the case in the contemporary US and UK.

Draw some contrasts: the UK does not lay claim to Eire and France, backed by military 'patrols' into their territory several times a day, and interference with their economic affairs. If it behaved as China is now doing, it would be doing exactly that, because it once possessed Eire and large parts of western France, which to the Chinese way of thinking would count as a clear ground of current ownership. And if England were growing rapidly in economic and military power, the likelihood that it would use both to get its way would keep pace. How do we know? Because in the past it actually did it, overpowering Wales and Scotland and Ireland and claiming a big chunk of France and, in due time, even bigger chunks of the rest of the world.

If our headlights remain dipped, we had better fasten our seatbelts more tightly. We can judge people by the company they keep, and so with states: think of China's friends – the likes of Burma and Sudan – and imagine what they would be like if they had China's money and guns. Would they be restrained, responsible, good neighbours? Raising the headlights shows that what the world needs is a different kind of politics in China, making it more responsible, more responsive, more benign: a state that is a better world citizen, and certainly a better neighbour in its region. The great hope, accordingly, is China's indigenous democracy and human rights movement, which merits every ounce of applause and support it can get from the rest of the world.

When China Rules the World

In the preceding essay I asked: when China is the world's biggest state in terms of population and GDP, will it be tempted to exercise its dominance in military terms? China's leadership wishes us to believe the contrary; their emollient and peaceful asseverations tell us that their country will follow what some commentators see as its historic example of being a benign hegemon, accepting the tribute of lesser powers and peoples and once again basking in what it has always believed to be its racial and cultural superiority. This view of China's past and what can be inferred from it for its future – insofar as anything can – merits questioning; I return to it below.

Commentators like Martin Jacques say that we should see China as a 'civilisation-state' rather than a nation-state, something that Jacques in particular (in his book *When China Rules the World*, 2011) is keen to make us see as an exceedingly important fact. A key aspect of his analysis is that China is developing in its own distinctive way, contrary to the over-confident expectation of Westerners that every economically developing country must inevitably become democratic and Westernised. 'It is clear that Chinese modernity will be very different from Western modernity,' he writes, and that therefore

'China will transform the world far more fundamentally than any other new global power in the last two centuries.' In his view this is because the Chinese model of non-democratic state capitalism is one that much of the rest of the developing world might come to find more attractive than the Western model; think for example how attractive to a number of African countries is China's combination of dictatorial politics with successful market capitalism.

To substantiate this thesis Jacques cites China's extraordinarily rapid economic growth, its massive hunger for energy and raw materials, its consequently significant economic relationships across Asia and Africa, its vast ownership of US debt, its demographics, its foreign policy interests, its out-stripping comparison to performance in the rest of the global economy, and its impact on perceptions elsewhere in the world. The statistics iterate the story we are now all familiar with: that China's economy has undergone in the last thirty years what the universe itself was said to have experienced in its first few seconds – a vast and ultra-rapid, indeed explosive, expansion.

Is the world unaware of what is portended by the fact that the sleeping dragon has so dramatically awoken? Consider Jonathan Fenby's *History of Modern China*, 2008, and I have myself been arguing in print for nearly two decades (starting with a book jointly authored with Xu You Yu, *The Long March to the Fourth of June*, first published pseudonymously in 1992 under the joint name Li Xiao Jun) that China's rise requires that the West pay careful attention, not least because a world power which cares nothing whatever about human rights is a profoundly uncomfortable prospect.

The account Jacques gives of China's spectacular economic gallop since 1978 is overall a positive one. But an alternative and less comfortable story tells us that the ingredients of China's economic success are these: state enablement on a massive scale – imagine how well any business fares with big tax exemptions, a state-granted monopoly, preferential prices for raw materials, every obstacle levelled and every opportunity levered open by government – no health and safety standards, no pollution controls, availability of wage-slave and actual slave labour, theft of patented ideas from abroad, limitless unlicensed copying of Western technology, unscrupulous friendship with and aid to delinquent regimes such as Burma, Angola and Sudan in exchange for access to cheap raw materials and oil, an aggressive irredentism and territorial policy.

Then add the following: corruption and nepotism are rampant – nearly half the members of the present Politburo are the children of former Politburo members. In 2007 China's State Auditor said that $7 billion had been stolen by corrupt officials from public project funds; this is almost certainly a huge underestimate. In 2007 the head of the national food and drug administration was executed for taking bribes to issue licences for unsafe products. This relates to a well-known problem about the general quality of Chinese manufactures; about three-quarters of the world's toys are made in China, and there are frequent scares over their safety.

China's human rights abuses are among the worst in the world, and on a scale that dwarfs the rest of the world. Corneas, kidneys and hearts from executed prisoners are purchasable on the open world market, and the supply is not restricted (there are over sixty capital offences in China's criminal law; since they include embezzlement, corruption and unmarried sex construed as 'rape' they give plenty of scope for removing undesirables – first removing their body parts). The abortion of female foetuses, the resulting imbalance in the number of women available for marriage, and the further resulting kidnap of girls for wife-hungry men, constitute one standing scandal among many others.

Let us dwell a little more on just two of these points, though all of them merit fuller exploration. First, actual slave labour (as opposed to the already familiar wage-slave labour in China's sweatshops). All the great economies of the world took their rise from slave labour: the British and the American are two of the more recent and egregious examples, but no major historical empire has been any different. Today's China follows suit. It is difficult to quantify how many people are subjected to forced labour in China's gulag, the 'laogai', situated mainly in the western provinces of Qinghai and Xinjiang; conservative estimates say 20 million. (The authority on the laogai system is Harry Wu, who spent twenty years in it, and whose health was broken by it: see his books *Laogai: The Chinese Gulag*, 1992 and *Bitter Winds*, 1994.) To give a sense of the laogai system's importance to the Chinese economy, one need only reflect that almost everyone in the West will probably touch something at least once a week made in one of the laogai camps – a chopstick, a label, a plastic widget of some kind, a toy, a pen. Almost all the slaves in these camps are there on 'administrative detention' (which means: without trial) in order to undergo 're-education through labour' (which means: slavery). How membership of the World Trade Organisation was given to a country whose economy benefits from slave labour on such a scale would be a mystery if morality ever played a part in monetary considerations.

Second, pollution and the health and safety of workers. As to the latter, let anyone search the internet for the weekly death toll in China's mines and factories, some reports citing 6,000 deaths per annum in China's mines alone – and on average two new coal mines are opened every week. As to pollution: it is estimated that China has hundreds of billions of dollars worth of clean-up to do of its poisoned rivers, soil, air and cities, caused by the heedless rush to industrialise as fast as possible, without a thought to any human or environmental cost. In 2007 the World Bank nominated Linfen in Shanxi Province as the most polluted city in the world; nationally nearly half a million annual deaths are directly attributed to pollution.

A quarter of a century ago, walking across the ice of the Songhua River in Heilongjiang Province to the dachas on the islands in midstream, I turned to look at the city of Harbin on the opposite shore, and could not see it for the toxic smog enshrouding it. That, to repeat, was twenty-five years ago: imagine what it and all of China's other industrial cities are like now. In 2005 when the Songhua River itself was profoundly poisoned by an explosion (no surprise there) at a petrochemical plant, decanting vast quantities of benzene and nitrobenzene into the water, the Chinese government tried to hide the incident. It failed to do so; think how often it succeeds in covering up such incidents.

Jonathan Fenby points out the essential instability of Chinese society. In 2007 there were 70,000 incidents of unrest each involving over 100 people, requiring suppression by the police. A huge and restive population of unemployed migrant workers constitutes a continual headache for the security services. The increasingly rich middle-classes in the lucky and mainly coastal cities of China's economic boom are no longer so uninterested in the political arrangements by which they live, at least when these show any signs of flagging, as when growth dips and wages experience upward pressure.

These last points are of great significance. China's staggeringly rapid growth has been and continues to be fuelled by two political imperatives that trump all other considerations for the ruling Party. One is the recovery of the national pride which China regards as its due because of the undisputed regional superiority and hegemony it enjoyed for much of its history. But the other more immediately important one is that the Party's hold on power depends on a growth rate of 8 per cent or more so that employment levels and standard of living can keep pace with population increase. Growth of 6 per cent or lower would undermine the Party's acceptability to the people. But a drop in the growth rate is bound to happen: the current level of growth is unsustainable. At current rates, China's need for energy and raw materials will, in just a few decades, be greater than the entire world can produce. So a slow-down is inevitable, and with it a crunch for the Party's tenure of the 'Mandate of Heaven'.

Add further the interesting facts, carefully reported by Jacques, that China's output consists largely of low-tech cheap goods, that 80 per cent of its exports are produced by foreign-owned firms in China, that their presence there is premised on the plentiful cheap labour supply China offers, that wages in the coastal economic zones are rising, and that therefore industry is moving into the hinterlands to exploit the supply of cheap labour there. What of the higher expectations among those in economic zones now pricing themselves out of the employment market? This imposes a need for China to raise its technological game and to move into higher-value production, following the lead of the developed West. In some respects necessity has already pushed it into such development: its immense energy-hunger has encouraged it to become an innovator in alternative energy, and its automotive industry promises to lead the way in hybrid cars. But the question is a crucial one: a Big Bang expansion of low-end manufacturing is one thing, but can its scientific and technological research and development catch up with a West which is already so far in advance?

In short, there are plenty of bumps on the road ahead for China and its ruling caste's aspirations to become a world power, still less the world's economic (and even less still its military) hegemon. Too little of this is emphasised by commentators, even when they are careful enough to place the occasional 'if' in their prognostications, only then to forget them and to assert with confidence that China's economic development will transform the future.

Yet these remarks about the home-grown bumps on the Chinese road need to be supplemented by some major considerations: by pointing out that the US and Europe, to say nothing of India, the Middle East and Africa, are scarcely going to sit placidly by while China races ahead. For, first, it is a little early to be speaking of US decline, and, second, Europe is only at the beginning of an equally inevitable though long-term journey to greater unity, ultimately towards a federation on the US (or German) model, the consequences of which have yet to be thought out. And even closer trans-Atlantic political and economic ties are on the cards too, as one likely response to the emergence of Asian giants.

Third, India's economic lift-off will not take long in making it a major competitor, as Japan still is, to China's ambitions to be even so much as a regional hegemon. Fourthly, Africa is already uneasy about the barrier to its own progress represented by being a dependent exporter of raw materials to China and an importer of its finished goods – a reprise of the old colonial economic imbalance that ultimately works to the detriment of the weaker partner in the exchange.

One could go on, but these points – again, too infrequently discussed – should by themselves be enough to suggest that although China is soon bound to be a very big fish in crude GDP terms as it already is in population, there are no inevitabilities about what follows from this fact apart from the mentioned problems it entails. Viewed in this light, we might reach a different conclusion: instead of saying that China is tomorrow's superpower, wielding a history-changing influence on models of statehood, economies and cultures, we could describe a coming massive problem for the stability and health of the world economy and the balance of international political arrangements, as an autocratic polity with an over-heated economy and a bloated population runs out of control and implodes.

This alternative is suggested even by the description, accurate in all essentials, that, as a proponent of the more optimistic view, Jacques gives of China today. His different conclusion is based on the claim, mentioned earlier, that China represents a new form of modernity. Arguably, however, it represents no such thing; arguably it is an essentially nineteenth-century industrial-revolution state with essentially nineteenth-century ideas about power and world status – among which are ideas about the ultimate utility of 'hard power' military capability.

Jacques also emphasises the length and continuity of Chinese history as a factor in its uniqueness. Arguably again, Western civilisation is as ancient and continuous, its originating civilisational framework having been forged as long ago as China's was – namely, in classical antiquity, whose language we still use in the conceptual vocabulary we think in today ('politics', 'democracy', 'ethics' and so on: not just Greek words but continuingly vital ideas). 'Christendom' was a more unified domain than he allows; and interestingly, its partial post-Reformation fragmentation resulting in the Westphalian settlement was a precursor to its industrial and technological rise, not a barrier to it.

Moreover Jacques ignores some striking parallels: in the same period from the sixteenth century CE onwards in which Europe was acquiring empires, so China was doing the same – conquering vast abutting territories and extending its own empire over neighbouring peoples and lands. The fecundity of the Han gives today's appearance of homogeneity in today's Chinese land empire, but as Jacques himself points out in passing, the cultural and linguistic diversity of today's Chinese empire is not much different from Europe, though both China and Europe are internally also much more linked than they are different.

But: will today's China always remain a single entity, or are there centrifugal forces at work in the far western provinces, in the 'minority regions' of the south-west, even of the nation-sized and rich Guangdong Province?

These thoughts suggest that China is not as exceptional, in the end, as Jacques wishes to insist. Any casual visitor to today's China of Western-style skyscraper cities, Western-dressed people, with its Western-style industry and Western-style business, would be a bit puzzled by his insistence on a 'different modernity'. What is different is the continuation by another name of China's traditional form of governance –

in name a Politburo, in function an Emperor – and the question is: will a growth rate of less than 8 per cent show that it or indeed any country can, in the end, really do without Western-style political institutions? That is a question Jacques does not ask, but to which Fenby implies a negative answer.

But even if Jacques is right about China as a future world-changing superpower, perhaps even as *the* world superpower, the next and final question is: will that be a good thing, if it does not also start caring about human rights, civil liberties such as personal autonomy and free speech, and the rule of law? Since the answer that any rational person must give is No, it follows that if Jacques is right, we had all better sit up and take twice the notice.

China and Human Rights

China was desperate to get the 2000 Olympics, because it wanted the 'face' that would thereby accrue, allowing it to walk tall on the international stage and show off its extraordinarily rapid development and re-invention as a modern, major world-influencing state. When Sydney was awarded the 2000 Games instead there was crushing disappointment in Beijing. What then went into its renewed efforts to get the 2008 Games is anyone's guess, given that China does not observe norms of law or morality in going after what it wants; but by the time of the Moscow meeting at which the 2008 Games decision was made, Beijing was a clear front-runner over Paris and Toronto in the minds of the IOC committee, whose then-shortly-to-retire chairman, Juan Antonio Samaranch, was as keen for China to win as any Politburo member in the Forbidden City's Zhong Nan Hai complex.

At the time many of us engaged in campaigning about China's human rights record lobbied hard against Beijing's candidature. One thing we understood was that success for Beijing, conjoined with China's effect on glazed-eyed salivating Western businessmen and their governments seduced by the 'vast potential market' promise, would almost completely stifle interest in protests about Chinese human rights violations – and so it proved. Indeed the fact that in China's poverty-stricken hinterlands, hidden behind the glittering economic success of the Special Economic Zones, there is frequent harshly repressed turmoil and rioting, is barely mentioned in the Western press, who do not have correspondents in the rural depths of Hunan and Gansu or the 'minority regions', and who ignore the samizdat news reports that filter out of them.

It would take too long to list the many respects in which the human rights of Chinese citizens are persistently and comprehensively abused – but that in any case is common knowledge: any number of reports in the public domain from Human Rights Watch, Amnesty, the United Nations, the US government and other agencies, rehearse the data in detail. I shall mention just one: that the 'laogai' – the vast gulag of over 1,000 forced labour camps, which Harry Wu's Laogai Research Foundation calculates has had over 40 million inmates since the first camps opened in the 1950s – continues its output of slave-made products. Like all economic miracles in history, China's miracle also depends on slavery.

The luckier victims of China's oppressions are not those sent without trial to 'education through labour' in the laogai where death is slow, but those shot for any of the more than sixty capital offences on China's books (they include fraud, tax evasion, smuggling, bribery and 'splittism', i.e. advocating independence for Tibet, Taiwan, or anywhere else) – providing of course they are also lucky enough not to have their corneas or kidneys removed for transplant purposes before being shot. China executes more people annually than the whole of the rest of the world put together – and the families of the victims pay for the bullets. I have personally seen a truckload of those about to be executed in a public stadium being paraded through the streets of a Chinese city, tied up and with banners pinned to them announcing their crimes.

The occupation and repression of Tibet peaked in the news during the run-up to the Beijing Games as Tibetan activists used the occasion to get the outside world's wavering, short-term, Attention Deficit Disorder notice back to their terrible plight. Western press coverage might rather feebly mention that there is unrest in the provinces of Qinghai, Sichuan and Xinjiang also: and yes, at the very least craniums are being cracked and kidneys kicked there too, and the trucks heading for the laogai were even fuller than usual in the run-up to the Games – and not just because of the typical and predictable re-run of the notorious 'Strike Hard' campaigns to 'clean up' Beijing and other major cities before the influx of foreign visitors, aimed at getting rid of dissidents or 'liu meng' or just anyone whose jib is not cut as the Party and the Gong An Ju (the 'Public Peace Bureau' *aka* police) like.

China's Games

However churlish it might seem to say it, the fact that little Lin Miaoke mimed the solo at the Olympic Games opening ceremony in Beijing in 2008 is still the perfect metaphor for contemporary China: all cosmetic, masking deception. China's self-presentation is a continuous act of deception, which matters because the victims of it include the Chinese people themselves. So well known is this that I cannot imagine anyone was surprised to learn that Lin Miaoke was miming not to her own pre-recording, but to the sweet tones of the even younger Yang Peiyi, who had been deemed insufficiently pretty to take the stage. For this is just par for the Party course.

Other elements of that deceptive moment might not have registered with the watching billions. The Chinese flag was carried to the squadron of goose-stepping soldiers by a large cohort of children, all dressed in the traditional costumes of the so-called 'minority peoples' of the Chinese empire – the Zhuang, the Manchu, the Hui, the Miao, the Uighur, the Yi, the Tuja, the Mongols, the Tibetans, the Buyei, the Mosuo, the Naxi, and so on – there are fifty-five such groups recognised officially by the Chinese government, and a number more who claim ethnic difference from the Han Chinese but are not recognised.

Almost all these people live in territories occupied by the Chinese empire. For that is what China is: it is as Europe would be if Napoleon or Hitler had won their respective wars of conquest, and unified Europe under a single rule. Then imagine that the conquering nation had grown in population to be 90 per cent of the continent's ethnicity, leaving the

Czechs and Hungarians to be 'minority peoples' obliged to attend national ceremonies in quaint ethnic dress.

Just to give a sense of what is involved here, let me relate an anecdote. While teaching at the Chinese Academy of Social Sciences in Beijing some years back, I was asked by the members of another department of the Academy's Institute of Philosophy to give a lecture on 'the nature and origins of consciousness'. Rather bemusedly I said that I'd be happy to talk about the difficulties we face in understanding the nature of consciousness, but was not sure what could be said about its origins. And I asked them whether the origin of consciousness was a subject of research among them. Oh yes, they said; we take our clipboards and visit minority peoples in the outlying areas of China, and we study them, because they have more primitive levels of consciousness than Han Chinese, so from them we can infer something about the evolution of consciousness among humans.

Enough said. At the oasis of Turfan in the Takla Makan desert I once asked a Uighur for his view of Chinese rule over his region. After a significant pause he said, gesturing at the well next to which we stood, 'A Chinese will take the bucket from the well and put it down on the sand.' Nothing could be worse for a desert-dweller than to have dirt introduced to well-water; the comment was intended as a sweeping metaphor.

In fact neither of these tales is fair to the Chinese people themselves, but both speak volumes about official or governmental China. Here is a generalisation, to be tempered by remembering that people are much the same everywhere: the Chinese seem to me a good-hearted, hard-working, courageous, sentimental, humorous, vigorous, highly likeable people, and I have the deepest affection for many friends made in years of living and travelling there. Bureaucratic China, government China, is an utterly different matter. Because China is going to be a world superpower in a generation's time, it matters that China should rectify its human rights record, give up its irredentism, think again about its forcible occupation of Tibet, Xinjiang, and the 'minority areas' along the Vietnamese and Burmese borders, stop supporting hideous regimes like Sudan, Burma and Zimbabwe, and become a good neighbour to Japan and a good world citizen generally.

Only think: on most of the items just listed, the world's current sole superpower, the US, has never been wholly perfect, and yet if you put a gun to most people's heads and forced them to choose between living in the US or almost anywhere outside the 'first world', they would choose the US. If China becomes as the US is today in world power terms, yet keeps its current regime and outlook, US history will look like a legend of saints. That is why the pressure has to be kept on China to reform its political institutions and human rights record – systematically one of the worst in the world.

In the interests of the future what we do not want is an apparently sweet-faced Chinese government singing saccharine melodies while behind the scenes all is fraud.

Opium

There were, one has to admit, many who said that if there is a living refutation of the saying, 'If the fool would persist in his folly he would become wise', it is former President George W. Bush. This especially applies to the conduct of war in Iraq and Afghanistan, and the associated failure of social policies operated in both countries in an effort to prepare for post-conflict peace. One example cited is his demand that the Kabul government destroy the poppy crop of Afghan tribesmen. The aim was to 'deprive the Taliban of funds' thereby; the result was to further alienate struggling tribesmen whose livelihood was destroyed with their crops.

Yet the infinitely better solution was obvious: buy the crop, don't destroy it. Buy it for a generous price, thus simultaneously (a) depriving the Taliban of a money-maker, (b) cheering the Afghan tribesmen, and laying the basis for them to diversify economically, away from poppies, when peace comes, (c) getting control of the opium supply, using as much as is necessary for medical opiates, and stockpiling or burning the rest. In comparison to the billions being spent on bombs, this looks like a comparatively cheap as well as sane and effective way to solve a number of problems in one blow.

But no: Washington's choice was to lay waste the crops and with them the hearts and minds of their growers, adding to the recruitment pool of the Taliban, lengthening the war, costing the world far more in lives, money and misery. Surely there are statesmen and women somewhere able to understand the better course of action, able to do the sums showing that buying poppies to help stop a war has to be a far cheaper option than using them to commemorate war dead.

In the short term the move would encourage poppy growing, of course, and naysayers will argue that this exacerbates a different problem. This different problem was originally created by outlawing certain kinds of drugs (not nicotine or, save for the criminal-industry-creating folly of Prohibition in the 1920s, alcohol, two of the worst), and there is a powerful case for legalising all drugs and managing their accessibility and quality exactly as nicotine and alcohol are controlled.

The 'quality' point is essential. Some years ago the son of an acquaintance of mine died from a massive heroin overdose on the first occasion he experimented with the substance, because he did not know how much to take and did not know that the heroin he had been supplied was very pure. If heroin could be bought in Boots it would have a consistent potency, there would be instructions on the box about the right quantity to take, and that boy would now be a young man.

Why are some drugs illegal? The answer will come that it is because they are bad for people, and that anyway consuming narcotics or hallucinogens is a contemptible resource for finding release or getting a high, for making life more colourful or more bearable. I agree with this latter point, but cannot agree that society has a right to stop people (adult people) from harming themselves if they wish, providing that they do not expect the rest of society to clean up after them. By bracketing a range of drugs as illegal, society has created a rod for its back; it has potentiated a criminal industry and assumed the vast expense of policing it, thereby creating an equally vast public problem where before there had been personal and medical problems only.

'Sights you seldom see' include a cabinet meeting waking up to the futility and absurdity of laws that, from gangland shootings in Manchester to the Taliban in Helmand Province, create problems we do not have to have.

A Christian Nation?

It is sometimes rather lazily said that the British are a 'Christian nation'. At its best this characterisation is meant to draw upon those magnanimous and liberal characteristics that – at certain times and in certain places: alas, not everywhere or always – were connoted by the term 'Christian', as when people talked of 'the Christian thing to do' to mean being tolerant, forgiving and kind. The 'Christian gentleman' was an oxymoron, in twice overusing epithets that denoted someone courteous and considerate, modest, helpful and generous.

No doubt users of the phrase also mean to refer to the historical fact that from the early seventh century of the common era, following Augustine's mission to Britain's shores commencing in the year 597, Christianity was the dominant religious outlook of England, and eventually of the whole British Isles. That hegemony over thought and belief lasted until the eighteenth century, during which a more ambiguous attitude to religious dogma increased among educated minds. England (not the whole UK) has remained *officially* Christian since, having an established church.

But it is of the first importance in any pluralistic society that we should not allow the use of such phrases as 'a Christian nation' to pass without challenge. First, Christianity not only does not have a monopoly on tolerance, kindness and generosity – these are attitudes of individual human beings of any religion and none – but in a bloody and tumultuous past it has often exhibited the opposite of these characteristics, and that must not be forgotten.

Second, 'being Christian' was enforced on the residents of the British Isles for many centuries, on pain of punishment up to and including death. Church attendance, the payment of tithes, and adherence to the doctrines of the church, were legal requirements. It is an open question whether enforced belief and practice qualifies as making us a Christian nation. Until the repeal of the Test Act in 1824 only those who were prepared to subscribe to the Thirty-Nine Articles of the Church of England were allowed to go to university or hold public office. The Dissenting communities of Britain – in fact comprising the most vigorous, innovative and entrepreneurial of all Britons – were excluded from these fiefdoms of privilege.

A related point is this. In the Christian church's early centuries as an accepted and very quickly dominant force in the Roman Empire – that is, from the fourth century CE – much of the effort of the Church Fathers such as Jerome, Ambrose and Augustine was devoted to 'apologetics', which means the explanation and justification of Christian teachings in an attempt to persuade a sceptical world of their truth. By the period of the church's greatest temporal power and influence, the late Middle Ages, apologetics was an outdated genre, for by then it was no longer necessary to try persuading people about Christianity: it had become a capital crime not to believe it. Religions are ever thus.

Third, for most of the time since the seventeenth century, Britain and its growing empire were run by graduates of the ancient universities. The main studies at those universities were the classics. That means that the British governing class was brought up on the literature, philosophy and history of classical civilisation – ancient Greece and Rome. This was a fine education – in government, military strategy, ethics, political theory, historical examples of good and bad rule, management of an empire, social conditions, how to mitigate popular unrest, educational theory, institutions of law, and much besides. Aristotle and Cicero, Homer, Aeschylus and Virgil, the ancient myths and legends, the examples of Horatio and Mucius Scaevola, had as much if not indeed more influence on the minds of the British ruling class than the etiolated beliefs of Christianity, which provide very little in the way of instruction or guidance – beyond a few generalisations about being nice to people – for dealing with the complexities of life.

And it is not surprising that this should be so. Only consider: if you go to the New Testament for instruction on how to live, you are told to give away all your possessions, make no plans for the future, reject your family if they disagree with you, and stay celibate if you can (see respectively Matthew 19: 21, Matthew 6: 25, Matthew 12: 48, and 1 Corinthians 7). This is the outlook of people who sincerely believed that the Messiah was going to return next week or next month, anyway very soon. It is an unlivable ethic, and when after several centuries the Second Coming had still not materialised and hope of it had been deferred *sine die*, more was needed in the way of ethics. Where did it come from? From Greek philosophy – not least from the Stoics – and from the Roman Republican virtues of probity, honour, duty, restraint, respect, friendship and generosity that Cicero, Seneca, Virgil, Horace and countless others wrote about and enjoined ceaselessly. 'Christian values' are largely Greek and Roman secular values. So Christianity is not even Christianity.

An associated point reinforces this. The early Christians, like St Paul, were Jews. They believed that when you die, your body sleeps in the grave until the Last Trump, at which point the graves open and all the dead rise to be judged. St Paul said that the faithful will 'see no corruption' – that is, their bodies will not rot in the grave. But anyway at the Last Trump when all rise, the faithful will be clothed in 'new bodies', resplendent and fine.

But when Christianity had become the official religion of the Roman Empire (which it very quickly did; it was legalised by Constantine's Edict of Milan in 313, and made the empire's official religion by Theodosius IX in 381; within the next few decades all other religions were proscribed) and churches were being built apace, all requiring relics of the martyrs and saints, these latter were found to have rotted ('seen corruption') in their graves. This embarrassing problem was quickly got over by importing another useful idea from Greek philosophy: Plato's doctrine of the immortal soul, which entered Christianity via the Neo-Platonism of Plotinus and his followers. That is why, starting from several centuries after the lifetime of Jesus of Nazareth, Christians believe in such a thing. Once again, Christianity is not Christianity but borrowed Greek philosophy.

Those who ignorantly claim that Western civilisation has its roots in Christianity and therefore 'we are Christians' would in fact be more right to say that 'we are Greeks and Romans' and mean thereby that we are defined by the following words – and therefore concepts – of pre-Christian classical Greek and Latin origin: *democracy, liberalism, values, history, morality, comedy, tragedy, literature, music, academy, alphabet, memory, politics, ethics, populace, geography, energy, exploration, hegemony, theory, mathematics, science, theatre, medicine, gymnasium, climate, clone, bureaucracy, dialect, analogy, psychology, method, nostalgia, organ, encyclopaedia, education, paradox, empiricism, polemic, rhetoric, dinosaur, telescope, system, school, trophy, type, fantasy, photography* … take almost any word denoting political and social institutions, ideas, learning, science and technology, medicine and culture, and it derives from the languages – and therefore the ideas and the history – of ancient Greece and Rome.

In fact, Christianity attempted to suppress this heritage! and for a time succeeded. The Emperor Justinian closed the schools of Athens – the institutions founded by Plato, Aristotle and others – in the year 529, because they taught 'pagan' philosophy ('philosophy' then meant everything – science, history and the rest included). There was little learning worth the name in the first seven centuries of Christianity's dominance, because it had suppressed it, leaving only the thin pickings of 'scripture' as the source of knowledge; later it persecuted those who advanced scientific ideas in conflict with scripture: Giordano Bruno was burned at the stake, and Galileo nearly so, for not accepting that the Sun goes round the Earth as Psalm 104 and Joshua 10: 12–13 says it does. If the list of words just given provides us with the terminology that we use to describe ourselves today, then the mighty endeavour of Christianity to obliterate all those words and what they mean makes us anything but a Christian nation.

We who protest against the description of us as 'a Christian nation' have in mind the fact that we are a highly pluralistic nation, with many faiths and none, and that the 'nones' are net contributors to our society and culture in major ways that does not deserve having the fact of their principled rejection of religious belief overlooked.

It goes without saying that the description 'a Christian nation' is deeply misleading if taken to imply a nation of believers in Christian doctrines and legends. Generally it is not taken to mean this, but instead to imply the existence of

Christian roots. As the foregoing shows, this is itself an error – and one that the churches and religious folk generally are, with very unchristian lack of respect for truth, too keen to foster.

Unjust Justice

In the atmosphere of outrage that followed the end of war in 1945 it was relatively easy to get consensus, in the nascent United Nations, for the idea that there are universal human rights. One of the good ideas that Mrs Eleanor Roosevelt's committee for drafting the UN Declaration of Human Rights came up with, in enjoying that supportive tide of opinion, was to enshrine the idea of equality before the law – unqualifiedly implying equality for anyone anywhere in the world before any properly instituted and administered law.

About the only thing now universal about human rights is the irritation they prompt in governments. How inconvenient human rights are, how difficult it makes prosecuting undesirables or deporting them or otherwise flicking them off the sleeve of society because they are disagreeable or plain bad! The idea that even those suspected of the worst crimes have a right to get the fullest possible hearing has come to be regarded as a nuisance, as if it is plain in advance that the processes of the law are mere window-dressing for what everyone already knows about this rabble-rousing mullah or that aged celebrity and his sexual tastes, viz. that of course they are obviously guilty and that's that.

In some jurisdictions it is proposed that illegal immigrants can only appeal against deportation in their country of origin.

This is a bald-faced piece of trickery: it exploits the fact that the difficulty and expense of appealing from abroad would stop most such folk mounting a challenge to their expulsion. Worse, it introduces a very unhealthy change to the principle of equal treatment before the law, by enshrining discrimination against a class of people in effect judged to be less deserving of a full hearing on the same terms as everyone else because already supposed to be in the wrong.

Consider what is at stake. The point is not the independently correct one that each individual has the same right as every other individual to the same treatment at law, for to insist on this is to invite the rejoinder that in immigration cases the defendants are not, or not yet, recognised as citizens and therefore do not have the same rights that citizens automatically enjoy. To get into a debate on this ground is a distraction. This is clear from the fact that whether or not a person is a citizen, if he is indicted for a crime in the jurisdiction he can be tried and if found guilty punished for it there, and accordingly any such person is being treated equally by the law.

The real point in the case of deportation appeals is the law itself: that it should be indifferent to facts about an individual who comes before it other than those germane to the case in hand. People appealing against a deportation order on the grounds that they have a right to stay should expect the law to consider and decide on the merits of their cases, without the law front-loading major disadvantages to offering them its remedies. To do this is to enshrine injustice in statute.

Mere self-respect should be enough to require of people in developed countries that they have a legal system that is scrupulous in what it offers to anyone who comes before it, and for whatever reason. There is no difference in principle between having differential laws according to, say, your race (Aryan or Jewish? Caucasian or not?) and whether one has the same opportunity as people in non-immigration cases to appeal against an adverse decision.

The explicit intent to make it more difficult to seek a review of a court decision because a person belongs to a singled-out class of appellants is accordingly wholly unjustifiable. A legal system should not merely dispense justice, but should do it justly. It would be interesting to know what lawyers who found themselves in such a regime think about politicians who tell them to be unjust in the administration of justice, and what they would do in response. If anyone should be expected to uphold the rule of law, it is the law's own servants.

What We Owe the Dead

Do we owe the dead respect, even if we disagreed with them profoundly, even if we were harmed by them in some way, even if we think that their influence on their times was largely negative, and their legacy damaging?

When the controversial Margaret Thatcher died there were street parties celebrating the occasion, and they were condemned for bad taste. They are certainly unprecedented in Britain at least, and they manifested an unappealing similarity to television images of people dancing on the fallen statues of dictators in parts of the world where nothing like the institutions and practices of British political life exist. In suggesting a comparison, the British did themselves no favours.

But bad taste and false comparisons aside, the question remains: must we respect the newly dead merely in virtue of their being dead? We might be mindful of the grief of family and friends, but still feel that a judgement about the life and legacy of a prominent individual should be an honest one.

The standard trope is: *de mortuis nil nisi bonum* – 'of the dead say nothing but good'. Why? Why should one not speak as one did when the person was alive? The story of a prominent individual's life cannot be complete without the truth about what people felt at the moment of summing up, whether it is in mourning or rejoicing. Let us say what we think, and be frank about it: death does not confer privileges.

An outburst of pleasure at the departure of someone who was deeply polarising and gave expression to callous attitudes is both perfectly understandable and justifiable. No quantity of apologetics about the good effects on the economy or the military situation in the world will satisfy someone who saw whole communities devastated by unemployment, livelihoods lost and neighbourhoods turned into wastelands: the felt quality of life is the final measure of the effect on individuals, and they have a right to their say.

Respect for the dead is a hangover from a past in which it was believed that the dead might retain some active influence on the living, and that one might re-encounter them either in this life or a putative next life. Once a year the people of China go in their millions to the graves of ancestors to perform the annual ritual of putting paper money and cakes on them. Honouring the dead is not only a form of remembrance but also propitiation. In our more rational age we know that the only thing left of the dead is influence and memory in the minds of the living. It is the influence which is the target of praise or condemnation when summings-up are offered.

Future historians will be glad that people have begun to speak frankly of their estimations of major figures when they die. Frank opinions explain far more than the massaged and not infrequently hypocritical views expressed in obsequies. The democratic value of frank expression of opinions about public figures and public matters should not be hostage to squeamishness or false ideas of respect – let us respect ourselves instead, and say what we truly feel.

Black Poison

'Postmodern thought' (if the phrase is not already a contradiction) consists in the intellectual licentiousness permitted by taking cognitive relativism and causal over-determination to be the only two permissible explanations of things. A more responsible and reflective attitude sees cognitive relativism and causal over-determination as, simultaneously, factors and constraints that must be taken into account in the search either for truth, or at least for the most stable and robust account that can be given of a subject matter. But to regard them as all of the story leads to mistakes or – more usually – nonsense.

Over-determination is a particularly interesting phenomenon as it besets efforts to arrive at explanations in the social sciences. It is the reason – to take three not too random examples – why historians can disagree, why understanding other people is an art rather than a science, and why politics is necessary. It certainly means that one cannot nominate single culprits for the world's present discontents: too many factors, too many layers of history, too many conflicting rights and wrongs jostle in the claustrophobic space of explanations for that.

And yet: in the heaving crowd of causes one can pick out a few tall malefactors, ubiquitous and malevolent, diffusing noxious, maddening, riot-provoking odours as they dart about to spread their evil. One is mentioned so often that the curse of its putatively holy name can be given momentary rest here. Another is mentioned far too infrequently, though frequently still. It is the black, toxic, planet-sickening ooze on which the world is so utterly drunk that it has become insane – lusting for the ghastly poison because burning it belches out wealth, and wealth means power and influence. A dithyramb beckons invitingly on this subject, saying: power struts itself in armaments and armies, big buildings, motorcades, visiting heads of state, motorways lined with flags, all the show and pomp which from time to time feels that it needs a war or a massacre or two to sustain itself, and to keep hold on the power that leads so often to abuse of power.

The stuff in question is of course oil (and let us add gas to the equation too), and it is why the world is hostage to (a) the lust for it in the huge economies that consume oceans of it daily in the mad rage of their thirst – think USA, China – and who buy it from (b) countries run by questionable regimes – the Saudi, Iranian, Russian, some Central-Asian regimes – where disturbing human rights records, dictatorships, sometimes bullies and zealots, are the suppliers, paid by each of us in the oil-consuming economies every day of our lives so that they can variously and according to taste buy weapons, flog or stone adultresses, fund jihadi-producing madrassas, threaten the world with more conflict, and generally keep world affairs inflamed.

If there were a sudden outbreak of rationality in the world, or at least in our parts of it, the major Western economies would turn their attention, on something like a total war footing, to finding alternative sources of energy – a massive effort to harness clean renewables and to find other technological solutions, to break dependence on oil and therefore on the parts of the world it comes from. Think what would happen to those regions if no one wanted oil any more. Try to imagine what the world might become if cheap clean home-grown sources of energy quickly became available to the major economies, and they no longer needed endlessly to consume the poison from those places, corrupting themselves in the process.

Is there really no chance of ending the oil lust? People will say this is not a 'realistic' option because we are far too heavily invested in it. The oil companies with their hundreds of billions of dollars committed to oil wells, refineries, fleets of tankers, scores of thousands of petrol stations: they do not want the world to cease being addicted to oil, and it would be surprising if they did not use their muscle to ensure that politics plays along. So we are each of us hostage to someone else's determination to keep making profits, at whatever cost of war, terrorism, and other charming spin-offs – not to mention the catastrophic effect on the environment, where the black poison does its other destructive work.

Would genuine and sensible alternatives only become realistic if oil becomes too costly to extract? Sunni Saudi Arabia would probably try not to let oil become too expensive if only to limit Shi'ite Iran's income, but not even Saudi's oil-taps are limitless in their power to control world energy prices. As we see in connection with problems over oil prospectors wishing to explore Antarctica, the cost of finding and extracting the stuff will play its part. But we are still some way from being forced by money (only money) considerations – forget war, forget deaths, forget the environment: only money will force the change – to seek alternatives to oil.

Two questions press. What is our answer to this vast weight of inertia and vested interest that keeps us all victims of the black evil? And: I wonder what the cost of the Iraq and Afghan wars would have funded in the way of research into alternative energy sources?

Death and Taxes

Death and taxes are said to be the two great inescapabilities of life, and sometimes the implication is assumed to be that they are the only two worth mentioning when one is marshalling one's reserves of stoicism to counter life's vicissitudes. But there are others, some positive: I think kindness or fellow-feeling is a far more common trait among human beings than cruelty, as proved by the normal daily functioning of society, and I think – quite consistently – that selfishness and its even less appealing manifestation as greed is more common than sentiments of social responsibility when it comes to attitudes towards anonymous others. That sometimes seems to be all too true of people whose lives are dedicated to the imperatives of Wall Street and the City of London.

These latter borrow shares, currencies or contracts, sell them to push down their value, buy them back at the lower price they reach, and return them to their original owners with a profit in their pockets. Suppose they do this with bank shares. The bank's share value drops, depositors become anxious and withdraw their money, credit rating agencies lower the bank's standing which means that it has to borrow money at higher interest to cover its obligations. As a result it begins to teeter. Depositors might lose some of their money, most forms of rescue entail job losses from the bank's staff, people seeking mortgages to buy a home or loans to start up a small business find life harder ... but those who have profited are not among them.

Such forms of capitalist activity as short-selling and other techniques to make money out of money – conducted by people operating in the financial sector to graze upon, exploit, finesse, manipulate, and ultimately profit from the money transactions going on at the level of the 'real' economy – are said to be vital to the 'real' economy, and in many ways this is true. For one thing City profits are a major component of the UK's standing as one of the world's wealthiest countries (and therefore the City's activities are very much part of the 'real' economy). For another, the money generated does not all go on imported luxury goods, thus benefiting other economies, but serves the rest of our own economy through investment and credit facilities.

At the same time, though, some of this activity really does have a big downside, and it was obvious in the financial crisis of 2008 and the following years. Financiers resist government attempts at regulation and oversight, they are endlessly inventive in the ways they can make money out of money and the movement of money, creating tradeable 'assets' – even out of dodgy debts, as we saw with the cancer at the heart of the

2008 crisis: sub-prime mortgages in the US – and artificially manipulating the financial marketplace for short-term gain, as in short-selling. The good that the market can do in being an open arena of trade and opportunity is thus threatened by the vices of its virtues.

There is no surprise in the fact that the 2008 crisis started on Wall Street, because American capitalism is much less regulated than European capitalism. The lesson learned from the Great Depression of the early 1930s is that governments and central banks cannot stand by and let everything fall to pieces. So we see central banks pump billions of dollars into the financial system to maintain availability of credit for its institutions, we see nationalisations (even by the US government: a whole New Deal) and abrogation of competitiveness legislation – in short we see action that should theoretically be the very opposite of capitalism, the very opposite of reliance on 'the wisdom of the markets', to save our skins.

A nice reckoning was afoot there. The paladins who resisted the state's interference in the money markets proved unable to manage them well without the state's help. But the state cannot go too far in sitting on the goose that, in good times, lays golden eggs. It had to find a way of limiting the goose's more noisome efflations while keeping the eggs coming – a finger in the right dyke, so to say – and that is a delicate matter. Over-correction in the regulatory direction might do opposite harms; yet the robber-baron mentality of speculators cannot be allowed to destabilise the entire economy on the grounds that nothing but the profit motive counts.

One place to start is with short-selling. The Financial Services Authority banned short-selling for four months at the height of the crisis. This was an admission that part of the reason for the crisis is a sharp practice. For consider: these activities amount to gambling on a certainty. With central banks and governments loth to let a bank go under, the cowboys can manipulate matters knowing that they are in no danger of losing out, though lots of other people will do so – and, in the end, mainly the taxpayer. They know, in effect, that at the limit they can put their hands in the public's pocket: their own pockets are safe. The then Chancellor of the Exchequer, Alistair Darling, said that the short-selling ban was temporary because in normal times the technique is acceptable and indeed useful for providing liquidity and funds for investment. But then it was damaging and irresponsible; and that moment is always waiting to repeat if the reckless push to maximise profits overrides all other considerations, not least among them stability.

The only thing that prevents greed is a guaranteed danger of burning your fingers to the knuckle if you go too far. One simple idea: for every x percentage drop in a publicly quoted bank's value directly attributable to short-selling of that bank's shares, the tax on the profits thus made by short-sellers jumps in increments of 20 per cent to the maximum 100 per cent. Such a provision might do the trick.

Religion and Education

Facts do not always speak for themselves, but they can sometimes shout. In a speech not long ago the Archbishop of Canterbury quoted the saying, 'teaching children is like engraving in stone', meaning that what is learned early is what sticks. It is therefore relevant to note that 33 per cent of all primary school teachers in England, and nearly one in five of all secondary school teachers, receive their teacher training in Church of England colleges. There are 4,470 Church of England primary schools – 80 per cent of the country's Church of England schools are primary schools. There are 2,300 Roman Catholic schools in England and Wales. In Scotland Catholic schools are wholly funded by the government. At time of writing there are sixteen 'faith-led' institutions of higher education (is this not an oxymoron?) in England and Wales, between them admitting over 100,000 students a year. (Most of these institutions are now called 'universities' according to the new definition of what counts as such, viz. that it has more than 4,000 students and awards 'degrees' – this latter word being a homonym of a term that used to denote something rather different in quality and status. If you think this a tendentious remark, consider the following fact: that 0.28 per cent of students who take the International Baccalaureate achieve the highest marks possible in that examination, whereas over 25 per cent of students who take A levels achieve three A grades. Something spectacularly fishy there; and the fishiness feeds all the way through the system into the newly described universities and the degrees they award.)

The facts about Church of England institutions of higher education are reported in the absorbing and troubling 'Christian Universities: A report into the Higher Education Institutions founded by the Church of England' prepared by Joe Gladstone for the National Secular Society. He tells us that in these institutions more than half the governing body is appointed by the church, that the Chancellor of each has to be a communicant member of the church, and that each has to have a Church of England chaplain. All the mission statements of these institutions make reference to their 'Christian foundation' and state their aim as 'service, worship and the serious study of Christianity'. Gladstone adds, 'All the institutions have committed to the "Engaging the Curriculum" project which has aimed to make available ideologies of Christian faith into subjects where there was none before.' And he further adds, quoting a Church of England publication entitled 'The Way Ahead' (2001, p. 67), 'Although there are many statements of inclusivity found in the universities' literature, they also make sure their chaplaincies *ensure that worshipping Christian communities lie at the heart of the colleges*, and that all institutions *offer a Christian influence to all staff and students*.' Apart from the intrinsic objectionability of religious skewing of education – and, to add deep insult to injury, education funded by the taxpayer at that – there is yet another concern: 'by [the church's] own admission the student intake [of the Anglican universities] has now broadened due to wider course choice so that *practising Christians [are] probably in the minority*' ('The Way Ahead', p. 68) – which means that the church is using a largely state-funded institution to proselytise people of other faiths and none into its own version of the creed.

Only imagine if the educational institutions were 'Conservative Party primary schools … Labour Party universities' for propagating the outlook and beliefs of each in the young. And what do we think about those madrassas that teach hate and jihad – not just in Pakistan, but here in our midst? If such are not acceptable, why is C of E or RC inculcation of religious superstition in three-year-olds more acceptable? Surely not because neither has ever burned anyone at the stake when they were in a position to do so.

Much more might be said. But two other quotations included in Gladstone's report should suffice: '*We consider it essential that all those appointed to senior positions in the colleges should be in sympathy with, and willing and able to support, the mission of the colleges as Christian institutions*' ('The Way Ahead', p. 70); and '*We would go further and so we recommend to the colleges that as a long term policy, the head of the teacher training should be a practicing Christian*' (ibid.).

Remember that all this Christian teacher training is aimed at Christian indoctrination of the young, not least the very young. Without indoctrination of the young religion would wither and die of its own implausibility. The religions – all of them – depend on recruitment by this means of capturing the minds of children. As a result of it you either have the person for life – Islam's grip is almost always totalising: its votaries are taught that abandoning the faith is a terrible crime, in not a few places punishable by death – or if they rebel for a time in adolescence it will only take divorce, a spell in prison, the death of a loved one, failure or illness, to make some reach for the comfort and support of the tales once told. Odd, isn't it, that someone in psychological need who was indoctrinated with Christianity in primary school rarely becomes a Zoroastrian or a worshipper of the Japanese Emperor (and so for the vice versa): which is proof, were it needed, that it is not the religion but the indoctrination which is at work.

Children should be taught about religion as a sociological and historical fact, and left to make up their own minds about the merits, such as they are, of each when they have reached maturity. That this simple and indisputable suggestion is anathema to the religions themselves speaks – shouts, screams – volumes about them and what they are doing. And we with our tax money are complicit in allowing them to get away with it.

'Many Faiths, One Truth'

There was in recent years an op-ed in the *New York Times* by the Dalai Lama, headlined 'Many Faiths, One Truth'. He is of course right: there are many faiths, and there is one truth: viz. that all the faiths are bunkum. We all like the Dalai Lama, who in this article iterates the claim that no one heeds, viz. that tolerance is required for a peaceful world – except that he does not extend that warm sentiment to the limit: 'Radical atheists issue blanket condemnations of those who hold to religious beliefs,' he laments, alongside mention of murderous inter-religious strife and religion-inspired mayhem – as if 'blanket condemnations' and mass murders were somehow on a par. Anyway: the point of mentioning this is to suggest that we never allow passage to the claim that the many faiths are all the same at bottom. Supporters of religion hope that repetition of the claim will make it seem true; in response we should endlessly iterate the obvious, and state it frankly on the tragic evidence of history and our own troubled times: that the various religions are mutually exclusive, mutually blaspheming, mutually hostile, bitterly and deeply divisive, and thus a rash of open sores in the flesh of humanity.

An equally questionable point in the Dalai Lama's article is that he calls Buddhism a 'religion', and indeed in the superstitious demon-ridden polytheistic Tibetan version of it that he leads, that is what it is. But original Buddhism is a philosophy, without gods or supernatural beings – all such explicitly rejected by Siddhartha Gautama in offering a quietist ethical teaching; but he has of course been subjected to the Brian's Sandal phenomenon in the usual way of time and the masses.

Religion and Public Service

Not long ago a Mr Andrew McClintock, Christian and ex-magistrate, appealed against an employment tribunal decision which went against him when he sought redress for having, as he claimed, been forced to resign from the magistracy because he was not granted exemption from sitting in hearings in which children might be given into the care of gay couples, something that offended his religious scruples. He wished to be allowed to keep his job and his prejudices simultaneously, and to be allowed not to comply with the law of the land, because the sexual morality of shepherds 3,000 years ago, keen on the increase of their flocks, made it taboo for sex ever to be about anything other than reproduction.

This principle resulted in the killing of Onan by God in the Book of Genesis (38: 9) for 'spilling his seed' instead of impregnating his brother's widow, and the Catholic Church's long-time view that rape is less bad than masturbation because it can result in pregnancy. It also resulted in the millennia-long oppression and persecution of gays, who were put to death by the devotees of a gentle and forgiving god, an oppression that Mr McClintock wished to keep alive.

Well: Mr McClintock did exactly the right thing by resigning. If his prejudices interfered with his responsibility to serve the law as one of its officers, he was evidently much better employed elsewhere. Think of a votary of any other religion allowing his personal beliefs to prevent him from carrying out his public duties in the UK: an orthodox Jewish fireman who would not carry a woman from a burning house because he is allowed to touch no other woman than his wife and daughters; a devout Muslim in a council education department refusing to let girls into a certain school because there are boys there, or working for an adoption agency and refusing to countenance applications from gay couples; a doctor who is refusing to help a woman at the scene of an accident for the same kind of scruples – odd how all the examples that spring most readily to mind involve prejudices about women and gays.

The point is an entirely general one. When individuals cannot allow their religious loyalties to be trumped by their public responsibilities, they should resign; the alternative is for the public domain to be invaded and disrupted by a Babel of claimed individual religious sensitivities, or even worse, by various religious organisations whose prejudices, taboos, anxieties and antipathies distort the overall public endeavour for a decent and equitable social order which is as inclusive as possible. The McClintock case is another powerful argument for saying: if you are serious about your religion, be consistent and honest and accept the consequences, as Mr McClintock rightly did by resigning. What he then did wrong (apart from allowing his life to be controlled by ancient religion and its prejudices) was to complain about the rest of us thinking that he did the right thing.

The Power of the Press and the Press of a Button

When in office President Sarkozy of France was contemptuous of the media. His treatment of it suggested that the French Fourth Estate in his time – and maybe still – is not what it was as a force in political and social affairs. Evidently Sarkozy felt no need to woo it, explain himself to it, or have it on his side: he treated it with disdain, as if it were irrelevant.

And perhaps it was then indeed becoming so, at least as regards the political process. There were two connected reasons for thinking this. One is the internet and in particular the twin phenomena it has created of blogging and interactivity, by the latter meaning the comment threads that accompany most op-ed pieces on media websites.

The other reason, in no small measure following from the first, is the loss of trust and credibility that the media have suffered in recent years.

There is much that is good, and something bad, about the effect that the internet has had in these respects. The good effect is the great democratisation of opinion and debate that the internet has enabled, and the way it has made the world porous to information. We might be living through an information honeymoon: how long before nervous governments begin to emulate China in policing the internet more vigorously and eventually castrating it? But at present much information gets arrowed around the world in fractions of a second, a lot of it such that someone somewhere would rather it were kept quiet. In these respects the internet is like the agora of old, except that everyone can attend and have a say.

The downside is the volume of rubbish, the anonymous viciousness and sneering, the *ad hominem* attacks, the paragraph-long pretensions to authoritativeness, the degrading of debate it encourages, making the internet what I've before now called the biggest toilet wall in history. Well: it takes a lot of compost to grow flowers, so we have to put up with this; and anyway, some things deserve trouncing with the gloves off, even if not everyone can tell the difference between justified and irresponsible versions of that process.

The media have always been a much weaker presence politically in the United States than in Britain and elsewhere in Europe. This is a function of the US's size, and the fact that although all newspapers and TV channels are local to constituencies of readers and viewers, in the US newspapers are mostly local to geographical regions too. Moreover whereas the broadcast media in Britain tend to take their cue on national (not on international) news and opinion from the print media, the sheer variety of media outlets of both kinds in the US makes the news and opinion landscape there considerably less uniform – except on the lowest common denominator material which focuses on celebrities, sports and spectacular murders. Only where there is a genuinely national press such as in Britain has it been able decisively to influence policy and elections – think Murdoch's *Sun* and its electorally damaging opposition to the Labour Party.

But if the power of the press is weakening in the way here surmised, is it a bad thing? It might be that a diminution of political influence can allow the more valuable functions of the Fourth Estate – which are to inform, to challenge, to explore and to debate – to emerge more strongly, for the reason that the cacophonic Babel of voices created by the internet makes the need for 'expert filters' all the greater, as forums where a degree of responsibility, reliability and accountability places positive constraints on the quality of content. If a media organisation gets it wrong in some respect, say by libelling someone, it can be brought to book. The anonymous insulters or liars on the internet are (in the literal sense of the term) irresponsible, and so there is no constraint on their output. This big difference will get bigger with time, as the geometrically increasing uptake of the agora-like potential of the internet progresses.

One can see the promise, and in fact already the presence, of a mutually positive relationship between the media and the blogosphere, chiefly in the latter's hawk-eyed challenge to the former. Columnists and leader writers once pontificated with the luxury of hearing no raspberries blowing back; individuals who disagreed might write a letter to the newspaper or the individual journalist, a practically silent protest with little effect. Now the entire world can know what responses a piece of journalism has evoked, and when it gets things wrong or is egregious in view or stupidity, it can be publicly castigated. This drastically diminishes the standing of the press, but can and should have the effect of making the press ever more careful. And that enhances its function, described above, of serving as a more reliable, better informed, clearer voice than most voices in the overall tumult of noise.

So whether or not the media are losing their political clout, one must hope that they will retain the better part of their purpose as just described. For however good it is that the sans-culottes are everywhere in today's versions of Alexandra Palace and Printing House Square, it would be a dismal thing indeed if they were the only occupants.

Irrationality, Immaturity, Braggadocio, Putin

One of the marks of irrationality is failure to profit from experience. One of the marks of immaturity is a knee-jerk desire to get one's own back even at the expense of harming oneself. One of the marks of braggadocio is posing in front of a phalanx of press photographers without a shirt on, brandishing a gun or something equally ithyphallic, such as a very large fishing rod. Join up all these dots and you get a picture of Russia's posturing, pouting, pectoral-flashing Mr Putin.

Mark one: Russia, despite violently denying self-determination to Chechnya, has encouraged and rewarded it in Abkhazia and South Ossetia, the break-away regions of Georgia, and has taken the Crimea from Ukraine and actively attempted to detach East Ukraine from the rest of that country. Not long ago, to the amusement and delight of observers, it appeared that little Tatarstan, the oil-rich region in the very heart of Russia, wished to become independent after the model of Abkhazia and South Ossetia. And no doubt other regions – including Chechnya again, when it has recovered from the pulverising Russia has given it – will begin to ask for the same courtesy that Mr Putin has extended to the former regions of Georgia.

Put this another way: Russia's efforts to weaken its neighbours and incrementally recover the empire lost upon the demise of the Soviet Union is proving to be its own undoing, because the more it nibbles at those neighbours by such means as it has used over Crimea and East Ukraine, the more it will encourage just such break-away movements from within and around itself.

So there is a lesson here: what you do can backfire. Now let us apply that lesson to Russia's aid to Iran to build a light-water reactor in Bushehr, capable of producing weapons-grade plutonium, and to train Iranian nuclear scientists in Moscow. This strengthening of ties was seen at the time by commentators as a Russian reaction (getting its own back; mark two) to US and Western support for Georgia. But (mark one again) 'what you do can backfire': Russia is helping Iran become a nuclear-weapons nation; Russia is helping a mullah-dominated state (perhaps forgetting its own Muslim populations – for example in Chechnya – who might wish to secede, and who might invoke the aid of co-religionist neighbours in doing so) to acquire nuclear weapons. Any chance that this might backfire too, literally as well as figuratively?

And now (mark three) as to braggadocio. Some, including Mr Putin, think it admirable that he ordered the invasion of Georgia while reclining at ease in his VIP seat in Beijing's Olympic stadium. He can ignore most of the international community's objections because he has his fingers on the taps of the pipes that send gas to Europe: if Europe gets too uppity he can turn his hand, and Europe will squeal. This though (back to mark one yet again) can backfire: his pipeline westwards transmits gas, but the invisible pipeline running in the opposite direction transmits money. If he turns off the gas, he thereby turns off the money; and like the Middle Eastern countries waxing fat and pursy on the money that the West lavishes on oil and gas, he is as drunk and dependent on the cash as Europe is on the energy.

Anyway, the point of mentioning all this is that in Putin's Russia we see the ballooning strength of yet another delinquent power. With China, Russia, religious fundamentalism, and the prospect of the Republicans' desired version of the US blundering around the crockery shop, most of the possibilities for our fragile world seem to be shattering ones.

But one forgets! – one is not allowed to criticise Russia in this way, because of the crimes and follies of the US and the West in invading countries and encouraging break-away states and doing what it can to annoy its enemies. That is, I forgot the principles of blogic (i.e. the logic of the blogosphere): that if the West does anything wrong, then no one who lives in the West can criticise anyone else.

Except – note this: Westerners can and do disagree with what their own governments do, and their investigative journalists can investigate and criticise without the risk of getting murdered as a result – unlike journalists in Mr Putin's Russia. In this little fact lies a big difference, relevant to deciding which side one would take if forced to take sides.

Spain and Rome

Those who are indifferent to, or sceptical about, the degree to which the churches still work to exercise political influence need only look at the unsubtle battle that the Catholic Church waged against the Spanish government when José Luis Zapatero was Prime Minister and instituted a bold reforming agenda to dilute church–state ties. His policies were aimed at ending direct government subsidy to the church, introducing same-sex civil unions, easing divorce laws, and encouraging greater participation and opportunities for women in Spain's society and economy. He also openly condemned the fascist

Franco regime and honoured those who had resisted it, something that beforehand was regarded in his country as too contentious and divisive to attempt.

None of this pleased the Catholic Church either in Spain itself or in the Vatican, showing by this (if showing were needed) the reactionary colouration of church politics. In a highly unsubtle gesture of opposition to Zapatero the Vatican conducted its largest ever mass beatification, honouring 498 pro-Franco 'victims of religious persecution' during the Spanish Civil War. Those victims were fascists and their church supporters, and included 7,000 members of the Catholic clergy killed between 1931 and 1939 in an uprising against the staggering oppression by church and state that had kept the population poor, benighted, ignorant, exploited and suffering.

Look at most Catholic countries until the 1960s and beyond, in South America and Ireland and Spain: the picture of the social, political and economic effects of Catholicism is in essentials the same. Women condemned to bearing large numbers of children, over-large families perpetuating poverty and ignorance, backward social policies and the iron grip of a clergy acting like the Stasi in controlling the minutiae of private lives through the confessional and the influence of fear – fear of hell, among other things. The small and in the end ineffectual 'liberation theology' rebellion among some South American clergy was quashed by the church, not interested in salvation for anyone in this life except for the church itself as an institution whose principal aim, like the Politburo of the Chinese Communist Party, was (and is?) to stay in control at any cost.

The savagery of 1930s anti-clericalism in Spain, with its deplorable murders and violence, is a mark of how bitterly clerical oppression was felt. Anti-clericalism had been running strongly in Catholic Europe ever since the Inquisition and Counter-Reformation, when it was the priests who did the murdering, and Spain was not the only example of an anger-prompted violent response to priestly oppression.

Some might think that murder *by* priests is worse than murder *of* priests because priests are most particularly not supposed to murder, and if murdered (in the right circumstances, that is; not in bed with their mistresses or – more usually of late – choirboys) can claim martyrdom. But obviously murder by anyone of anyone is wrong, and the Spanish revolution of the 1930s would have been better effected, *per impossibile*, without the mayhem. Anger towards the church explains but does not excuse the violence unleashed on it; from this perspective of history, the reason why the church provoked such violence is the significant point.

The immediate reason for the church's action in beatifying Franco fascists as a way of confronting Zapatero's liberal policies was that in Spain's schools that same year new civics courses were beginning, explaining and discussing the Spanish constitution and the rights of the citizen. Because of what the constitution accords to gay people and women, the church was bitterly opposed to it, and to children knowing about it. The nun who was the church's liaison to the education ministry in Madrid told the press that this new civics course was 'a frontal assault on the Catholic religion' and 'part of a clear persecution … of the Catholic faith'. One's response to her first complaint was 'good', and to the second, 'so: a bit of your own medicine; and salutary medicine at that – for everyone else'.

The Catholic right-wing in Spanish politics, with Vatican assistance, was determined to reverse the social gains that

Spain made under Zapatero's premiership. Their hopes were understandably high; by law the Catholic version of Christianity was still taught in Spain's schools (though this was to be a target for Zapatero reforms too) and the church remained a large presence in the country and its life. So the battle-lines were drawn, and one of the last major conflicts of the Counter-Reformation appeared ready to be played out there, as if in a corrida between the future and the past, freedom and oppression, sanity and superstition. The question is: who has won?

Superstition

It is both the glory and the tragedy of humanity that it never forgets anything. Like the layers of geological strata that go deep down into the earth beneath our feet, the beliefs and superstitions accumulated by humanity from its earliest infancy remain buried in all our minds, just like those geological layers. And because everyone's biography from childhood onwards is a kind of reprise of mankind's history, those early layers are vivid in childhood, and by their vividness leave a shadow on the mind thereafter. This is the source and explanation of superstition, including its organised form as religion.

The single most significant of those early geological layers of the mind is the belief that everything is animate – that is, is in some sense an agent, an actor: the rock that trips your foot, the tree that sways in the forest, are somehow conscious things with purposes or intentions that we instinctively feel might be malevolent. More so are the ghosts and demons that come out at night. This is the direct result of early man's effort to understand the world around him. He was conscious of his own agency; he picked up a stone and threw it, and was therefore the motive force behind the stone's flight. He projected from his own felt capacity as an agent to everything moving, growing, happening around him in the world, for – he thought – everything that happens must have a motive force behind it, a will or an intention, just like his own, even if he could not see the agency responsible for it.

He therefore explained the thunder as an invisible and mightier version of himself walking on the clouds. Lightning was a spear hurled by that being, in threat or punishment. The sound of the wind in the trees was whispering, the trees themselves observed him as he crept through the forest, and he might knock on their trunks to propitiate the spirits within. (We still knock on wood to avert bad luck.)

Every superstition has its origin in ancient tales and beliefs about the myriads of agencies swarming throughout nature, many of them antipathetic to humans and therefore in need of being placated by little rituals or invocations. We do not now see these superstitions as our earliest science and technology (science: explanation; technology: prayer, ritual) because the organised religions have swept up the powers of nature and removed them – first to the mountain tops, then outside space and time altogether, as education increased and better understandings of nature supervened.

One of the pleasantest feelings is getting rid of one's superstitions, by boldly ignoring them – go on: walk under that ladder, don't throw a pinch of spilled salt over your shoulder, step on the pavement's cracks. The resulting sense of liberation, of maturity, is a refreshment.

Are direct arguments against superstitions and – more importantly – religious beliefs likely to dissuade their votaries? The anecdotal evidence seems to suggest otherwise; robust full-frontal attacks by Richard Dawkins and Christopher Hitchens, it is said, only annoy the faithful and make them dig in further.

I am not so sure about this. In my personal experience waverers and Sunday-only observers can find forthright challenges to religious pretensions a relief and a liberation; it gives them the reason, sometimes the courage, to abandon those shreds of early-acquired religious habit that cling around their ankles and trip them up.

Still, Charles Darwin had a point in thinking that 'direct arguments against [religion] produce hardly any effect on the public, and freedom of thought is best promoted by the gradual illumination of men's minds which follows from the advance of science'.

The Advantages of Atheist Political Leaders

In our present uncomfortable climate of quarrels between religionists and secularists it would be a great advantage to everyone to have atheists in leading government positions. Here are the reasons why.

Atheist leaders are not going to think they are getting messages from Beyond telling them to go to war. They will not cloak themselves in supernaturalistic justifications, as Prime Minister Tony Blair and President George W. Bush came perilously close to doing when later talking about the decision to invade Iraq in 2003.

Atheist leaders will be sceptical about the claims of religious groups to be more important than other civil society organisations in doing good, getting public funds, meriting special privileges and exemptions from national laws, and having unelected seats in the legislature and legal protection from criticism, satire and challenge.

Atheist leaders are going to be more sceptical about inculcating sectarian beliefs into small children separated into publicly funded 'faith-based' schools, risking social divisiveness and possible future conflict. They will be readier to learn Northern Ireland's bleak lesson in this regard.

Atheist leaders will by definition be neutral between the different religious pressure groups in society, and will have no temptation not to be even-handed because of an allegiance to the outlook of just one of those groups.

Atheist leaders are more likely to take a literally down-to-earth view of the needs, interests and circumstances of people in the here and now, and will not be influenced by the belief that present sufferings and inequalities will be compensated in some posthumous dispensation. This is not a trivial point: for most of history those lower down the social ladder have been promised a perch at the top when dead, and kept quiet thereby; and the claim that in an imperfect world one's hopes are better fixed on the afterlife than on hopes of earthly paradise is official church doctrine.

Atheist leaders will not be tempted to think they are the messenger of any kind of Good News from above, or the agent of any Higher Purpose on earth. Or at very least, they will not think this literally.

If an atheist became prime minister in the UK, the prospect of disestablishment of the Church of England would come closer. This is a matter of importance, for two chief reasons. The first is that the Church of England's privileged position gives other religious groups too much incentive to try elbowing their way into getting similar privileges, such as the ear of ministers, tax exemptions, public funding for their own sect's faith schools, and the big prize of seats in the legislature.

Second, the C of E has far too big a footprint in the public domain, out of all proportion to the actual numbers it represents: just 2 per cent of the population go weekly to its churches. Yet it controls the primary school system – 80 per cent of C of E schools are primary – and a substantial proportion of the secondary school system, including academy schools. It is entitled to have twenty-six of its bishops sitting in the House of Lords, plus a number more who have been made life peers on retiring; and it has the automatic ear of government – do not suppose that if an Archbishop of Canterbury phones Number 10 he is told no one is at home.

Having a publicly atheist British prime minister would make it more likely that the functional secularity of British life and politics, the foregoing exceptions noted, would become actual secularity. 'Secularism' means that matters of public policy and government are not under the influence, still less control, of sectarian religious interests. The phrase 'separation of church and state' does not quite capture the sense in which a genuinely secular arrangement keeps religious voices on a par with all other non-governmental voices in the public square, and all the non-governmental players in the public square separate from the government itself. It means that churches and religious movements have to see themselves as civil society organisations exactly like trades unions, political parties, the Boy Scouts, and so on: with every right to exist, and to have their say, but as self-constituted interest groups no more entitled to a bigger share of the public pie of influence, privilege, tax handouts and legal exemptions than any other self-appointed interest group.

As things stand, religious groups get a slice of the pie vastly larger than their numbers or merits truly justify. The big advantage of an atheist prime minister or head of state would be that he or she would see that fact, and act accordingly. An atheist is not going to have the lingering sense that because someone has chosen to believe one or another ancient dogma, and put on funny clothes, he is to be respected and honoured, listened to, given the public's money to bring up other people's children in the same beliefs, and exempted from some of the laws of the land.

Religion is a matter of choice in that, unlike your race, age, gender or disability if you have one, you can change it or not have it at all. True, most people believe because they were made to believe as small children, and belief can be hard to shake off if your community threatens to reject you or in some cases even kill you for your apostasy. But it is still fundamentally voluntary. As such it should pay its own way and take its place in the queue along with all other voluntary things. That is something that an atheist political leader might say aloud, and we might all breathe a great deal more easily as a result.

Despite appearances, the world is not seeing a resurgence of religion, only a big turning-up of the volume of religious voices, which is happening in response to increasing secularism tired of the disruptions, obstructions and conflicts religion so often causes. Public acknowledgement of atheism by a senior politician would be just one more indicator of the fact that the tide is actually running in the opposite direction: and that would be a welcome and hopeful sign.

Hard-Wired for God?

Recently I had occasion to debate – if the sound-bite culture of radio news permits that description – with a member of Oxford University's Centre for Anthropology and Mind, on the 'findings' of its Cognition, Religion and Theology Project, to the effect that children are hard-wired to believe in a 'supreme being'. The research is funded by the Templeton Foundation, an organisation keen to find, or to insert, religion into science and to promote belief in their compatibility – which, note, comes down to spending money on 'showing' in the end that the beliefs of ancient goatherds are as good as modern physics.

The Centre for Anthropology and Mind says on its website, 'Why is belief in supernatural beings so common? Because of the design of human minds. Human minds, under normal developmental conditions, have a strong receptivity to belief in gods, in the afterlife, in moral absolutes, and in other ideas commonly associated with "religion" … In a real sense, religiousness is the natural state of affairs. Unbelief is relatively unusual and unnatural.'

That children have an innate tendency when small to interpret what happens in the world as the outcome of purposive agency is indisputable. I, an atheist funded by no organisation but keen on promoting atheism, agree with the Centre on this. Children's earliest experiences are of purposive agency in the adults and other people around them – these being the entities of most interest to them in their first months – and for good evolutionary reasons they are extremely credulous, not only believing that things must be acting as their parents do in being self-moving and intentional, but also believing in tooth fairies, Father Christmas, and a host of other things beside, in almost all of which they give up believing before puberty, unless the beliefs are socially reinforced – as with religious and, to a lesser extent, certain other superstitious beliefs. Intellectual maturation is the process in important part of weaning oneself from the assumption that trees and shadows behave as they do for the same reason that one's parents, other humans, and dogs and cats do; it is every bit as natural a fact about children that they cease to apply intentionalistic explanations to everything as that they give them to everything, on the model of their parents' behaviour, in the earliest phases of development.

But the Templeton-funded proponents of religion's innateness go very much further: they infer from the first half of these unexceptionable facts that children are hard-wired to believe in a Supreme Being. Not only does this ignore the evidence from developmental psychology about the second stage of cognitive maturation, but it is in itself a very big – and obviously hopeful – jump. Moreover it ignores the fact that large tracts of humankind (the Chinese for a numerous example) have no beliefs in a Supreme Being, innate or learned, and that most primitive religion is animistic, a simple extension of the agency-imputing explanation which gives each tree its dryad and each stream its nymph.

The Centre claims that children are hard-wired to believe that nature is designed. This it infers, apparently, from asking small children such questions as 'why is this stone pointed?' It does not seem to have occurred to them that the semantics of 'why' questions is such that they demand an explanation in terms of reasons or causes in response – the language game is constrained to that pattern: 'why is/did?' prompts an automatic 'because' – and that even small children know that 'just because it is' does not count as satisfactory. So of course, from the limited resources they have in which reasons are vastly more familiar than causes (the causes that natural science most fully discerns by investigation), they come up with what they know the questioner wishes to hear – an explanation – but in the absence of knowing very much about causes, they give it in intentionalistic terms. A small child might know why something might be made sharp, and for what sort of purpose, but not as readily how it might become so, especially if it is a natural object. All that this shows, therefore, is that the question was ineptly framed, not that the Centre and the Templeton Foundation has proved that religious belief is innate.

'Religious belief' and early childhood interpretations of how the world works are so far removed from one another that only a preconceived desire to interpret the latter in terms of 'intelligent design' and 'a Supreme Being' – the very terms are a giveaway – is obviously tendentious, and this is what is going on here. It would merely be very poor stuff if that was all there is to it; but there is more. The Templeton Foundation is rich; it offers a very large money prize – a bribe? – to any scientist or philosopher who will say things friendly to religion, and it supports 'research' as described above into anything that will add credibility and respectability to religion. Its website portrays its aims as serious and objective, but in truth it is just another example of how well funded and well organised some religious lobbies are – a common phenomenon in the United States in particular, and now infecting the body politic in the UK too.

But the Templeton Foundation would do better to be frank about its propagandistic intentions, for while it tries to dress itself in the lineaments of objectivity it will always face the accusation of tainting the pool, as with the work of this Oxford University institute.

Indeed one might question the advisability of Oxford University taking funds from the Templeton Foundation for this or any kind of work unless it were transparently in support of the cause of religion. My alma mater might be the home of lost causes, but this cause deserves to be lost.

The Prophetess

When Ayn Rand addressed a meeting of her publisher's sales staff shortly before the appearance of *Atlas Shrugged* in 1957, one of the salesmen asked her to summarise her philosophy while standing, as Rabbi Hillel had done to explain the Torah, on one leg. She did so: 'Metaphysics: objective reality. Epistemology: reason. Ethics: self-interest. Politics: capitalism.' Anne Heller tells us that the sales staff applauded, and so have many others since. Ayn Rand's books between them regularly sell half a million copies a year, and her influence has reached high places: egregious examples of her fans are Ronald Reagan and former US Federal Reserve chairman Alan Greenspan. The latter belonged for many years to her inner circle, and wrote articles for her newsletter *The Objectivist*. Her influence continues; actress Charlize Theron is said to have planned a television mini-series of *Atlas Shrugged*, and there is an Ayn Rand Institute which promotes her ideas and books and offers courses on her philosophy.

On the Ayn Rand Institute's website there is a video of its heroine being interviewed. In it her emphatic, confident, heavily accented phrases roll unhesitatingly off her tongue in perfect prose (few people, *pace* Molière, speak in prose), and her interviewer appears too overwhelmed to challenge anything she says. In the interview she gives another encapsulation of her ideas: her philosophy, she says, is based on 'the concept of man as an heroic being, with his own happiness as the moral purpose of his life, with productive achievement as his noblest activity, and reason as his only absolute'. She always used the word 'man' in speaking of the egoistic, self-assertive, independent hero who was her ideal – Howard Roark in *The Fountainhead*, John Galt in *Atlas Shrugged* – and correlatively held that it is women's work to worship the masterful hero, even to submit with pleasure (as in *The Fountainhead*) to being raped by him.

Many find attractive the idea of individualistic self-interest coupled with disdain for anyone who cannot assert himself likewise. Those who embrace such views find it easy to accept their corollaries, which are that the only morally acceptable social and political system is free-market capitalism, and that individual self-interest positively outlaws altruism. 'Do not confuse altruism with kindness, good will or respect for the rights of others,' Rand wrote. 'The issue is whether you do or do not have the right to exist without giving [a beggar] a dime.'

She attacked those who located the basis of rights in need rather than achievement; for her this was to stand both reason and morality on their heads. She saw promotion of individualism and opposition to collectivism as the only legitimate morality, not only in politics 'but within a man's soul'. This, she wrote in her notebooks, defined the theme of *The Fountainhead*, the story of the morally autistic architect-hero Howard Roark's struggle with lesser human beings.

The close identification of these ideas with Ayn Rand's name shows how intimately her life and thought were one thing. Biographies of her confirm what one surmises from her novels and essays themselves: that she was a brilliant but repulsive person, who inveighed against tyranny but was a tyrant, and who demanded loyalty from the disciples of her philosophy of individualism and independence, oblivious to the stark paradox involved. The members of her inner circle called themselves 'the Collective' as a joke; some of them came to realise too late just how ironic the label was, for Rand in effect organised her devotees into a cult from whose teachings any deviation – least of all into the individual independence she vaunted – was regarded as an unforgivable crime.

Indeed the microcosm of the Randian cult was a reprise of every historical example of actual or would-be revolutions that have devoured their own, most notably in the case of her standard bearer in the high years of her fame, Nathaniel Branden. At first every bit as tough and tyrannical in the cause of Rand's ideas as Rand herself, and moreover Rand's lover though considerably younger than she, Branden was the activist and exponent who turned Rand from a novelist-prophet into a designer label, a phenomenon and a force. He had been at her side for nineteen years, ever since he was a young college student. But he crashed from favour when he no longer wished to have sex with her after falling in love with a beautiful young woman who had, in Rand's view anyway, neither the intellect nor the spirit required to match Randian ideals. When Rand discovered Branden's 'betrayal' she exploded into a jealous fury, anathematising him as completely and violently as any Congregation of the Inquisition equipped with bell, book and candle. In the *Objectivist* magazine, which Branden had started on her behalf, Rand wrote that he (and his former wife Barbara) were no longer associated with the magazine, with her, or with her work and thought, and that she repudiated them 'totally and permanently as spokesmen for me or for Objectivism'.

As the Branden affair shows, Rand's life was indeed exemplary of her thought. It was, in line with her avowed principles, an entirely selfish life, to which she sacrificed her family, her good-natured husband Frank O'Connor, her friends, and all but the last of her devoted followers, Leonard Peikoff. Whoever was not wholly with her was against her. This too was in line with her philosophy, only this time not with its principles but its character: it was black-and-white, without nuance or flexibility, harsh, angry and simplistic. Its appearance of unyielding logic was employed as a smokescreen for absence of compassion and kindness, for the inability or refusal to accept that most people cannot be Roarks and Galts through no fault of their own, and that therefore an educated generosity of sentiment can and should figure among the premises of our choices and the actions that flow from them. Such a thought would have seemed to her too disgusting to contemplate; which in the view of anyone with a shred of social conscience makes her thought too disgusting to contemplate in return.

Rand's beliefs emerged from her early experiences. Born Alissa Zinovievna Rosenbaum to middle-class parents in Saint Petersburg, Russia in 1905, she lived through the revolutions of 1917 (she supported Kerensky and the Mensheviks) and the subsequent eight years of Bolshevik hardship before getting a visa to visit America, where she had relatives. She never returned to Russia, but changed her name to Ayn (rhymes with 'wine') Rand, and began a career on the margins of the Hollywood movie industry. Ascending from wardrobe worker to bit-part screenwriter to playwright to novelist she developed her very considerable talents to a pitch of genius, which resulted in her first major triumph, *The Fountainhead*, published in 1943. It was made into a film in 1949, based largely on her own screenplay for it, but she quickly became dissatisfied with it.

The reputation that the novel earned for her made her a significant enough figure to be called to testify before the House Un-American Activities Committee in Washington concerning communism in Hollywood. It also initiated the gathering of supporters and admirers who became the slave army of her cult.

Rand's principal work is *Atlas Shrugged*, which tells the story of John Galt, a businessman who, irritated by regulations that impede his getting rich, goes off in a huff to a secret valley, taking many of the business community with him. Without them the world collapses and its tiresome little lesser men, the collective-minded wishy-washy liberals, come running to ask them back. (This is scarcely a caricature of the book.) Rand devoted many years to its composition, and her devotees believed, as she did, that it would revolutionise the world. But on publication it met with a storm of critical abuse. One critic described it as a nightmare, another as the 'howl' of a harpy, a third as a 'display of grotesque eccentricity' that one could not find 'outside an insane asylum'. As Rand's sales figures permanently testify, readers did not share the critics' views. But the almost uniformly hostile critical reception plunged Rand into a deep depression, and she never wrote fiction again.

Still, Rand's growing celebrity – much abetted by Branden's indefatigable marketing of her and her ideas – made her an iconic figure from the 1960s onwards. Students at universities gave her standing ovations, and some professors – most of the rest were dismissive of her – rallied to her too. She was given an honorary doctorate, and appeared on prestigious television interview programmes. Decades later her books were still being cited in polls of American readers as among the most influential they had read, in one case placing *Atlas Shrugged* second only to the Bible in a list of the most important books of the twentieth century.

I can testify personally to her influence during the heady decade of the 1960s. As a high school junior I had a friendship with a woman some years older than myself, who was a student at a local teachers' college. She and her peers were avid followers of Rand, and I count myself the happy beneficiary of a sentimental education that was, presumably, a by-product of the young lady's Randian self-interest. Despite her efforts at proselytising me into Rand's tenets I did not succumb; I was, as all youth should be, on the Left, and too far so to find Rand's ideas other than appalling.

What is wrong with Rand's views is what is wrong with Gordon Gekko. The unregulated market coupled with unbridled individual self-interest adds up to something far from heroic in the would-be Roark/Galt mode; instead it adds up to the strong trampling the weak, to the callousness of the jungle – and eventually to a mightily ironic paradox, which is that the weak have to rescue the strong because the latter's unrestricted rampaging has consumed their own hunting-grounds. Only look at the moneymen of autumn 2008, who because of their reckless gambling with other people's money, in a market deregulated by Rand's epigones, had to be bailed out by the sacrifice of the small guy losing his job and his home, and that small guy's tax dollars funding the gargantuan bail-out that rescued the oh-so-heroic Galts of the financial markets.

Life is Rand's refutation. Unless you are prepared to embrace the brutal view that you care nothing about the inequalities and injustices which make the many start their race far behind the few, you cannot see the world as a place where the individual must stand alone or starve to death. The impulse that makes a woman comfort her crying infant generalises into the impulse most people have to help someone who trips and falls, or is stricken by grief, or is starving. And that impulse is educable into one that sees the need for food aid to starving populations, and human rights campaigns on behalf of prisoners in secret policemen's cellars in tyrannous countries. It is not one jot admirable that Rand did not grasp this, or refused to.

The philosopher Sidney Hook reviewed Rand's non-fiction account of her Objectivist philosophy, *For the New Intellectual* (which Gore Vidal in another review described as 'nearly perfect in its immorality') thus: 'I am confident that even at some danger to herself, Miss Rand would not rush out of a burning building and leave a helpless child behind.' He argued that she was wrong to think free minds could not exist without free markets, and that it had to be ignorance or wilfulness not to recognise that capitalism had created many evils, such as (for just one of a million examples) child labour in Victorian Britain.

Hook also pointed out that Rand misunderstood a philosopher she claimed to admire, namely Aristotle; and one should add that she also grossly misunderstood a philosopher she claimed to despise, namely Kant. These are illustrations of what Hook meant when he remarked that 'although a writer need not be a professional philosopher to write an interesting book about philosophy, substituting indignation for analysis was not the way to do it.'

Rand's novels are melodramatic – they are somewhat like circumstantial film treatments with long speeches inserted – and the ideas in them are simplistic, but (as I rediscovered on re-reading the two major ones lately) they are powerful page-turners, with much that is striking in them. One should regret the overweening sense of importance Rand encouraged some architects to acquire, to the detriment of too many urban landscapes, and the deformed morality of greed and selfishness she extolled, of the type that resulted in millions losing their jobs in the recent financier-induced recession; but it ought to be possible to recognise the merits of her novels while disagreeing with the line they seek to sell. She had enormous talents, great charisma, courage and dedication – all as apparent in her work as in her life, and all acknowledged by biographers – and not all of her ideas were wrong: her secularism merits applause, as does her opposition to the use of force in world affairs, and as does her championing of liberty – or rather, this latter might merit applause if it were not in fact a coarse and callous libertarianism merely, which means liberty only for the few strong enough to trample on the heads of the rest.

Ayn Rand wore a gold dollar sign as a brooch on her lapel. At her funeral in 1982 – she died aged seventy-seven – a six-foot-high floral dollar sign was placed by her open coffin. Alan Greenspan stood nearby. She once said that death would not be the end of her but of the world. She was right that it was not the end of her; she lives on in her legacy and influence, and in her book sales. But Rand was wrong about the end of the world; it endures too, more than ever in need of something more humane and constructive than the crude brass egoism of her philosophy.

The New Puritanism

If you have ever been in a car driven by someone who alternates repeatedly between accelerator and brake, making you jerk along, you will appreciate how change occurs in our society's moral attitudes.

To illustrate the point about oscillating uncomfortably back and forth between liberal and moralistic periods, consider the last two centuries. The Victorian era of prudery and (therefore) hypocrisy followed the unbuttoned Regency age. It was followed in its turn, after the catastrophe of the First World War, by the party mood of the Roaring Twenties. The interruption of another war led, by contrast, to a decade of dreariness in the 1950s, marked by social constraint and a savage police crackdown on homosexuals, one consequence of which was the suicide of the mathematical genius Alan Turing.

But any revival of puritanism invites a backlash by more liberal and open-minded people, chiefly the young, who do not want to be told what they can and cannot do by finger-wagging nay-sayers. The reaction to the closed atmosphere of post-Second World War Britain was the 1960s, an epoch of triumphantly claimed liberty, which of course the moralisers blame for everything they consider to have gone wrong since.

The truth is that what actually happens during moralistic periods is virtually the same as what goes on in more liberal times; what differs is the lack of openness about people's behaviour and the hidden nature of any harmful consequences. In moralistic periods, sin, crime and vice get pushed so far under the carpet that moralisers, believing (rather as children do) that what they cannot see does not exist, feel great self-satisfaction. The honesty of more liberal times, and the fact that everyone can then see harm when it occurs, affronts the moralisers; and they hasten to force it back into darkness.

Take drugs as an example. The sale and use of opium and its derivative heroin, and of cocaine and marijuana, were made illegal in the course of the first three decades of the twentieth century, first in an effort to stop the troops in the First World War trenches using them, and then in an effort to stop anyone else doing so. Until then drugs were legal, and could be bought at any pharmacy. The first laws relating to narcotics were passed in the 1860s to regulate their sale, giving pharmacies a monopoly. This had the useful effect of ensuring that drugs were of a reasonably safe standard. Society did not collapse because of them, and at the time people used opium (in the form of laudanum) for their headaches.

The moralistic Victorian-originated prohibition movement that sought to ban drink and all forms of intoxicants had its greatest triumph in 1920s America. A whole nation was criminalised, a vast criminal industry sprang up and the police found themselves at war with machine-gun-carrying mafiosi. When the ban on alcohol was lifted the prohibition of other drugs remained, and with it a continuing industry for the crime gangs. By pushing drugs underground, the effective management of society's use of that other dangerous drug – alcohol – could not be applied: the results are evident today.

Tabloid prurience about sex has always been with us, but the note of hysteria in reports about the romps of footballers, politicians and celebrities always threatens to push moralism up a notch or two. Sex has ever inflamed the sensibilities of moralisers; proponents of contraception in the nineteenth century were regarded as monsters, and if they tried to publish contraceptive advice they were sent to prison for obscenity. Books depicting sex were prosecuted until the Lady Chatterley trial of 1960. The onset of the Aids epidemic was a hook for another wave of moralising against gay people and sex workers. Now it is 'trafficking'.

To kidnap, trick, force into any kind of work, whether it is slaving in a sweat-shop or sexual services, is a serious crime and should be punished. There are laws against any kind of coercion and slavery, and in the case of forced sex work the rape laws apply also. So 'trafficking', if it means people-smuggling under false pretences into another country to be coerced into any kind of industry against someone's will, is a horror and deserves the full application of the laws that already exist to deal with it.

But 'trafficking' has been defined to mean much more than this, and it has been conceptually entangled with sex work to the exclusion of all else. For example: homosexuality is punitively treated in Poland, a Roman Catholic country, and many gay men have therefore emigrated to live in more liberal places. Some of those who come to Britain take work in the gay sex industry. If a friend has given them accommodation while they look for a home, or arranged a meeting with someone who can give them work, they have officially therefore been 'trafficked'. Their clients and friends have become criminals, and the police have yet more work to do.

Let us suppose a genuinely kidnapped or tricked woman is forced into sex work, in a country where her clients are criminalised for having any dealings with her. Her clients and her pimps are for that reason going to make it vastly harder for her to be found or helped; she will be deeper in the undergrowth precisely because of the greater risks that now attend her servitude. Such is the effect of criminalisation.

Politicians in England and Scotland, perhaps having reached that middle-aged point defined as happening when narrow waists and broad minds change places, have elected to follow the punitive prohibitionist line of Sweden and Norway in relation to the sex trade. They would have done far better to look at the example of New Zealand, which has moved in the other direction, with liberal laws giving sex workers greater protection, better access to health and welfare services, and which go some way towards removing the moralising stigma that erects a barrier between sex workers and the rest of society. Official and unofficial reviews of the New Zealand approach have consistently praised its benefits. Almost every public opinion poll in the UK shows majorities of people in favour of the same kind of liberal common sense. It is the political class which, on the basis not of good research, humane principles and mature attitudes, but of personal prejudice and moralism, or (more commonly still) fear of the tabloid press, pushes matters in the opposite direction.

There are undoubtedly people in sex work who are there unwillingly, because of debts, drugs or the malign persuasions of pimps. These people need to be helped. Making them more invisible does not benefit them. To the disbelief of moralisers, however, there are also people in the sex industry who are there willingly, and who prefer it to other kinds of work. What happens between them and clients – between consenting adults, where the interaction observes the same standards of acceptable behaviour between any people anywhere – is their business and theirs alone. Poking the interfering fingers of law into their private choices is worse than unjustifiable; it is wrong.

This is the expression of a general principle. The law has no place in the private lives of consenting grown-ups, whether they are playing Scrabble or having sex, and whether they are doing the latter for cash or for the long-term project of building a home and a family together. When the cycles of moral fashion swing back towards prohibition, criminalisation and the interference of law in private lives, and when this results in Canute-like efforts to stop people doing, seeing or being something that the moralisers themselves happen not to like, and which makes them wish to stop everyone else doing, seeing or being it, they need to be challenged – challenged on the facts, and urged to keep a level head. Alas, when it comes to sex and drugs, there seem to be few level heads around to deal with them sensibly.

The Global Financial Crisis

One reason for the global economic meltdown that began in 2008 – so we are told – is that bankers did not understand the complicated financial instruments they had created; they did not know what they were packaging and trading. When they finally grasped that they had invented large quantities of toxic nonsense, they froze: mistrusting each other because they knew they were untrustworthy themselves, they refused each other and everyone else credit, and the world teetered on the brink. We the taxpayers bailed them out, and they are now back at their work again, rescued at others' expense, almost as if they had learned nothing – indeed almost as if nothing bad had happened.

So: if the bankers themselves did not know what they were doing, if they could not distinguish between securitised bad debt and tax aid so long as either keeps them in bonuses, to whom should we look for an explanation of what happened, what it says about the state of capitalism, and what should be done to put it right?

To whom else but Joseph E. Stiglitz, the Nobel laureate professor at Columbia Business School, former Chief Economist at the World Bank, former Chairman of the President's Council of Economic Advisors at the White House, and the man asked by the United Nations to chair a panel of experts on the global meltdown's causes.

The answer Stiglitz gives to 'what went wrong' in *Freefall: Free Markets and the Sinking of the Global Economy* (2010) is, in sum, that the meltdown was caused by a combination of greedy bankers, deregulation of the financial markets and cheap money. Between them they created a bubble, in which vastly over-valued real estate funded unsustainable levels of consumption in the US. When (and the procession of outsize adjectives has to continue) huge financial institutions with huge bad debts found themselves slipping over the edge into *de facto* bankruptcy in 2008 as a result, the rest of the world went with them.

Stiglitz's warnings about the dangers implicit in under-regulated financial markets are on public record, and they were there for any number of years before the crash happened in 2008. At the 2007 World Economic Forum in Davos, when continuing world-wide growth seemed to rebut his Cassandra-like prognostications, he warned that the delay in the crash's arrival only meant that it would be bigger when it came. Within months he had been proved right.

His scepticism towards the piety that markets do better if left unregulated is not only vindicated beyond peradventure by the meltdown, but should have been shared by others. The evidence was clear for all to see: there have been 125 financial crises in various countries around the world since 1970 – that is, in the era of growing deregulation mania – whereas in the quarter-century after 1945 economies were stable and flourished under sensible regulatory regimes adopted in response to the 1929 crash. With the debacle of 2008 as the capstone, these facts illustrate once and for all that the biggest single flaw in recent economic orthodoxy is the mantric belief that regulation interferes with the supposed innate self-adjusting wisdom of markets.

Regulation of financial markets is needed, Stiglitz argues, for the obvious reason that they are so intertwined with the rest of the economy that any misbehaviour in them is guaranteed to drag everything else (the 'externalities') into trouble. 'The bankers gave no thought to how dangerous some of the financial instruments were to the rest of us,' Stiglitz writes. 'The current failure has affected everyone: millions of homeowners have lost their homes, and millions more have seen the equity in their homes disappear; whole communities have been devastated; taxpayers have had to pick up the tab for the losses of the banks; and workers have lost their jobs. The costs have been borne [all] around the world, by billions.'

In his *Freefall* Stiglitz describes the rescue of the banks by the taxpayer as 'the Great American Robbery'. He is withering in his attack both on the financial institutions and on the rescue packages provided to them by the Bush and Obama administrations alike. Together the packages amount to 80 per cent of US GDP, around $12 trillion: the sheer size is flabbergasting. Government acted as a garbage can for the banks' rubbish; it gave the banks zero-interest loans that the banks then re-lent at interest or gambled with; bankers and bank shareholders were rescued, but not individual homeowners and workers; and to add insult to injury, the government 'provided that money', Stiglitz writes, 'in non-transparent ways – perhaps because it didn't want the public to be fully aware of the gifts that were being given, perhaps because many of those responsible were ex-bankers and non-transparency was their way of doing business'. In part this last scornful remark alludes to the methods by which bankers hid bad debts in order to keep the rating agencies gold-plating the risky instruments they created, and in part to the general ethos of private greed that caused public disaster.

Early on Stiglitz alludes to the distorting bonus-incentive culture of Wall Street as attracting 'more than its fair share of the ethically challenged'; here he points out the magnificent irony of government refusing to regulate as it massively bailed out the banking system, on the grounds that doing so 'would interfere with the workings of a free market economy'. The only thing free about an economy in which banks are bailed out by taxpayers, is the ride given to the bankers.

Stiglitz's disappointment, in particular, with President Obama's failure to improve on President Bush's efforts turns on the unfulfilled expectation that a Democratic administration would look first to the little guys being thrown out of their homes and jobs. Instead, by continuing with bank bail-outs rather than giving help to borrowers and employees, Obama's government engaged in 'privatizing gains and socialising losses'.

The examination Stiglitz subjects the crisis to is frank and unsparing, and he is not shy about naming names where he feels it is appropriate: Tim Geithner and Larry Summers, Obama's top economics men, come in for as much criticism as Alan Greenspan for the role he played during the Bush years. But the book is not all explanation and attribution of culpability. It also strongly argues a case for what should be done next. Foremost among the proposals is a fully global and transparent system of financial regulation that tackles such big problems as the incentive schemes which lead to undue risk-taking, gambling and short-termism, and the question whether the world can continue to afford too-big-to-fail financial institutions.

Although the G-20 as a collective body, and governments individually, have so far done too little to address these questions, says Stiglitz, doing so will eventually prove inevitable. 'September 15, 2008, the date that Lehman

Brothers collapsed, may be to market fundamentalism (the notion that unfettered markets, all by themselves, can ensure economic prosperity and growth) what the fall of the Berlin Wall was to communism. The problems with the ideology were known before that date, but afterward no one could really defend it.'

Market fundamentalism never served the poor well; now it has threatened hundreds of millions more with poverty, and cost the world economy dear. In Stiglitz's emphatic view a small adjustment to the system is not the answer. So far all that has happened, he says, is that to keep things from getting worse 'we called in the plumbers who installed the plumbing' (and they have 'overcharged us for the repair'). This does not seem to augur well for sufficiently radical reform; but it is surely – and sorely – needed. Moreover it must include breaking up the too-big-to-fail banks, curbing excesses of leverage, curbing outsized bonuses rewarding outsized risk, and putting an end to 'over-the-counter derivatives'.

There has been a rash of books since the crisis began, but Stiglitz's book has the most distinguished author, the clearest prose, and the most authoritative and uncompromising take on matters. Everything he says is leavened by an admirable concern for the ordinary men and women who are the true victims of the bankers' greed and unaccountability, and the lack of protection afforded them by regulation. The fact that Stiglitz has for years been warning that the free-for-all financial system was heading for trouble adds weight and value to all he says. If one had to choose a single must-read about the great economic crisis of our times, this is it.

Climate Change

When discussions of climate change dominate the news, the question of how to minimise its dangers takes centre stage. There is widespread consensus that because the scale of the problem is so great, the remedies have to be likewise: production of greenhouse gases by industry, agriculture and transport, and the destruction of forests, have to be tackled on a world-wide scale. At least – there is widespread consensus among those who accept that climate change is being caused by human activity. By far the majority of responsible scientists are among their number. But their warnings and advice are being undermined by climate change sceptics.

The sceptics' main concern is that if there is no global warming, or if global warming is not 'anthropogenic', then the efforts made to mitigate its supposed effects would not just be a waste of time but – worse from their point of view – a waste of money. Their chief aim is to avoid the inconvenience and expense of taking climate change seriously.

Some quite influential and respectable people are climate sceptics; but their stance is questionable for two reasons. First, the overwhelming weight of scientific opinion is against them, and second, even if the dangers are overstated, it is still prudent to do everything sensible to mitigate possible effects. Sometimes the sceptics seem to be trying to will the problem away, sometimes they seem unconscious that they might merely be offloading the problem onto future generations to save themselves bother. If the latter, it would be a moral scandal of the first water.

Only concerted international action by governments can really deal with the problem. But what about individuals? Can changes in habits at the individual level make a difference? It is argued that individual efforts to be 'green' would contribute no more than a tiny bit to any solution. That is probably true; but they would not be nugatory. At very least they would embody a collective will to make a difference – and expressions of collective will can be effective in persuading governments to do better.

The practicalities of individual green awareness come down to one thing: restraint. That is not a comfortable term for those used to the high-octane (in all senses) lifestyle that consumes at a fast rate and measures success by that rating – the size of house, the number of cars and foreign holidays, the wattage of the lifestyle. Part of the deficit represented by such a manner of living – living to consume lots rather than consuming enough to live well – is said by the philosophers of restraint to be that people lose touch with valuable simplicities. This is a teaching (a preaching?) that sits especially badly with the bling-encrusted high-roller flashing his wad in the back of a limo. All that Thoreau and Emerson high-mindedness, all that loincloth piety – so they say – is the solace that have-nots give themselves because they have not.

Yet the sad truth is that if the big consumers refuse to rein back a little, everyone who survives the coming climate crunch will have to accept the teaching of restraint willy-nilly. And no one likes having to learn forced lessons.

The Force of Nature

Earthquakes and tsunamis remind us of something we are very quick to forget when the news switches to other subjects: that the earth is a theatre of immensely powerful forces always at work around us. Some of those forces are the opposite of catastrophic. For example, as spring approaches in our tranquil islands, millions of birds are building nests, billions of buds are opening on twigs, tons of sap are rising in trees, together constituting a vast wave of change over the country. This is benign, and welcome; far different are the forces of nature which are just as normal and commonplace, but inimical to mankind.

From the devastating tsunami-prompting earthquake that happened off Japan's coast, thousands of times more powerful than the one that not long before caused so many tragic deaths in New Zealand, have come many video images of what an earthquake and tsunami are actually like as they happen. The images are horrendous: the irresistible power of the tsunami sweeping everything before it, the violence of the quake beforehand, the reactions of people as they realised that this was not just another medium-sized event of the kind that Japan is used to, all brought the horror home.

From the planet's point of view, however, the events were just part of the natural round. Consider: the Himalayas, the world's highest mountains, are getting higher all the time at about the rate our fingernails grow. This is because the surface of our planet is a mosaic of gigantic geological plates always in motion. Look at a map of the Atlantic Ocean with Africa to the east and South America to the west, and you see how the two continents once fitted together. The Himalayas are formed by the Indian plate pushing underneath the Asian plate, lifting it up, the great mountains with it.

The same is true of the Andes in South America; here likewise the movement of plates is lifting the mountains. And incidentally, as this happens so more islands form in the Galapagos archipelago, as volcanic activity released by plate movement boils up through the sea and solidifies into new islands.

The Pacific rim is the most active of the earth's earthquake regions. From New Zealand to Japan and round to California earthquakes are frequent and sometimes huge. And yet millions of people choose to live along these fault lines, demonstrating that great and fatal human ability to know but at the same ignore the fact that they live in mortal danger of nature's stupendous powers.

For this is the uncomfortable truth, from the human point of view: that our knowledge of the world and our skill at controlling and utilising so much of it, impressive as both are, remains puny compared to what nature can do. We have little defence not just against earthquake and tsunami but against volcano, flood, lightning, drought, plague, and extremes of cold and heat, when these occur beyond the limits of our competence to deal with them. We live from day to day with the comfort-inducing falsehood that the normal state of affairs is a quiet planet, orderly and predictable. But only think of the natural disasters of recent decades that have killed so many and destroyed so much: Tianjin, San Francisco, Chobe, Thailand, Sri Lanka, Sichuan, Christchurch, and again Japan. Even the aftershocks in the latest Japanese earthquake are bigger than most of those mentioned.

The thought of how an earthquake happens, with millions of tons of rock jarring against each other underground as the earth's crust splits and moves, is terrifying from our tiny human perspective, but an ordinary phenomenon for the planet. If a meteor crashed into our planet, as meteors continually crash into planets and moons all the time in our galaxy, it would be catastrophic for the tiny creatures crawling about the planet's surface, but just another day at the office for nature.

It is this difference of scale which makes the phrase 'force of nature' so ominous to human sensibility. We ignore nature's benign forces – those tons of sap rising in the trees all round us – but we also and more foolishly ignore the all too frequently proved fact that the earth can open and swallow all that clings precariously to its surface, or that the sea can heave thirty feet into the air and sweep across the land, blindly indifferent to what lies in its path.

Of course there is no choice but to accept the puniness of mankind in comparison to nature. But it remains a puzzle why millions of us build our homes along known major fault lines, and insist on hoping that when the big one happens, it will be when we are not there.

CONSTRUCTIONS
and
CREATIONS

The Public Intellectual

If it was once said that the word 'intellectual' made despisers of the term reach for a gun, the term 'public intellectual' assuredly makes them reach for two guns. To critics the term connotes the cheap and easy option of pontification, of commentary without responsibility, rather like the luxury enjoyed by a political party in opposition – the luxury of having to move nothing but your lips.

To those who, on the other hand, see the importance of a lively public conversation about all that presses, it is Emerson's idea that recommends itself: the idea of individuals who are acquainted with both history and the history of ideas, who can take from them insights of relevance to the present, and who can effectively communicate new ideas and insights as a result.

Without people who are alert and engaged, who are eager to debate, and who have some expertise to offer from their studies or experience, the public conversation would be a meagre thing. What such people offer is exactly what the public conversation needs: ideas, perspectives, criticism and commentary. What anyone who offers them should expect in return is robust examination of what they offer. Whether ideas come to be accepted or rejected, everyone gains by having them discussed.

There is no bar to anyone's being a public intellectual other than having nothing to say. One thing this implies is that public intellectuals are, generally speaking, a self-selected group; they are those who step voluntarily forward, as enfranchised citizens of ancient Athens once did in the agora, to make a point. The internet has thrown open the possibilities of such self-selection, with some commentators becoming known for the incisiveness and good sense of their comments on discussion threads and blogs. Despite the fact that most of what appears on threads and blogs is anonymous ranting and vituperation, the democracy of the web has proved its worth, reviving the agora on the grand scale.

Some public intellectuals have a committed political stance. Others, siding with Edward Said's view that the aim of the public intellectual is to 'advance freedom and knowledge', try resolutely to occupy neutral ground. Of the two stances, the latter is hardest to maintain, and least plausible to outside view. Can anyone really be detached enough, emotionally uncommitted enough, unmoved enough by the injustices, follies, mistakes and depredations committed in the world, to rise above them to true dispassion? Arguably, engaged intellectuals have grist to their mills, whereas those who claim to be disinterested (not of course uninterested) lay themselves open to charges either of fundamental indifference to the things that matter to the rest of us, often urgently so, or concealment of a purpose they hope to gain through its unobviousness.

There is a danger in the fact that people who are publicly salient as a result of major contributions in some special field – in science or literature, say – come to be regarded as oracles on every other subject too. There are fields of endeavour which lend themselves to generalism – politics and journalism especially – where the essence of the task is to take a broader view, factoring in considerations from a range of subject matters. But anyone whose self-election as a public intellectual is accepted by the public, and whose initial claim is based on achievement in a specialism, needs to be alert to the risk of only seeing things through its lens. (As it is said: if your only tool is a hammer, every problem looks like a nail.) For the basis of the public intellectual role is the possession of informed and considered views about many things that integrates them and offers to make sense of them. It is about breadth of interest and application to it of a worked-out perspective.

Can one give a catch-all definition of 'public intellectual'? Consider this list: Bertrand Russell, Albert Einstein, Edmund Wilson, Lionel Trilling, Stephen Jay Gould, Norman Mailer, Susan Sontag, Noam Chomsky, Richard Dawkins, Christopher Hitchens; they have very little in common other than their intelligence and engagement, and the fact that they have spoken out. Those three things, accordingly, might be taken to capture the essence.

Whether the utterances of members of this heterogeneous group make a difference, large or small, is a matter of history rather than judgement, but it would be very surprising if in at least some cases they did not, because ideas are the cogs of history, and drive its changes forward. Isaiah Berlin wrote that the philosopher sitting in his study might alter the course of events fifty years after his time – he had Locke and Marx in mind, two paradigms of public intellectuals – and there is much truth in that, if the word 'philosopher' is given (as it should be) its widest application, perhaps as the appropriate substitute for the term 'public intellectual' itself.

Wisdom, Mind and Brain

I s there such a thing as wisdom – a thing, stuff, an abstract entity – or are there only wise individuals and wise actions and attitudes, these latter not exclusively the possession of the individuals in question given that even fools can sometimes be wise?

This question is a significant one, because it bears on the enterprise of 'wisdom studies', a parallel endeavour to the 'happiness studies' now big in the neuropsychologically-informed social sciences. (And there too the question has to be: is there such a thing as happiness, or only happy individuals and happy times and experiences, the latter not the exclusive property of the individuals in question, given that even the gloomiest of us can occasionally be happy?) If you aim to study wisdom, or happiness, presumably in the hope of finding out how we can all be wiser and happier, you had better be clear about the object of study; not an easy thing to do, given the vagueness of the concepts at issue.

First there is the problem of defining wisdom. This is where the opening question bites. If the word 'wisdom' is one of those nouns that misleads us into looking for an abstract entity (like 'redness' if such a thing is supposed to exist independently of individual red surfaces: the medieval Realists followed Plato in taking such a view, to the justified amusement of their opponents the Nominalists), then the whole enterprise has started on the wrong foot.

In *Wisdom: From Philosophy to Neuroscience*, Stephen S. Hall gives a first and avowedly tentative attempt at a definition as follows: 'Many definitions of wisdom converge on recurrent and common elements: humility, patience, and a clear-eyed, dispassionate view of human nature and the human predicament, as well as emotional resilience, an ability to cope with adversity, and an almost existential acknowledgement of ambiguity and the limitations of knowledge.' Note that this is not a definition of an abstract thing called 'wisdom' but a sketch of the personality characteristics of what one might consider a typically wise individual. Given that context makes the same action wise in one setting and foolish in another, one needs to know more to distinguish patience from passivity, dispassion from fence-sitting, emotional resilience from insensitivity, and so for the rest. Generalities are fine: social scientific investigation needs to get to particulars. The definition just suggested does not get near the particulars.

It would seem natural to inspect the biographies and personalities of individuals conventionally held to be wise. How does one decide who to regard as such? A questionnaire to members of the general public yielded predictably conventional nominations save for a couple of weird surprises: Gandhi, Confucius, Jesus Christ, Socrates, Mother Teresa, Solomon, the Buddha, the Pope, Oprah Winfrey, Winston Churchill, Nelson Mandela, Ann Landers, Queen Elizabeth II (all mentioned by Stephen Hall). In my view a sturdy case can be made for just one of these as an exemplar of wisdom: Gautama Buddha. A couple of the others were smart, which is a different thing, and they did a wise thing or two as a result of being so; but that is not enough to make them wise as such. (As to which if any of them were good: well, that is a question for a different time, and the answer is by no means straightforward.) As both this and the first attempt at a definition show, the business of getting started on examining wisdom is very fraught: as the countryman said on being asked the route to a distant town, 'Well, I wouldn't begin from here.'

One big problem that infects the social scientific, and especially neuroscientific, study of diffuse and vaguely specified phenomena such as wisdom and happiness is that much of what happens in such study results in expensive and polysyllabic confirmation of what common sense and received wisdom long ago knew. For example: the Stoics of antiquity were strongly in favour of something that was old hat even in their own day, namely, emphasising the importance of managing one's emotions by thinking about why one feels them and what the consequences of their unconstrained expression might be. By being reflective and considered, said the Stoics, one can attain 'ataraxia', which means 'peace of mind' or emotional stability.

Now read the above-quoted Hall again: 'even-keeled … "emotionally resilient" [people] apparently use their pre-frontal cortex, the front part of the brain, which governs reasoning and executive control, to damp down activity in the amygdala, those twin almond-shaped regions deep in the brain that process emotional content.' Actually this is not merely a restatement of the Stoic view, but it goes further in attempting to give the impression of high science by mentioning a couple of brain structures whose inner complexity and functioning are as yet understood only in the crudest and most approximate terms. This use of modern anatomical terminology does not disguise the ancient – and vague – insight in question.

A good deal else of what neuropsychology says has this character – for example, that being optimistic is good for health, that older people are wiser than younger people because their awareness of the approach of life's end detaches them from distractions and trivialities – all obvious, all attributed to brain function, but with the same helpfulness as directing someone to a particular street address in London by pointing at a postage-stamp-sized map of London and saying 'there'.

The repetition of such insights in long technical words and after massively expensive fMRI brain scanning is not, though, entirely without point. Leaving aside the necessary sceptical doubts about what fMRI actually shows – correlations mainly, which is not the same thing as causal explanation; and most fMRI work is done on tiny samples of (usually) college students, the 'lab rats' of this new discipline – the fact is that confirmation of received wisdom is by itself a gain.

And sometimes research on commonplace assumptions can overturn the latter: solitaries in old people's homes were once assumed to be in some kind of trouble because they were not engaging fully with others; it turns out they are often the more alert and intelligent ones, who are solitary by choice because they dislike the imposed conformity of life in an old age home. That is just one example: others, of perhaps greater significance still, concern our beliefs about free will and decision making; I return to this point.

First, though, one must point to another and quite general difficulty with contemporary research in the social sciences and neurosciences, namely, a pervasive mistake about the nature of mind. Here is a truth that neuropsychology appears entirely to overlook: *minds are not brains.* Please note that I do not intend anything non-materialistic by this remark; there are only brains, and minds are not some ethereal spiritual stuff *à la* Descartes. What I mean is that minds are the result of the social interaction between brains. As essentially social animals, humans are nodes in complex networks from which their mental lives derive most of their content. A single mind is, accordingly, the result of interaction between many brains, and this is not something that shows up on an fMRI scan. The historical, social, educational and philosophical dimensions of the constitution of individual character and sensibility are vastly more than the electrochemistry of brain matter by itself.

Neuroscience is an exciting and fascinating endeavour which is teaching us a great deal about brains and the way some aspects of mind are instantiated in them, but by definition it cannot teach us everything of what we would like to know about minds and mental life.

I think the Yale psychologist Paul Bloom put his finger on the nub of the issue in a recent number of *Nature* (No. 464, 25 March 2010, p. 490) where he comments on neuropsychological investigation into the related matter of morality. Neuroscience is pushing us in the direction of saying that our moral sentiments are hard-wired, rooted in basic reactions of disgust and pleasure. Bloom questions this by the simple expedient of reminding us that morality changes. He points out that 'contemporary readers of *Nature*, for example, have different beliefs about the rights of women, racial minorities and homosexuals compared with readers in the late 1800s, and different intuitions about the morality of practices such as slavery, child labour and the abuse of animals for public entertainment. Rational deliberation and debate have played a large part in this development.' As Bloom notes, widening circles of contacts with other people and societies through a globalising world plays a part in this, but it is not the whole story: for example, we give our money and blood to help strangers on the other side of the world. 'What is missing, I believe,' says Bloom, and I agree with him, 'is an understanding of the role of deliberate persuasion.' Contemporary psychology, and especially neuropsychology, ignores this huge dimension of the debate not through inattention but because it falls well outside its scope. This is another facet of the point that mind is a social entity, of which it does not too far strain sense to say that any individual mind is the product of a community of brains.

This thought poses challenges for the neuropsychological enterprise. Brain-scanning evidence sometimes does the reverse of confirming old common sense, by cumulatively suggesting that free will, the nature of decision-making in circumstances of uncertainty, and what has to happen so that we can override our natural impulse for immediate rewards in order to reap greater gains later, is not what we commonly assume. For example, fMRI scans suggest that decisions and choices are made quite some time (seconds are eternities in neurology) before we are ourselves conscious of them. This research focuses on simple time-defined choices, and it records brain activity assumed to constitute the decision before the subject reports the decision himself. Leave aside the fact that there are questions about what this research really shows, and note that no fMRI scan is going to track correlations and time-delays in brain activity associated with thinking about a marriage proposal or which college to apply to. Put this together with the thought that mind is more than brain, and the scale of the task in understanding one desirable feature of mental life – the making of wise choices, the possession of wise attitudes – becomes yet more apparent.

The complexity of understanding brains and minds – and the wisdom exemplified by some of the latter – does not entail that questions about these topics are permanently unanswerable; rather, the endeavour itself forces us to think afresh about what questions we are asking and what phenomena we are investigating. If I were to say (as I am inclined to) that the wisdom of an individual consists in maturity, intelligence ('there is no method but to be intelligent' said T. S. Eliot) and self-possession (understood as resistance to blandishments from without and overweening appetites within), this would seem to indicate that wisdom relates to character and behaviour in a social setting, and that we are therefore more likely to learn about it from literature, history and philosophy than from other sources. This is not to downplay the importance of the new neurologically informed social sciences, which are highly promising; but it is to insist that our enquiries into them need to connect with other studies, and that some of these latter might still merit taking the lead even though the former now have superb new machines to aid them.

Neurophilosophy

As the previous shows, the development of neuroscientific tools for investigating real-time brain functioning brings interesting new dimensions to the study of mind. Questions about the relation of mental states to brain states, not least in respect of subjectivity, consciousness and representation, have been central to the philosophy of mind ever since dualism and non-materialist monisms (various idealisms and 'neutral monism') were rejected as serious possibilities. But a raft of further questions – about morality, intention, free will, selfhood, rationality, and philosophical aspects of learning, memory and emotion – have also become amenable to investigation with the greater empirical depth offered by functional magnetic resonance imaging (fMRI).

Accordingly we have a promising combination of neuroscience, psychology and philosophy giving rise to a new field of enquiry with a new name: neurophilosophy. The armchair speculations of traditional philosophical enquiry here yield place to something with a more solid basis and some surprising and suggestive findings already to hand. Even before fMRI studies on decision and volition began to suggest that these are pre-conscious processes, we knew that people whose brain hemispheres had been separated by commissurotomy seemed to have two sometimes competing centres of selfhood; and studies of brain chemistry have provided insights into the nature of mental disturbance, emotion and social bonding.

It is however not to be either sceptical or critical of this project to say that a sense of proportion has to be kept regarding its philosophical promise. For when one thinks about persons, their characters, what they know and believe, the frameworks of concepts that organise their view of the world and their attitudes and responses to it, and the way they give weight to competing reasons for action, the neurophilosophical approach is only part of the story, because in principle it cannot be the whole story. The reason is given in the previous essay: minds are more than brains, not in the sense of being some sort of ghostly stuff, but in the sense of being the result of the brain's interactions and relationships with other minds and the surrounding world.

In other words minds have to be understood 'broadly' as opposed to 'narrowly', in the same sense that we speak of 'broad content' and 'narrow content' in relation to mental content generally, as when we say that individuating referential thoughts *necessarily* involves mention of the referents of the thoughts; thus, to individuate the thought of a chair from the thought of a book necessitates reference to the physical chair and the physical book outside the thinker's head.

In saying that the character and content of one's mind is the result of its interaction with its social and physical setting, one is saying that any individual mind is accordingly the product of a community of minds and of input from the world. It develops by continuous feedback in interaction with parents, teachers, the community and the physical environment. Therefore to identify what a person knows and believes, and to describe how he thinks, is to see him as a node in a complex of relationships with other minds and a manifold of accompanying external stimuli. The point might illustratively be put by saying that a mind is the product of many brains in interaction; that externally caused excitations – many of them from other brains – of some subset of sensory surfaces (fingertip dendrites, rods and cones, taste buds, ear drums) are necessary conditions for mental life, to which ineliminable reference must be made in explaining mental content. In short, mind is brain plugged into two kinds of environment, social and physical, and a brain not thus plugged in is not the seat of a mind.

These considerations do not seem to have been given full weight even in the preliminary indications that fMRI gives us about the nature of volition, decision, the place of emotion in reasoning, and like matters of philosophical significance. For example: experiments which suggest that decisions are reached some time (split seconds are aeons in neurological terms) before a subject is aware of having made a decision, take the form of choosing which button to press after receiving a given stimulus. Such decisions are a far cry from deciding where to invest one's savings or whether to accept a certain job offer. Likewise, the suggestion that moral responses are hard-wired and amygdala-based fails to take into account the way moral attitudes change in individuals and societies over time and as a result of discussion and information.

Again: this is not to call neuropsychology and neuro-philosophy into question; it is merely a reminder that questions about mind are not exhaustible by investigation of the brain; there is here still work for philosophy, without a prefixed 'neuro', to do.

The Brain and History

There is something magnificent about the ambition of Iain McGilchrist's *The Master and his Emissary: The Divided Brain and the Making of the Western World* (2009). It offers nothing less than an account of human nature and Western civilisation as outcomes of the competition between the human brain's asymmetrical halves. All the way through there is a single recurrent theme like a drumbeat, a theme McGilchrist thinks we urgently need to understand and do something about. It is that once we understand the structure and function of the brain, we see that the wrong half of it is in charge of our civilisation.

Thus baldly described, the endeavour doubtless seems implausible at least. And alas, for all its erudition and ambition, it is. The chief reason is that far too much is made to turn on a far too suppositious and slender basis, this latter being the current state of knowledge in brain science. Although a great deal of intensely interesting work has been done and is being done in brain science, with volumes of knowledge and insight accruing from the application of amazing technologies and brilliantly designed experimental work which together make this one of the most exciting and rapidly evolving areas of science – and McGilchrist tells us about it in fascinating and lucid detail – nevertheless it simply does not permit such claims as that 'the right hemisphere underpins our sense of justice', 'only the right hemisphere understands metaphor', 'the left hemisphere closes most routes to reality', and the overarching claim for which McGilchrist argues, namely, that the narrow, fragmenting, thing-based, mechanical, overly self-confident, black-and-white, unempathetic, even zombie-like left hemisphere is dominating our civilisation to its cost.

As this characterisation of the left hemisphere implies, the right hemisphere is McGilchrist's favourite. Chapter after chapter is devoted to explaining and exploring the contrast between the two hemispheres, a contrast which McGilchrist finds in the experimental work, by far chiefly to the right hemisphere's credit. This hemisphere, he claims, is more in touch with reality and life; it is global and integrating in its activity, creating a holistic view of the world; it recognises individuals, and is the seat of most forms of attention; it is the home of emotion and therefore of empathy and its offspring morality. To it belong music, art, religion and social connectedness. It is, or should be, the master hemisphere, but its quondam servant, the left hemisphere, whose job should be the instrumental and subordinate one of focusing on details and applying rational calculation when needed, has usurped it – principally because the left hemisphere's chief interest, says McGilchrist, is power: it wants to divide and rule, and by underpinning the emergence of the analytic philosophy, science and bureaucratic organisation of the Western world in the last half dozen centuries, has succeeded in doing so.

And as this further implies, McGilchrist wishes us to return to a right-hemispheric way of being. That means getting in renewed touch with our emotional and empathic sides, and allowing instinct and religion back onto centre stage. He thinks that modern art is an example of the left hemisphere's attrition of the values that the right hemisphere would prefer us to live by, including the beautiful art of the past, the legends and myths, the metaphors and larger openness of feeling and belief – the inclusive and numinous vaguenesses, one might say – that characterised life in most of our civilisation's earlier history.

On reading McGilchrist's prescription for reasserting the right hemisphere's influence on our lives I found myself, no doubt because I am quite considerably a left-hemispheric creature, shuddering. At the end of his book he gives a detailed picture of what an entirely left-hemispheric world would be like, an unappetising portrait of a kind of utilitarian, even emotionally fascist, wasteland which is as narrow as it is bleak and desiccated. He does not offer a right-hemispheric world portrait, but he obviously intends us to assume that it would be a much gentler and happier place, more realistic and more connected with others and with nature. Unfortunately, if one accepts the logic of his argument that our Western civilisation has declined from a right-hemisphere to a left-hemisphere dispensation, we do not have to imagine what the former would be like, because history itself tells us: in it most of us would be superstitious and ignorant peasants working a strip-farm that we never leave from cradle to grave, under the thumb of slightly more left-hemispheric bullies in the form of the local baron and the priest.

I do not mean to caricature McGilchrist's argument, but it does really come down to no more than the claim that the left hemisphere of the human brain has become damagingly over-powerful in the affairs of Western civilisation. His argument might have been framed in quite different terms, closer to the standard counter-Enlightenment tropes that promote the authority of emotion, art, religion, ethnic feeling and the like (including *das Volk*, the Fatherland, blood, the gods, the glorious past ... we are altogether too familiar with such objects of invocation) over the supposed reductive barrenness of reason. But oddly, McGilchrist is not anti-reason or anti-science – far from it: his book is an exercise in applying both by the bucketload – and he is at pains to insist that human life needs both the brain's hemispheres, and that both are anyway engaged in all aspects of mental life. Early in the book he insists that claims to the effect that the left hemisphere is the specific home of language and logic while the right hemisphere is the specific home of spatial ability and emotion are mere popular misconceptions. But then he proceeds to go much further than these popular misconceptions in assigning whole rafts of highly complex functions and capacities to one side of the head or the other, building the pictures just sketched of the two different worlds that the respective hemispheres generate for us, with the radically different value implications of each.

The fact is that the findings of brain science are nowhere near yet fine-grained enough to support the large psychological and cultural conclusions McGilchrist draws from them. His argument does not persuade one that returning our Western civilisation to the government of such supposed right hemisphere possessions as religion and instinct would be anywhere near a good thing.

The Triumph of Science

Is science and its successes somehow inimical to the quest of the arts and humanities to uncover 'the secret of man'? Is science taking the poetry from human experience, and substituting for it the dry austerity of equations? Is science an enemy to the meaning of human life, and its possibilities, because it reduces it to an object of study in laboratory terms? In what follows I offer not just negative answers to these questions, but a reason for thinking that science is a coadjutor, even an exemplification, of the artistic and humanistic quest itself.

At an ever-increasing rate since the seventeenth century in the Western world, and latterly in the world as a whole, the natural and social sciences have been transforming both the daily lives and the self-image of humankind in dramatic and irreversible ways. For some – those who are invested in traditional, and often typically religious, views of the nature and destiny of man – this indubitable historical fact is not a matter of celebration. Even some of those who have a secular and generally modernising outlook are alarmed by what they see as the reductive tendency of science, reductivism at its worst being the propensity 'to see nothing in the pearl but the disease of the oyster'.

These fears are misplaced. The truth is that in revealing much of great value about the world and humankind, science invites a transformed and imaginative response in those aspects of humanity's conversation with itself that science does not pretend to address. These aspects are art, literature and the humanities, which between them explore human relationships and experience as they are perceived from the perspective that most deeply and revealingly captures them – namely, the intensely subjective perspective which gives them their fullest meaning in our lives. It is love and friendship, creative play and artistic expression, learning, literature, the quest for philosophical insight, the building of institutions that enhance our ethical possibilities, that matter in all the most thoughtful and constructive human endeavours. To them science is neither a threat nor an alternative, but a component and an adjunct.

It really matters that one should see that this is so, and that there is no conflict of interest in the pursuits that lie under the encompassing labels 'science' and 'humanities'. There are two areas of natural science, and one of social science, that are most relevant in penetrating to the heart of humankind's self-image and self-understanding in a way that causes concern to the traditionalists anxious about their effect. They are biology, cosmology and psychology. It is largely ignorance concerning the content and aims of these sciences that generates anxiety in traditionalists, who in rightly thinking that poetry and subjectivity are the true sources of the understanding we seek, are fearful that these sciences will displace and corrode their effect. A note on each of these exemplary sciences is therefore instructive. I believe that once we understand their content and purposes, the notion of a conflict between them and what matters to us in the humanities will be recognised as mistaken. Let us take each in turn.

Biology is the science of life. It is arguably the most important of the sciences for the question in hand, in the sense that some of its subdivisions and offshoots – not least genetics, the theory of evolution, and sociobiology and evolutionary psychology – are at the frontier of changes in medical technologies and practices, and in human self-awareness, developments which unquestionably present new ethical and social challenges.

Biology has a wide remit, reflecting the variety and complexity of all the many forms of life that exist. Its deepest unifying concept is *evolution*, without which – so it has been rightly said – nothing in any of its domains of enquiry makes sense.

The roots of biology lie in the pursuit of what was once called 'natural history', which received its first organisation as an enquiry in the work of Aristotle (384–322 BCE) and his successor Theophrastus (died 287 BCE). They engaged in direct observation in both zoology and botany, and were arguably the first to introduce systematicity into taxonomy, which is the classification of plants and animals into rational arrangements by similarity of form and other criteria.

A second source of biological science was medicine, not just as a result of enquiry into human anatomy and physiology as first systematically conducted by Hippocrates (born 460 BCE) and Galen (c.130–200 CE), but in the collection and examination of plants which had come to be recognised as having medicinal properties. Because of this, and because of the practical knowledge gained in thousands of years of agriculture, botany was an advanced science even before Carl Linnaeus (1707–78) undertook his work of classification in the eighteenth century. Indeed, detailed herbals existed in medieval times, and nearly three-quarters of today's modern pharmacopeia is derived from substances known to herbal or traditional medicine.

But it is with Zacharias Janssen in the seventeenth century and Linnaeus in the eighteenth century that modern biology properly began. The invention of the microscope by Janssen and its continuing improvement was essential to progress in the study of cells (cytology) and tissues (histology), which in turn laid the foundation for biology's rapid advances thereafter – most particularly in embryology, heredity, and therefore evolutionary theory itself.

Among the twentieth century's many advances in biology, including the identification of viruses and the first application to evolutionary theory of genetics (Gregor Mendel's discovery of genes in the nineteenth century was only fully appreciated in 1905), the undoubted chief was the identification of the structure of DNA by Rosalind Franklin, Maurice Wilkins, Francis Crick and James Watson in 1953.

The revolutionary impact of DNA's discovery was profound. In less than half a century it resulted in the mapping of the human genome, and with it wonderful prospects for great advances in medicine and a cornucopia of knowledge besides, including better and further-reaching understanding of humankind's history.

The sheer scale and speed of advances in biology explain the nature of debates in our time over questions of biodiversity and the environment, in bioethics generally but not least in medical ethics, and in sociobiology and evolutionary psychology as accounts of the nature of humankind.

These last are perhaps the main concern of those who fear that science threatens to erode traditional understandings of humanity. This is because they explicitly concern the place of human nature in nature. Charles Darwin's discoveries firmly placed humankind in the natural world, thus causing immense shock to his contemporaries, almost all of whom accepted the previous and long-prevailing orthodoxy that humanity is a divine and therefore special creation inserted into the world, of an order different from all other life in it, this other life having been provided by a deity for humanity's convenience and pleasure.

The fear and dismay generated by so reductive-seeming a finding that human beings are apes took a variety of forms. Whereas the physiological similarities between people and apes were sufficient to make the latter a symbol of the degenerate and beastly side of the former, the connection for a while was made almost entirely in the imaginative resource of film (think *King Kong*, *Planet of the Apes*) and lurid magazine stories. At first the evidence from palaeoanthropology, whose serious beginnings lie in the nineteenth-century discovery of Neanderthal Man, fed the ape-man myth.

But following recognition of the close relationship between humans and other primates in so many respects – resulting for example from ethological observation of chimpanzee tool-use, familial bonding and tribal warfare – genetics has revealed that today's higher primate species have a common ancestor in the recent evolutionary past (a mere 5 million years in the case of chimpanzees and humans), and so many commonalities persist that it has become impossible not to accept that study of non-human primates yields much insight into our human selves. Chimpanzees and humans have 98.4 per cent of their genes in common.

The word 'sociobiology' was coined in 1975 by Edward O. Wilson, who described it as a 'new synthesis' of biology, sociology, ethology, anthropology, population genetics and other associated disciplines. Its premise is that animal behaviour has been selected under evolutionary pressures to enhance reproductive success. As applied to monkeys, sheep and the like, the idea is illuminating. As applied to human beings it is controversial, because its critics see it as premising genetic determinism, which overlooks the vastly powerful influence of culture and intelligence in shaping human behaviour in all its intricacies.

Sociobiology's critics especially dislike the implication that if certain patterns of behaviour are genetically determined, we cannot do anything about them. Consider male aggression, which might often enhance male reproductive success (by fighting off rivals, and by frequent rape, say). If this behaviour is hard-wired, does it mean that we are helplessly unable to do anything about it? Surely sociobiology cannot mean to suggest that because a given form of behaviour is 'natural' it is good?

Critics of sociobiology – among them Richard Lewontin and Stephen Jay Gould – say that the right reaction to it is to keep insisting that humanity is special because of its intelligence and its concomitant creation of culture, which they have an easy time describing as a far more significant prompt of our intricate behaviours than mere appeal to reproductive success.

It is obvious, in turn, why sociobiologists find reductive explanations in terms of reproductive success so plausible. Right across the mammalian world mothers are zealously and instinctively protective of their offspring, with culture and intelligence having nothing to do with it. Some sociobiologists claim that among their critics' motivations is a 'politically correct' distrust of anything that seems to imply a deterministic basis for differences between races and the sexes, for example in such respects as intelligence. In opposing this implication, sociobiology's critics point out that 85 per cent of all genetic variation among humans exists within populations, that historical and cultural factors are largely responsible for community differences in 'intelligence' as 'measured' by IQ tests, and likewise for inequalities and hierarchies in human societies and for many alleged male and female differences.

But what threat is really posed to human self-understanding by what biology teaches us about humanity's place in nature? One striking thought that undercuts any anxiety in this regard is that historical and cultural factors are themselves evolutionary adaptations of humankind. In place of fur and claws, sharp teeth or feathered wings, humans have evolved self-reflexive consciousness and high levels of intelligence, which allow us to invent many different and elaborate strategies for interacting successfully with the environments we encounter. Even if the most fundamental drive in humanity really is a genetic imperative to reproduce in such a way as to maximise the number of copies of our genes in following generations, and even if in all creatures other than humans the result of this imperative is a relatively inflexible repertoire of behaviours (chimpanzees do not write symphonies and construct scientific laboratories as part of theirs), it does not follow that sociobiological explanation is misleading in the human case. On the contrary, it seems to offer deep insights into aspects of the creative variety of human behaviour, and into human nature itself.

The naturalists of bygone times with their butterfly nets could not have imagined how controversial and exciting these descendants of their pursuit would be – until Darwin came along. To most of them, nature seemed to give testimony to the creative activity of a wise and bountiful deity. Accordingly, to them Darwin's ideas appeared as a blasphemy. Yet when they reflected on the evidence of their own eyes they could not fail to see what a challenge Darwinism posed to the tidy certainties of previous thinking. A poignant account of the conflict between the old and new biology occurs in Edmund Gosse's *Father and Son*, a memoir of his father Philip Gosse, who attempted to oppose Darwinian views with a creationist account of nature in which all the biological and geological phenomena cited by Darwin were explained as having been laid down, just as they appear, in the six days of creation. He was ridiculed in the press (jokes were made about God having concealed fossils in rocks to tempt scientists to infidelity), so he exiled himself from London and its scientific community. His son says that he sincerely believed that his book opposing Darwin, *Omphalos*, would show how Genesis is consistent with the fossil record; its comprehensive failure to do so settled matters on the eastern side of the Atlantic, but has yet to do so on the western side, where creationism and its disguised version as 'Intelligent Design Theory' still persist.

These remarks are intended to show that biological science has not refuted the view that there are large areas of our thought about humankind and its experience which remain the domain of art and the humanities. Instead, biology and its express application to an improved understanding of human nature *via* sociobiology are supplements, not alternatives, in this quest.

What, now, of cosmology? Before the sixteenth century the orthodox view was that our planet, and we on it, sat at the centre of creation. Astronomy, and in particular cosmogony and cosmology – the studies respectively of the origins and nature of the universe – have had an immense effect in changing human self-perception. Where once we were the apex of the universal creation, and at the centre of things, now we are inhabitants of a small planet orbiting an average star in an outer arm of one of many billions of galaxies. That is a remarkable change of perspective.

The 'Big Bang' theory is the best-known account of the origin of the universe, though in the evolution of cosmological debate it is undergoing major revisions even as these words are written. A summary of it, bringing together the idea of an expanding universe with influential ideas about how the first moment of that expansion occurred, offer a picture in which the universe came into existence about 13 billion years ago in a 'singularity' which, from an initial immensely rapid size 'inflation' in the first infinitesimal fractions of a second of its history, set the universe on a course which has resulted in its present character.

The origin of the Big Bang theory lies in the observation made by astronomer Edwin Hubble (1889–1953) that the universe is expanding. He saw that in every direction one looks in the sky, every galaxy is travelling away from us, and that the rate at which they are receding is proportional to their distance from us (Hubble's Law): the further away they are, the faster they are going. This implies that at earlier points in the universe's history everything was closer together; running the clock back eventually gives us everything compacted at a starting point. Proponents of the then-rival 'Steady State' theory which says that the universe exists eternally, with matter spontaneously coming into existence in the vacuum of space, sarcastically described this first moment of the universe's existence as a 'Big Bang'. As often happens with names that begin as criticisms, it stuck.

At the very beginning of the universe's history, says the Big Bang theory, what had a moment before been a vacuum was an enormously hot plasma which, as it cooled at about 10^{-43}

seconds into its history, came to consist of near-equal numbers of matter and antimatter particles annihilating each other as they collided. Because of an asymmetry in favour of matter over antimatter, initially to the order of about one part per billion, the dominance of the former over the latter increased as the universe matured, so that matter particles could interact and decay in the way our current theories describe. As the initial 'quark soup' cooled to about 3,000 billion degrees Kelvin a 'phase transition' led to the formation of the heavy particles (protons and neutrons) and then the lighter particles (photons, electrons and neutrinos). A more familiar example of a 'phase transition' is the transformation of water into ice when the temperature of the water reaches zero degrees Celsius.

Between one and three minutes into the universe's history the formation of hydrogen and helium began, these being the commonest elements in the universe, in a ratio of about one helium atom to every ten hydrogen atoms. Another element formed in the early process of nucleosynthesis was lithium. As the universe continued to expand, gravity operated on matter in such a way as to begin the process of star and galaxy formation.

Hubble's founding observation that led to the Big Bang theory can be understood by visualising the following: imagine that our galaxy is a raisin in a lump of dough swelling up in a hot oven. From the point of view of the raisin on which we ourselves are located, all the other raisins will be seen to be getting further and further away as the dough expands, and the further away they are the faster they will be receding, just as Hubble's Law states. Relatedly, the speed and distance of galaxies can be calculated by measuring the degree to which the light emanating from them is shifted to the red end of the colour spectrum. The greater the red-shift, the faster the source of light is moving away and therefore the further away it is.

The Big Bang theory received powerful support from observations of cosmic background microwave radiation, left over from the universe's earliest history. This observation won the 1978 Nobel Prize for physics for the two astronomers who made it, Arno Penzias and Robert Wilson. It is also supported by the observation that the most abundant elements in the universe are helium and hydrogen, just as the Big Bang model predicts.

The standard version of the Big Bang theory requires a consistent mathematical description of the universe's large-scale properties, and the foundation of such a description is the law of gravity, the basic force by which large structures in the universe interact. The standard theory of this force is Einstein's general relativity, which gives a description of the curved geometry of space-time, states equations describing how gravity operates, and gives an account of the large-scale properties of matter. The standard model premises that the universe is homogeneous and isotropic, meaning that the same laws operate everywhere and that we (the observers) do not occupy a special position in it – which in turn entails that the universe looks the same to observers anywhere.

These assumptions, jointly known as the 'cosmological principle', are just that: *assumptions*, and are of course challengeable – and there are indeed questions about them, not least one that asks how the universe's properties had sufficient time to evolve (especially in the very early history of the universe) to be as they now are. This is known as the 'horizon problem'. A currently persuasive answer to it is the 'inflationary theory' which hypothesises a much smaller starting point for the universe, and a much more rapid expansion from that point, together allowing the known laws of physics to explain how the universe's properties arose. There are other less conservative answers, some requiring adjustments to Einstein's equations, or more generally requiring acceptance of the idea that the values of what we now think of as the constants of nature (such as the speed of light) might have been different in the early universe.

One puzzle concerns whether the universe will continue to expand for ever, or whether gravity will eventually slow down its expansion and then pull it back into an eventual 'Big Crunch' – which perhaps, if the cycle repeats itself endlessly, will be a new Big Bang that starts everything over again. The answer depends on the density of the universe. This is estimated by working out the density of our own and nearby galaxies, and extrapolating the figure to the whole universe – which involves the assumption that the universe is everywhere homogeneous, something there is reason to doubt. This is the 'observed density'. The ratio of this density to the 'critical density' – the density of the universe which, so it can be calculated, would eventually stop it expanding – is known as Omega. If Omega is less than or equal to 1 then the universe will expand until it cools to the point of extinction (a 'cold death'). If it is greater than 1 it will stop expanding and begin to contract, suffering a catastrophically explosive death in a Big Crunch. For reasons of theoretical convenience, Omega is arbitrarily assigned the value 1, but measurements achieved by observation suggest that it is about 0.1, which if right predicts the continual expansion to a cold death scenario.

Although the Big Bang theory is the one most widely held by cosmologists, it leaves many questions unanswered, so that research into the origins of the universe remains a highly active field, and neither the theory itself nor the various supplementations and emendations of it are uncontroversial.

One historical rival to it, mentioned above, is the 'Steady State' concept put forward by Fred Hoyle, Hermann Bondi and others. This theory hypothesises that the universe exists infinitely in the same average density, with new matter being spontaneously generated in galaxies at a rate which equals the rate at which distant objects become unobservable at the edge of the expanding universe. (Hoyle and Bondi accepted that the universe must be expanding because in a static universe stellar energy could not be dispersed, and would heat up, eventually destroying the universe.) The rate of appearance of new matter required for the Steady State need only be very small – just one nucleon per cubic kilometre per year.

Apart from the discovery of the cosmic background radiation, which powerfully supports the Big Bang model, another reason for scepticism about the Steady State theory is that its assumption that the universe does not change appears to be refuted by the existence of quasars (quasi-stellar objects) and radio galaxies only in distant regions of the universe, showing that the earlier universe was different from how it is today. (Distance in space is equal to remoteness in past time; to look at far objects in space is to see into the history of the universe.)

There are a number of other rivals to the Big Bang theory, in the form of alternative models: the Symmetric theory, plasma cosmology, the 'ekpyrotic model', the 'meta model', 'subquantum kinetics cosmology' and others. These proposed alternatives have different degrees of plausibility – some of them are as exotic as they are imaginative; but one of them might be right. The universe is not guaranteed not to be a very strange place.

Such competitors to the Big Bang theory are motivated by the fact that it has many problems. Among the criticisms it faces are these. It has to adjust parameters, such as the cosmic deceleration parameter or those that relate to the relative abundance of elements in the universe, to conform to observation. It has to explain why the cosmic microwave background temperature is the residuum of the heat of the Big Bang rather than the warming of space effected by radiation from stars. It has to account for the fact that the universe has too much large-scale structure to have formed in just 12–15 billion years, thus needing the 'inflationary' hypothesis to render consistent, in a way that is ad hoc and untestable, the apparent age of the universe and the greater age needed for the formation of its structures. A particular example is that the age of some globular stellar clusters appears to be greater than the calculated age of the universe. Some observers claim that the most distant – and by hypothesis therefore the oldest – galaxies in the universe, those in the 'Hubble Deep Field', show a level of evolution discrepant with their supposed age. And perhaps most puzzling of all, the Big Bang theory requires that we accept that we know nothing about 80 per cent of the universe, which has to take the form of 'dark matter' to explain the distribution and relationships of observed galaxies and galaxy clusters, and moreover with another mysterious ingredient – 'dark energy' – pushing the universe apart.

What does all this tell us about the effort of humankind to make sense of itself in its world? Well: it very significantly reminds us of the power of the human intellect. Cosmology is a field that offers ample room for speculation, and science is as creative and imaginative an enterprise as any other, if not indeed more so. But it is not fancifully so: it is constrained by observation, evidence, publicly repeatable experiment, and mathematics. The Big Bang theory itself undergoes modification and adjustment constantly as new discoveries are made, new challenges and criticisms offered, and new hypotheses advanced in physics both at the cosmological and quantum scales. Whether it or one of its competitors – or perhaps a theory not yet put forward – is right, cosmology itself is a testament to the powers of observation and reason, and of creative intelligence, that drive the human mind to levels of understanding that are utterly remarkable.

But mention of the human mind reminds us that there is a social science – or rather: a science which combines as perceptively as it can the methods of both social and natural science – which expressly enquires into the nature of mind. This is psychology.

Of all the areas of human enquiry, psychology must be one of the broadest in scope. It means the study of mind and mental life, but the variety of approaches and methods, and the specialist subdivisions of psychological interest, are numerous. The work of educational psychologists, developmental psychologists, industrial psychologists, psychoneurologists, psychiatrists, psychotherapists of all kinds from the Jungian and Freudian schools to cognitive behavioural therapy, and more, makes this region of enquiry highly diverse and rich.

As this in turn suggests, the targets of these enquiries are diverse too, from every aspect of the development and normal and abnormal functioning of perception, memory, learning, reasoning, intelligence, emotion, sexuality and more, to the social expression of and influence upon them of education, work, family life and relationships, and further to their physiological and neurological underpinnings. In the recent development of powerful non-invasive means of studying brain function, for example by means of fMRI, a great deal has been learned in neuropsychology about the physical correlates of psychological phenomena, though it is accepted on all sides that there are aspects of enquiry in psychology that cannot rely on brain imaging alone.

The mind and its workings have undoubtedly been of interest to human beings since the dawn of human experience, and we can see psychological theories symbolised in the myths and legends of antiquity – not least in the highly sophisticated and insightful mythology of ancient Greece – as well as in the literature of all ages. But it is in the eighteenth century that theories of mind and mental functioning first began to emerge systematically; the 'associationist' psychology developed by David Hartley and employed by David Hume in his philosophy is an example of the wide acceptance of the view, dominant at the time, that mental activity consists in the linking of ideas by associations of similarity or habit.

In the 1870s Wilhelm Wundt brought the study of psychology into the laboratory, a departure which marks the beginnings of scientific psychology proper. Important contributions were made by William James in his *Principles of Psychology* (1890) and Ivan Pavlov (1850–1909) who demonstrated the conditioned response by – famously – training dogs to salivate at the sound of a bell.

A different impulse was given to psychology by Sigmund Freud and Carl Jung, younger contemporaries of James and Pavlov, in the direction of clinical psychology, addressing the ambiguous field of human experience between the 'normal' psychological range and the kind of mental pathology that could then be adequately handled only by putting its victims into lunatic asylums.

Whereas the diverse approaches of James and Freud relied on introspection and subjective data, another powerful school of thought, the behaviourist school, insisted on a different approach. As a technical term in psychology, 'behaviourism' denotes the thesis, first put forward by J. B. Watson in 1913, that mental phenomena should be explained wholly in terms of objectively observable behaviour, thus attempting to make psychology an empirical science. His most notable and more radical successor was B. F. Skinner. Their key idea was that behaviour, in humans as much as in animals, consists in conditioned responses to external stimuli, and that all psychological phenomena can be accounted for in these terms.

A major implication of their view for the debate about the relative importance of nature (innate mechanisms) and nurture (experience) in learning, is that it comes down strongly on the side of nurture. This means that what is learned is the result of conditioning, for which the mammalian central nervous system is in general apt, this being the only mechanism in play – contrast the view otherwise held, that a mind consists of many separate mechanisms adapted to handling different types of problems.

A distinction between 'methodological' and 'scientific' behaviourism is significant here. The former insists that psychology must be an empirical discipline reliant on publicly observable evidence, not on the subjective avowals of the human subjects being studied. 'Scientific behaviourism' is more stringent, in requiring that psychology should concern itself exclusively with the formulation of laws correlating input (stimuli) and output (behaviour), ignoring all talk of 'inner' mechanisms and processes. This means having to do without such concepts as intention and attention, motive and memory.

Today most empirical psychology takes its cue from 'methodological' behaviourism. The key advance in empirical psychology lies in cognitive science, which draws on advances in computing, philosophy and artificial intelligence as well as the various branches of psychology themselves, together with the development of brain-scanning techniques allowing real-time investigation of brain function correlated with the performance of mental tasks and the occurrence of emotional and cognitive responses. Along with greatly increased knowledge about the physical and psychological effects of brain injury and disease, these advances have pushed psychology and its related fields into an area far in advance of anything that could have been imagined by the eighteenth-century 'associationists'.

Do the advances in psychology threaten to displace the need for the humanities in achieving insight and understanding of human nature and the human condition? Again the answer is 'No', just as with the implications of biological understanding that places human nature in nature, and the cosmological perspective on our place in the cosmos. This is because the insights of psychology illuminate rather than diminish the richness of those aspects of our mental life which produce the ultimately value-bearing activities that we cherish. To know more about how we learn and perceive, remember and reason, does not undermine the objects of perception, enquiry and memory. To know more about how the intricacies of mental life can be disturbed by illness, injury and age, is to help us recover or retain the powers that make life most worth living. To enquire into genius and creativity is fascinating; more, it might help us to unlock yet further potentialities in the human psyche, so that we can educate better, and more abundantly benefit from what the mind can do.

My emphatic view is that just as science itself is the outcome of humanity's creativity and intelligence – is itself one wonderful form of a great artistic and humanistic achievement in its own right – so it is no threat to those other aspects of arts and humanities which more directly offer us the many interpretations of what we might call the poetry of life, its meanings and its possibilities: among which the furtherance of the scientific adventure itself is a central part.

Science and Democracy

Historians date the beginning of modern times to the sixteenth and seventeenth centuries, the period of the late Renaissance, the Reformation, and the scientific revolution. The outcome of these tectonic shifts in the Western mind is the Enlightenment of the eighteenth century and the liberal democracies that grew from it in the nineteenth and twentieth centuries.

This broad-brush picture is a familiar one, and it is, equally broadly, right; but interesting questions remain about the relationship between the strands of development involved. One argument is that the growth of science and the growth of liberal democracy were not merely contemporaneous, but causally connected; and that the causal link runs from science to democracy. A proponent of this view is Timothy Ferris (*The Science of Liberty*, 2010). He adds the further claim that science continues to underwrite the political freedoms enjoyed by developed societies today.

There is a lot to be said for this thesis. Science could neither have arisen nor flourished in circumstances of oppression of thought, and indeed the churches made strenuous efforts – including persecuting and even executing people – in the early phases of the scientific revolution in an effort to quell it; and those efforts had to be defeated to allow science to grow. As this shows, the science–freedom link is an intimate one. But an adjustment to this thesis is required: rather than taking the rise of science to be the literal cause of the growth of political liberty, both science and political liberty would be better regarded as the joint outcome of an antecedent cause. This antecedent cause is the freeing of the human mind from the trammels of doctrinal orthodoxy. I argue this in *Towards the Light* (2008): aspirations to liberty of religious conscience in the sixteenth century rapidly evolved into demands for liberty of thought and enquiry in all fields, including science; and once people had asserted the right to think for themselves without conforming to a dogma on pain of death, they were able to ask questions both about nature and about socio-political arrangements. On this view, science and democracy grew together from a fundamental impulse towards liberty, and are its joint fruits.

But it may not be wholly right to say that once an advanced degree of scientific understanding of nature is achieved, and applications of that understanding via technology begin to transform human experience, democratic structures are thereby enabled. Alas, there are social and political arrangements in the world that take the fullest benefit from scientific progress without accompanying commitment to democracy. Perhaps the cruellest paradox is seen in the use made of technologies – in the form of aeroplanes and computers and explosive devices – by people whose zeal is for a worldview that arose many centuries ago, and who seem to wish to return the world to that period's condition by making as much use of today's science and technology as possible.

Still, there is a hopeful sign for the world lodged in the fact that increased scientific understanding does have a tendency to make people think more, and more clearly, about their other assumptions and beliefs. Action to diffuse not just scientific knowledge but scientific styles of thought therefore recommends itself – not just as a way forward for humankind, but its best hope for a peaceful way forward. The dismaying consideration is that it might be the best hope because it is the only one.

Making Mistakes and Apologising

We can be the prisoners of our mistakes, especially if we do not learn from them; but when we do learn from them we can be their beneficiaries. Which do we most tend to be? No doubt we all wish the latter. We console ourselves that to err is human, and that, as George Bernard Shaw once remarked, it is better to make mistakes than to do nothing.

Shaw's point does not hold without exception; it depends on the nature of the mistake. Inadvertently leaning on the button that fires the nuclear missile is not preferable to having stayed in bed that day. Some mistakes teach lessons that come too late to apply.

In the larger spheres of life – politics and government, international affairs – it is less easy to regard mistakes as learning opportunities for the perpetrators. If government ministers start a war, get economic policy 90 degrees wrong, attempt reforms in healthcare, education or the armed forces in ways that turn out to make things vastly worse, we are naturally reluctant to entrust them with big responsibilities again. That is part of what elections are for.

Recently, Tony Blair made an outspoken speech about the dangers posed to global stability by militant forms of political Islam. Among those who think that he made a calamitous mistake in going to war in the Middle East are those who think his judgement should never again be relied on. A man who takes a nation to war on such a questionable basis does not deserve to be listened to.

Are they right? It depends. There are different factors at work in the matter of mistakes, even calamitous ones. At one end of the scale there is incompetence, at the other there is bad luck. In between there might be one or more of inexperience; unforeseen circumstances; pressures of various kinds; an assortment of motives some of which have the effect of clouding the vision or distorting the judgement. Can one conclude that someone is permanently untrustworthy because of a mistake unless one has looked at the circumstances of its making?

Compare it with how we think about people who have served a prison sentence. We say they have paid their debt, and we hope that they will be reformed by the experience, or at least disincentivised against repeating it. Can someone never recover from being the perpetrator of a mistake? In fact, is there not a presumption that – unless sheer incapacity is to blame – the perpetrator is less rather than more likely to repeat it?

If we never forgive and excuse, never allow second chances, we are not only being very harsh, we are losing the opportunity to benefit from what someone might have learned. If mistakes pave the road to insight, if mistakes are better tutors than always (and sometimes by accident) getting things right, then not giving second chances is a lost opportunity.

On the other hand, there is the question of risk. A perpetrator of a mistake has a known negative record. Is it not rational to act accordingly, by withholding trust? To do otherwise is to allow hope to triumph over experience (as Samuel Johnson said of second marriages). In relatively inconsequential things this might not matter too much. But in affairs of state? Of war and peace?

In Blair's case one might be inclined to think that his experience, both negative and positive, and what he has seen and done since, might give him an entitlement to be heard. He is not asking to be prime minister again, so the case is not quite parallel to mistrusting a mistake-perpetrator with a second go at the same thing. On the contrary: you might think that the views he holds now on aspects of the sequel to his earlier actions are all the more worth noting, precisely for that reason.

If we turn inwards and reflect on our own mistakes and the fallibilities that prompt them, we are sure to hope that we will be allowed second and even third chances; that we will meet with generosity when we err. It has been said that the saddest of all words are 'it's too late'. Not wishing to hear them said to oneself is a reason for being diffident about saying them to others. For after all, as the great Cicero pointed out: not every mistake is a foolish one.

In its Greek root 'apology' means a speech in self-defence. We sometimes still use 'apologia' to mean this, with perhaps a nuance in the direction of self-explanation rather than self-defence. But today an apology is an admission of fault as well as a statement of regret and conciliation towards an offended party. Words change their meanings and acquire different freight as usage carries them along; a politician accused of some great crime – corruption in office, massive failure of duty in affairs of state, or (in today's world) making amorous advances towards members of his or her staff – might have issued an apology in the form of a defence. To defend oneself now requires that one not apologise.

A major use of the concept of apology in Christianity's early centuries was defence of its claims against the dismissive scepticism of educated people. This was *apologetics*, the finding, invention, arrangement and insistence upon arguments and putative evidence in favour of the faith. The church's acquisition of temporal power rendered this effort unnecessary; once it became a capital crime not to believe, the effort of persuading people by argument and evidence was obsolete. Wherever the temporal power of religion has diminished in our world it is now the sheer weight of history that does the work of apologetics. A Mormon once said, on being taxed with the profound improbabilities of his religion, that 'it will not seem improbable in a thousand years' time'. He here hit the nail on the head: neither apologetics nor apologies will then be required, if the world continues in its present paths.

Politicians do not like to apologise for anything if they can help it, precisely because it involves admission of failure or guilt. Summon images of bowing Japanese prime ministers as they resign: figurative fallings on swords are there connoted. Another word that has acquired a negative cast in this domain is 'responsible': think of the difference between saying 'he is a responsible man' and 'he is the man responsible'. Being responsible for something means that one has a duty of care or obligation in regard to it; being responsible for something that has gone wrong means that one must apologise. This is why politicians dislike apologising; obviously enough and naturally enough, they do not like admitting that things have gone wrong.

Apologies have become a kind of political money. Descendants of slaves demand apologies from today's governments for the activities of two and more centuries ago. (They fail to recognise that every individual on the planet is descended from slaves *and* slave-owners: who apologises to whom, if we chase history back far enough?) But in one sense at least, they have a point. The psychology of the demand for an apology is that when one is wronged, one desires recognition of the fact as it applies to oneself, and acknowledgement by the perpetrator of the wrong done and the harm caused. There are good practical reasons for lancing the boils of resentment in this way, thereby teaching ourselves how to do better in future. In quotidian domestic life the giving and taking of apologies is a key regulator of affairs, like a thermostat or homeostatic device.

Our readiness to apologise to others for bumping into them in the supermarket or not seeing them about to enter the door behind us, is a marker of how right such philosophers as Mencius and David Hume were – despite large differences otherwise – in viewing human nature as more rather than less benevolent. For most people most of the time, the default attitude is an instinctive readiness to get on with whomever they encounter in the daily round. Because in our crowded warrens we have to navigate a dance of personal spaces and mutual adjustments, the reflex 'Sorry!' is a commonplace. It seems that it is only behind the wheel of a motor vehicle that this attitude changes to something different.

But politics is not a tube station or a supermarket. The rules of engagement are very different out there on the thin ice of political life. Occasionally a politician will apologise – the more easily if it is for something that happened centuries ago; indeed, he or she might get credit for bravely taking the rap for distant predecessors – but generally it is political suicide, or the next best thing, to do it in relation to a current matter. A game results: the less inclined a politician is to apologise, the more hounding by the press follows. The only invariable result of the game is that sooner rather than later it distracts attention from other things which might be, and (given what the press tends to hound politicians for) often are, considerably more important. When the press get it provably wrong, they print an apology. How easy that is: a little paragraph tucked away, sniffily implying the opposite of what it says, as it were rejecting while claiming to accept corporate blame.

There is something very unsatisfying about corporate apologies. The bigger the corporation, the less satisfying its apologies (for oil spills and the like) tend to be. This is why, I suppose, those who seek admission of responsibility from corporate miscreants prefer to have any resulting apologies in the form of hard cash.

Benjamin Jowett, the fearsome Master of Balliol College at Oxford in Victorian times, famously advised against ever apologising: 'Get it done and let them howl,' he said. In the very mixed alloy of real life this strategy has doubtful use – which is not to say that it has none: it can sometimes be appropriate, as for example when one has a clear view of the right thing to do and there is a gaggle of nay-sayers and enemies to cut through.

But since we are all fallible, we are quite likely to offend or do wrong at times, in lesser or greater degree: and then apology really is due. And the value of apology is immense, both for the apologiser and for any to whom his apology is owed. This is because the work that apology does is only partly about what happened beforehand. Its main benefit is what it does for the future, in relieving the feelings of all concerned and restoring relationships to a better footing.

A sincere apology involves a recognition of the wrong or hurt done to an injured party. It involves regret for the motives of an act as well as for its consequences. Often enough, people are not sorry for what they have done but only for being found out, and then their apologies ring hollow. Bankers and politicians are recent examples in this category; they can seem to be weepers of crocodile tears respectively over inflated expense claims and economy-wrecking greed. But what they are really sorry about is that they were caught; they are sorry only for themselves.

The point about recognition cannot be over-emphasised. Recognition that a wrong has been done is not only what makes an apology sincere, but is the key to the good that flows from it. That is why public apologies for major past wrongs such as slavery and forced child migration have a real value. They liberate victims or their descendants not from the injustice itself – time travel would be needed for that – but from the lack of closure that persists until a proper and fulsome public recognition of past harm has been written into the record.

One should never delay an apology when it is due. Humble pie is always better eaten warm, and there are few things worse than owing an apology and never being able to give it, as when an offended friend or a wronged fellow human being dies, leaving you with an uncauterised guilt. Feeling sorry does not come close to saying sorry from the point of view of making things better, or indeed from any point of view.

And there is another positive about apology: there is no better way of having the last word, even though you were in the wrong.

Does Government Know Best?

We are required by law to wear seatbelts in cars and crash-helmets on motorbikes, to refrain from smoking in public indoor areas, from injecting heroin and smoking marijuana – all in the interests of our health, our well-being and our safety. Such laws imply that government knows our interests better than we ourselves do, and has a duty to act accordingly. Given that government has the information, the experts, the commissions of enquiry, the ministries with teams of civil servants and special advisers and their responsibilities, could this be right?

What is at stake in this question? The answer is – liberty. When the authors of the Federalist Papers were debating whether to add a Bill of Rights to the then new United States Constitution, Alexander Hamilton objected that drawing up a list of positive rights would imply that they were the only ones to which citizens were entitled, whereas the absence of prohibition left open the whole field of what Isaiah Berlin later called 'negative liberties', defined as absence of constraint. Pertinently, Berlin declared himself wary of 'positive liberties' – those permitted or (worse) enjoined constitutionally or by statute – on the grounds that they are in the interests, as decided by those who know best, of those destined to enjoy them.

Once our legislators are endowed with the power to decide what is in our interests, it is not long before they begin to exercise it. We think it is a joke to say that sugar will soon be the new heroin, to be proscribed as injurious to health – but laws on the size of soda drink bottles in New York (a way of limiting corn syrup intake by the American obese) are a staging post on the way thither. It is accordingly important to distinguish between laws that require information about the content of foodstuffs – stating how much fat and sugar they contain – and laws that (might one day) ban sugar, because the former provide people with information on which they can choose for themselves how to act, whereas the latter embody the principle that nanny – the drafter of the relevant laws – knows best.

There is a difficult line to be trodden here, of course. Through its representatives in government a community might make rational decisions to do certain things that limit individual freedoms in the interests of all – such as requiring everyone to drive on the same side of the road, and not to do it under the influence of mind-altering substances like heroin and alcohol – but the temptation to paternalism and condescension in the form of other less evidently publicly beneficial laws that prohibit this or that behaviour because it is not in the interests of individuals to engage in it – the drug laws are a prime example – is another matter. The line in question is now regularly and in large strides overstepped by governments of all stripes, not least because of the passivity with which such tramplings on individual liberty are received by the trampled.

A high value attaches to the autonomy that individuals should have over decisions about their own lives. Such autonomy carries responsibility. Responsibility requires thought. Most people do not like to think. They thereby give an opening – too often, force governments to enter the opening – for governments to start taking decisions that should be each individual's to take.

Those who suffer most as a result are those who wish to, and can, take decisions for themselves. Because most of the rest will not do so, the autonomous are dragged into the queue that governments form on their behalf.

Obviously enough, questions and answers have an incestuous relationship: how the former are phrased determines how the latter are formulated. Controversies over the wording of census and referendum questions illustrate the point well. Consider, therefore, alternatives to the question. 'Under what circumstances *can* a person expect help from the state?' 'Under what circumstances should a person not expect help from the state?' 'Under what circumstances is there no reasonable entitlement for a person to expect help from the state?'

Perhaps the one question that sums up the concern behind them all is: 'How far is it morally acceptable for welfare spending cuts to go, in the light of their effect on people in vulnerable circumstances?'

There is a consensus, fuzzy at the edges but otherwise firm enough, in most Western European polities, that the state exists to provide basic securities and equities – using these terms in their non-financial sense of course: securities at very least in defence and the maintenance of law and order, equities in provision of health and education in quality and quantity sufficient to offer the least advantaged a chance to progress, if they will accept the offer – and in general to make a civilised distribution from the common purse, to all who wish to accept it, of the goods of health and education.

But the provision of security does not stop with the army and police. Subsistence and shelter for those who cannot pay their own way because of unemployment, disability, illness, age and like factors, are also forms of security. Much of the debate about levels of welfare spending concern *how much* such security should be provided, not *whether or not* it should be provided. The consensus in question is that the state has welfare responsibilities; the arguments are almost always about how much should be spent in discharging them.

The politics of that debate revolve around what we should devote resources to: is it to solving the underlying problems (say, the causes of unemployment) which generate a need for welfare spending, or palliation of the symptoms of the problem in the form of dole and housing benefit? After all, say this view's proponents, fixing the problem will obviate the symptoms. The response is to query the implication that this is an either-or matter: of course the underlying problem should be fixed, but in the meantime welfare should be maintained at civilised and compassionate levels, because allowing people (and especially children) to fester in poverty causes long-term problems of a kind that could and probably will make greater demands on future welfare budgets.

So the summary answer to the question posed above about what people should legitimately expect from the state is: that people should (are entitled to) expect help from the state when they are, for one or another reason, unable to attain by their own endeavours the basic securities and equities mentioned.

But there are other things people can legitimately expect of the state. Here is a list: protecting civil liberties; ensuring that economic life – work, trading, investment, manufacture, services, everything – is fair, safe and rewarded; responding sensibly to the myriad difficulties that spring up in a complex society; being an enabler rather than an interferer in citizens' legitimate activities, but interfering when justice requires; protecting minorities, and promoting the common good while respecting individual diversity, autonomy and privacy.

This is not an idealist's list, but a simple statement of basics, regarding what we should expect from the state in addition to its organisation of society's collective resources to provide a welfare net. We do not expect the state to moralise, to nanny, to over-protect, to make our personal decisions for us. But we do expect it to apply the shared resources of society to the interests of its members, and that fundamentally includes helping those who need it.

What about the freeloaders? There are doubtless some. If identified, they can be required to do their share. But their numbers are assuredly small: it takes a large lack of self-respect to be a parasite. Treat their thefts from the common purse as the charge we willingly pay so that no one in real need lacks their entitlement.

Beyond Subsistence

When societies move beyond subsistence level, giving their members time to reflect and debate, questions of principle emerge, and with them ideological differences in politics and ethics. These are closely connected for the obvious reason that individual projects of building good lives do better in the context of good societies, those which at the least safeguard the margins of liberty required for personal autonomy and chosen relationships while, as a background condition for them, promoting justice and stability. Because 'goodness', 'liberty' and 'justice' are essentially contestable concepts, they are inevitably the focus of ideological differences, the major forms of which are familiar staples of daily debate.

But underlying these familiar differences is a deeper opposition of thought, one that concerns this question: are individual human beings capable of overcoming such limitations of circumstance as birth, class, culture, deficits of education, and even the distorting pressures of history itself, to achieve by will and endeavour what they identify as good, granting that there are as many kinds of good as there are talents for achieving them? Or are people, or the vast majority of them, too weak, too fallible, too constrained by those circumstances, to be able to do this, meaning that they are essentially dependent, and need to be instructed and guided by the few who assume the role of leaders, teachers, those who know the right answers and possess the truth?

This great struggle of ideas is a modern one. It arises from the realisation, beginning in the sixteenth century, that the latter view, which had been dominant everywhere in history save for the enfranchised (adult male) communities of the

Greek city states of classical antiquity and the educated strata of subsequent Hellenistic and Roman (especially Republican) society, required challenge on the grounds that it not merely premises but actually works to achieve the permanent intellectual infancy of humanity. The monolithic ideologies require a dependent, submissive mass mind; in recovering the classical idea of individual potential for autonomy – the capacity of individuals to shape themselves according to their conception of such truly human goods as love, friendship, pleasure, kindness, knowledge and discovery, creativity and achievement – the modern Western liberal and secular mind has fought to break itself free from that imposed dependency.

This is not a merely abstract point. This deep divide in opinion about what human beings are and what they can do is at work in concrete ways in the daily reality of our world, from the quarrels between outlooks that divide us on this question to the bitterness and violence of too much of the world beyond. I assert this here with the brevity imposed by this medium, but have argued the different aspects and implications of it at length in two books (*What is Good?*, 2002 and *Towards the Light*, 2007) – a bit of advertising more for the argument itself than the books stating it, because the matter is so fundamental that it merits far more than bite-size examination. That examination might show why there can be such passionate opposition to anything that requires the entrapment of the human mind in the cage of One Big Truth that demands submission, the yielding of the autonomy that is our central human potential – think of the Christian tenet of 'dying to the self' and what is meant by the 'sin of pride' (viz. thinking one can get by without God), remember that 'Islam' means 'submission', think of Stalinism: they are all about obedience, heteronymy, dependence, tutelage, amounting even to a prohibition against thinking for oneself; for the first sin in Eden was disobedience, and the disobedient act – all too significantly – was one of acquiring knowledge. And what is this submission and heteronymy but the condition of slavery, the denial of the freedom to become and to be one's own master, and by responsible effort therefore to achieve one's own unique best, whatever form one's best might take, so long as it harms no other?

In turning on nothing less than the question of the nature of humankind, the significance of today's debates is ultimate. The shock of collision between outlooks has exposed the nerve of the issue, and that is why so many are taking sides, or announcing which side they are already on. The polarisation is alas as dangerous as it is inevitable, which is why it is worth iterating the hope that rational debate, respect for evidence, and clarity, will sooner rather than later bring a peaceful conclusion to this phase in what could be, and certainly should be, humankind's progress.

A Hard Choice

It was inevitable that the abortion debate would come to centre stage in the current inflammation of debate about the place of religion in public matters, expressed as the degree to which personal religious views can or should influence the public duties of those who have both – such as magistrates and doctors. To critical eyes, what is happening is a surge of effort by the nation's religious minorities to run everything and everyone their own way; to the votaries of one or another of the religions, the steam-roller of secularism, majoritarianism and law has gone too far for their tastes. To dispassionate observers it must at least be evident that activism in one of the major religions has encouraged some in others to be more assertive likewise, a case of roiling up, of hornets' nests.

Let's hope that the following is common ground: that in almost every case in which a pregnancy is terminated for almost any of the many reasons why a termination is felt necessary by the woman involved, the decision and its circumstances are serious and often difficult ones. There may be women who carelessly see abortion as a form of back-up contraception, but they cannot be the benchmark here.

What is not common ground is the claim that abortion is acceptable as a solution to the serious kinds of circumstances envisaged. For all supporters (me included) of a woman's right to choose what happens in and to her body and her life, the case is clear. Pregnancy is a vastly consequential matter, which is why abortion has to be a valid option. When faced with the task of considering the irruption of those vast consequences – typically unsought and unwanted if abortion is the contemplated remedy – into everything a woman has in the way of existing commitments and plans, she has to have that option, and in medically safe and legal ways.

This is accepted in UK society, and provided for in its law by a 1967 Act. But minorities continue to oppose it, and would like to see the law itself aborted – even though the consequence would be knitting needles in back streets, and the attendant horrors and greater tragedies that this would bring back.

The focus of present discussion is those medical personnel who do not wish to be party to terminations of pregnancy. The

1967 Act grants them exemption on grounds of conscience. The exemption has been further taken to imply that anti-abortion medical staff are not under a duty to refer women to practitioners who will perform abortions, on the grounds that this would make the objector instrumental in procuring them.

This makes the situation of medical personnel different from that of a magistrate who does not wish to act in conformity with anti-discrimination legislation in such cases as placing children in need of fostering into the care of gay couples. The anti-discrimination legislation does not provide exemptions on grounds of conscience, and quite rightly so; the legislation outlaws discriminating against people on grounds that are not matters of choice (ethnicity, sexuality, age, disability), whereas the 1967 abortion Act concerns a matter of choice. Some who support the idea of conscience-based exemption in general fail to see the difference, nor the injustice and chaos that would ensue if our legislators were incapable of drawing that distinction likewise.

The problem has since arisen, though, that medical personnel who oppose abortion have been using their position of authority and influence – both very considerable, for a distressed woman seeking help in a crisis – to try to persuade women not to have abortions. This is as disgraceful and unacceptable as someone using such a position of authority and influence to persuade a woman to have an abortion. Even if a conscientious-objector health worker simply refused to engage either way with a woman in crisis, relying on the 1967 exemption to have nothing to do with her and her problem, that would be a dereliction: it conflicts with the duty of care medical personnel have to those in need.

On the face of it this would seem to entail a serious dilemma for both sides of the equation – for troubled women who know only their local GPs and turn to them first for help, only to find (say) a devout Catholic in the chair opposite; and for the objecting practitioners themselves, because of the conflict between their personal conscience and their duty of care (unless they – falsely and irresponsibly – think that they serve the latter by persuading their patients on non-medical grounds to act in conformity to their own beliefs).

The solution is however simple, though it needs a coda to the 1967 Act to be made fully effective. It is that there should be agencies (an individual or unit in a health practice or hospital) devoted to advising women about all the options available to them in the case of an unwanted pregnancy – not to persuade them either way, but to inform them, and to put them in touch with the further agencies (support, adoption, termination) depending on the decision that the woman herself then makes. A conscience-objector doctor or nurse can have no scruples about referring a woman to such an agency, because they are not thereby acting as an agent to the procurement of an abortion. And they are not imposing their own personal minority view with consequences for a woman (and if they are successful in their propaganda, an ensuing child) when it is not their consciences and circumstances which should be the determiner of what happens, but that woman's. For women alone have the right to decide what happens in and to their own bodies and lives reproductively, and to exercise that right safely and lawfully.

Archiepiscopal Ethics

When Dr Rowan Williams was the Archbishop of Canterbury he gave a Wilberforce Lecture arguing that the state itself should be moral, among other things because by failing to be so it has the effect of making its individual members less than they might be. He further argued that this requires persuading 'those who run things in the public sphere that there are human values and ethical norms to which an entire society is answerable'. And then, in preparation for reasserting the claim if not of the Church of England then of religion to have leadership in identifying those values and norms, he said, 'In our relativist climate, this is very difficult.'

There is something right and something wrong about these thoughts and their implications. What is right is the closely allied idea that those who run the state machine, whether as politicians or civil servants, and those who influence them materially through NGO and interest group activities, should always be constrained by ethical considerations, and answerable to them. What is wrong is the idea that this unexceptionable claim entitles us to think of the state itself as an agent possessed of moral duties. The state is not an entity separate from those who run it and those who influence them, and so the expression 'a moral state' can only be shorthand for 'a state run by morally responsible people'.

Once one puts matters like this, it becomes hard to accept a further implication of the Archbishop's remarks, namely, that those running the state have a duty to identify and inculcate a morality so that the state – now, in a shift of focus, understood as consisting of the collectivity of its members – can itself be moral. What counts as a community's morality is always a double thing, consisting of the conventional morality of a previous generation in tension with the contested, evolving values under negotiation at any one time in the public debate. A living community has to tread this line, always; once a static moral orthodoxy is enforced, the effect on the community is a stifling one. Take the examples of divorce and homosexuality, both of which in living memory were regarded with distaste and opprobrium, and both of which have become acceptable and part of the mainstream, thereby liberating people to more generous possibilities for flourishing lives. This was not the result of moral legislation *de haut en bas* (and nor was it the result of leadership given by any religious group or church: indeed, the contrary!), but the outcome of the debate society has with itself about what is good and right, what is acceptable, and why.

That debate is a vigorous and responsible one, and it is disappointing but unsurprising that the former custodians of moral authority, the former arbiters of the good, namely officers of one or another religious group, insist on complaining that morality has gone to pot, is relativistic and thin, has been swamped by consumerism and individualism, and has collapsed in a welter of drink and pornography, threatening the end of the world. No such thing is happening; if anything, now that people are less distracted by such irrelevances as what they are allowed to eat and wear, and what they can and cannot do on different days of the week, matters of real ethical concern – war, poverty, injustice, the environment, child labour, human rights – have come to dominate an ethical agenda which once all but ignored them in favour of hand-wringing over Sunday shopping and unmarried mothers.

It is in fact a remarkable and heartening truth about the contemporary Western world that it has such a vibrant ethical debate as a distinctive part of its culture. Yes, the West does bad things – makes war, exploits and battens, pillages the environment, and much besides – but it also criticises itself about these very things, challenges itself, argues with itself, and sometimes makes things very much better for its denizens than almost anywhere else, at any other time, in the world and human history.

Think of it this way: would you rather live in a functionally secular Western country, or in one where the moral climate is much more influenced by what (among others, religious) leaders say it should be?

Free Speech

Liberty is not divisible; a society's members do not have it if they have only some of it in some spheres. That is why incremental reductions of aspects of civil liberty regimes are a danger; there quickly comes a point when the claim begins to ring hollow that members of a society have secure margins of freedom in their lives. The too-true cliché says that the price of liberty is eternal vigilance, which is why it is mandatory to resist, and resist vigorously, the early stages of assaults on liberty, not least those made by well-meaning politicians who earnestly, eagerly, sincerely desire to protect us from bad people and from ourselves, for these are the most insidious.

Yet though liberty is indivisible, regimes of liberties have a structure. The keystone of the arch is free speech. Without free speech one cannot claim other liberties, or defend them when they are attacked. Without free speech one cannot have a democratic process, which requires the statement and testing of policy proposals and party platforms. Without free speech one cannot have a due process at law, in which one can defend oneself, accuse, collect and examine evidence, make a case or refute one. Without free speech there cannot be genuine education and research, enquiry, debate, exchange of information, challenges to falsehood, questioning of governments, proposal and examination of opinion. Without free speech there cannot be a free press, which although it always abuses its freedoms in the hunt for profit, is necessary with all its warts, as one of the two essential estates of a free society (the other being an independent judiciary). Without free speech there cannot be a flourishing literature and theatre. Without free speech there are limits to innovation and experiment in any walk of life. In short and in sum, without free speech there is no freedom worth the name in other respects where freedom matters.

All this said, it is also true that there have to be limits to free speech at times. But it is absolutely vital that this be understood scrupulously and carefully, given what has just been said. The standard example of a case where limits to free speech are justified is crying 'fire!' in a crowded cinema. What is wrong with doing this, obviously, is gratuitously causing harm (to say 'gratuitously' or 'irresponsibly' adds little because there is no such thing as responsibly causing harm, as such; if harm is caused in achieving a greater good, as when one shouts 'fire!' in a crowded cinema when there really is a fire, it is the undesired by-product of intending to achieve good). Allowed too wide a reading, this can justify all manner of unjustifiable restrictions on free speech, as have occurred in our country in recent years ('glorification of terrorism', 'incitement to religious hatred'). Restrictions on free speech have to be extremely narrow, extremely specific, case by case, one-off, and only very rarely, on the best justification, prior to the speech itself.

The principle of freedom of speech promiscuously allows bad free speech, ranging from the stupid to the malicious and dangerous. If it is genuinely dangerous to life, as for example in direct incitement to murder, it invites a case-specific limitation. But generally the remedy for bad free speech is better free speech in response. In the case of libel and slander there is, as an instance of this, the post facto remedy of the courts. True, malicious mud-slinging is damaging even if a libel action is won, but free speech does not come free, and in a mature society we have to recognise that benefits carry costs, and this is one of them.

So vital is free speech to the health and liberty of a society that the plea of 'feeling offended' by what people say about one's choices and beliefs is not and can never be a reason for limiting free speech. Taking offence, followed by infantile demonstrations and infinitely more offensive threats of mayhem and death, has become a stock-in-trade of Muslim activists. This is unacceptable anywhere, but in Western liberal democracies especially so, for it strikes at the heart of what makes them both liberal and democracies. Censorship by coercion and special pleading is as big a threat to liberty in the West today as the actions by our own governments in diminishing our freedoms in the supposed interests of security. All who choose to come to live in a Western liberal democracy should be told that discrimination or insult directed at their age, ethnicity, disability if they have one, and sexuality – the things they cannot choose to have or be – will never be tolerated;

but their opinions and beliefs, the matters over which they have choice, are open season for cartoonists, satirists, and all those who disagree: and they must like it or lump it, or if they are too immature or insecure, or both, to do neither, they are free to leave.

All the above is directed mainly at the restrictions imposed on freedom of speech by our own governments in the last few years, in security measures and anti-terrorism laws. The stupid and objectionable girl misnamed the 'lyrical terrorist' is an unfortunate example of the wrong-headedness of restrictions on speech; how it sticks in the craw to defend someone who glorifies murderers in a 'poem', and yet consistency and principle demands it. How far we have come from a time, worse in many ways than our own, when one of our judges could resoundingly say, as the eighteenth-century Lord Mansfield did, 'So long as an act remains in bare intention alone it is not punishable by our law.' That has changed, for example with conspiracy and allied laws (some introduced in another period of panic, the late eighteenth- and early nineteenth-century scare caused by the French Revolution), and now with the proscription of 'glorification' of such inglorious things as terrorism; and our government has even sought to criminalise criticism of religion. The assault on free speech is well under way: it is the time for defence of it to get well under way too.

The Care and Maintenance of Friends

What is the highest and best form of human relationship, apart from the bond between a mother and her infant?

Without doubt it is friendship. To the champions of romantic love this might seem a calumny, but in fact romantic love is only the first step to what can become, if everything works out, the finest kind of friendship, for it is not an end in itself but a beginning to richer and deeper possibilities.

Think of it: if we can become friends with our lovers and spouses even as they remain our lovers and spouses, if we can become friends with our children and our parents even as they remain our children and parents, and likewise with our workmates and neighbours even as they remain these things too, then our relationships with them will have reached their summit. This is because of what friendship is: it is the vital connection that consists of trust, giving, support, enjoyment, sharing and caring, and is central to what makes life worth living.

The five key elements to friendship are mutuality, loyalty, readiness to help, readiness to challenge when necessary, and 'being there' as we say nowadays. Each can be illustrated from great examples of friendship in literature, legend and history.

Mutuality means the sharing of interests, concerns, pleasures and cares. In the tradition of philosophical debate about friendship, most writers have followed Aristotle in defining a friend as 'another self', but this is not quite right: respecting the other's difference, being complementary to one another, being a separate self, is important; it means each giving to the other what the other desires and needs in the bond of friendship. This is exemplified in the great friendship between Voltaire and the brilliant scientist Émilie du Châtelet, who began as lovers but soon became friends who supported each others' work and provided a creative foil helping each other to develop their ideas.

Readiness to help, to stand alongside one's friend, is illustrated in the story told by the poet Virgil of the love and friendship between Nisus and Euryalus, two soldiers in the army of Aeneas when he led his people to Italy after the fall of Troy. The pair were on a secret mission through enemy lines when Euryalus was caught, and although Nisus had already got through and was poised to carry the vital message to Aeneas, he saw his young friend in terrible danger, and plunged back into the fray to die at his side.

One of the oldest stories of loyalty is that of Ruth and Naomi in the Bible. When Naomi lost her husband and her sons she decided to return to her homeland, and told her daughters-in-law to do likewise since she had no more sons for them to marry. But Ruth would not leave her, and chose to convert to Naomi's religion so that she could remain with her. The two were inseparable thereafter, even when Naomi found Ruth a husband.

We have to challenge our friends, or be challenged by them, when either side needs admonishment, advice or warning. The point is best put by Oscar Wilde, who defined a friend as 'someone who stabs you in the front' – unlike an enemy who does it from behind. If we fail in the duty of giving our friends timely advice and admonishment when really necessary, we are not good enough as friends. But beware the 'toxic friend' who, under the disguise of being helpfully challenging, is really undermining.

Another way of describing the state of 'being there' for friends is keeping in touch and up to date with our friends' lives, remaining accessible, maintaining the flow of contact that nourishes the relationship and keeps it ready and apt in the ways just described. Here a good example is the torrent of letters that passed between members of the Bloomsbury Group – Virginia Woolf, Vanessa and Clive Bell, Roger Fry, Lytton Strachey and others – often half a dozen letters a day or more, which might seem excessive now but is easily replicable in this age of text messaging, Twitter and emails. A tweet can tell friends that we are thinking of them; when we know that we are in our friends' thoughts we are encouraged and warmed by it, especially at pressure-point times: going for a job interview, a medical procedure, a funeral, moving house, taking an exam.

Friends need as much if not more tending as a garden of flowers. Because friendship lies at the centre of good and flourishing lives, every one of us needs to be good at this special kind of gardening. The examples of Ruth and Nisus, Émilie du Châtelet and the Bloomsbury writers, show us how to do it.

But the question of definition remains: what is a friend? Since Aristotle there has been much debate in moral philosophy about this important question, but also – unusually for philosophy – much agreement. Friends, the philosophers say, are those who feel mutual affection and regard, who enjoy each other's company, have similar interests and tastes, help each other, share confidences, admonish each other when occasion calls for it, and always go the extra mile. To illustrate these qualities they cite famous literary and legendary examples of friendship: here are five examples to illustrate why.

Achilles and Patroclus are the famous friends of Homer's *Iliad*. There is the usual difficulty in classical cases of knowing whether they were gay lovers in addition to (or alternatively to?) being friends; most of history has regarded them as being such, though Homer tells us that when they went to bed in the same tent, it was each to his own couch, and each couch contained a beautiful young woman. You have to be good friends to choose this sleeping arrangement. The closeness of the bond between them is however most evident in the excoriating grief felt by Achilles when Patroclus was killed while personating him on the battlefield. In portraying them as intimately bound to each other, necessary to each, companions to each other in the deepest literal sense of the term, Homer offers a picture of friendship that sets the tone for much that followed in literature.

Jonathan and David are like Achilles and Patroclus in being men at arms, comrades both in circumstances of danger and in the world of affairs. David married Jonathan's sister, but this does not preclude the two men having been lovers also, as suggested by the fact that their mutual love is described as 'surpassing the love of women', and by the fact that the moment Jonathan first saw David he fell in love with him. So much did Jonathan love David that he not only opposed his father, King Saul, in order to protect David from Saul's jealous wrath, but went so far as to betray him in doing so, by telling David of his father's intentions and keeping David's whereabouts from his father's knowledge.

Ruth and Naomi offer one of the very few examples of friendship between women that literature and legend offer. The main reason is of course that women occupy the shadows of history, concealed from view in the harem or the inner courtyards, anonymously behind the men who figure in the stories that come down to us. No doubt the very nature of closeted and inward life forced on women made for richer, closer and more intimate friendships than men had – so it is an irony that the greatest arena of friendship might be hidden from us by the act of discrimination. But at least with Ruth and Naomi we see the loyalty and deep affection that make friendship a treasure, all the more so given that the choice that kept the two women together was a peculiarly difficult one for both.

Voltaire and Émilie du Châtelet might not seem an obvious choice for an example of friendship, and once again because there is sexual love in the picture; but after the honeymoon of the earlier phase of their relationship, these two highly intelligent and productive souls were friends above all else. Émilie translated Newton and made contributions to physics; here was a meeting of brains as well as personalities. Émilie protected Voltaire from the dangers he threatened to get himself into by his too acidulous pen; she fiddled the lottery to keep them financially afloat; in turn his wit and sharp mind interested and inspired her, and although they were too volatile a pair to remain together for ever, while they lasted they were a mutually enlivening combination in just the way that best friendships should be.

Vera Brittain and Winifred Holtby, both writers, the former the biographer of the latter also, were fast friends in their early adult lives, until the premature death of Winifred at the age of thirty-seven. They had met at Oxford and taken against each other at first, but when their friendship began in earnest they encouraged and solaced each other, growing together as writers in a world – the world of the two World Wars – still greatly inimical to women's chances. They both produced best-selling classics as a result of the support they gave each other, doing what friends so wonderfully do: giving each other permission to succeed, to aspire and to achieve. In writing of Holtby after her death, Brittain remarked that whereas a biography of a man could leave out his family life without having a material effect on the account, no biography of a woman could do that, because women are too closely defined by their relationships to husbands and children – or their absence. Rescuing Holtby from that occlusion was one of Brittain's greatest acts of friendship to her.

The Book of the Dead

One of the most pressing philosophical problems for early mankind must have been the question of what happens to the consciousness that each individual felt himself to possess; how could it just end and become nothing? In ancient cultures dreams, hallucinations and imaginings provided materials for an answer, resulting in entire mythologies and funeral traditions.

If an ancient Egyptian were rich enough when he died, his coffin would almost certainly contain a scroll with instructions, incantations and spells to guide him through the afterlife. This was the 'Book of the Dead', more accurately translated as the 'Book of Coming Forth to Daylight'. The scrolls were beautifully illustrated, although scholars say that in many of them the script was not always of the highest quality because they were prepared by undertakers, and in an age when literacy was a restricted skill, pictures were more significant than words.

The scrolls are therefore often exquisite works of art, as is the case with those in a recent British Museum exhibition 'Journey through the Afterlife', since recorded in a book preserving the images. It includes the Anhai Papyrus with its gold, pink and green hues, the outstanding Hunefer Papyrus likewise, and the longest Book of the Dead in the world at thirty-seven metres, the Greenfield Papyrus.

This Baedeker for the underworld illustrates how much importance the ancient Egyptians attached to their hopes for a posthumous existence. To reinforce the point, the British Museum exhibited the papyri along with painted coffins and gilded mummy masks, and with a remarkable panoply of the jewellery, trappings and statuary that accompanied them. Together the texts and artefacts expressed an entire universe of belief about a world regarded as vastly more significant than mortal existence.

A standard narrative for the Book of the Dead has the deceased entering the underworld, regaining the powers of speech and movement, proceeding to the place of judgement where his or her heart is weighed and, depending on the outcome, either being admitted to blessed occupancy of the afterlife, or being consigned to annihilation by the terrifying 'Devourer'.

In the Hunefer Papyrus the crucial sequence of events is shown in remarkable detail: the king's scribe, Hunefer, is led by Anubis to the weighing of his heart and, having passed the test, is taken by Horus to the throne of green-skinned Osiris, with the goddesses Isis and Nephthys standing behind. Above them sit the fourteen Egyptian gods arrayed as judges. It is cartoon, silent movie, high art and deep theology all in one.

Ancient Egypt was opened to the astonished and admiring view of the rest of the world by Napoleon's expedition there. Although Jean-François Champollion was the first to discover its treasures, he was quickly followed by other European scholars, among them Karl Lepsius, who invented the name 'Book of the Dead' for the funerary texts he found and published.

But it was the British who, having quickly ousted the French, accumulated one of the greatest collections of Egyptian antiquities, including the world's most comprehensive holdings of Book of the Dead manuscripts.

While Assyrian and Babylonian funerary practices included burying food and weapons to help the dead in their mysterious onward travels, it is only in Egypt that such elaborate preparations were made for that journey. It is as if the whole of existence pointed in that single direction.

This elaborate focus on an afterlife marks a great contrast: one acts very differently if the value of life is located after death rather than before it, and the respective art, thought and literature of cultures focused on these sharply opposed objectives are likewise very different. Funerary traditions are among the best resources on which to meditate on the difference: they are striking evidence of the fact that different phases in the history of humankind devoted very different thought, but similar time and wealth, to the visions at stake.

Darwin in Scotland

Charles Darwin's two years at Edinburgh University, passed there between the ages of sixteen and eighteen, were profoundly important for his later career. He was there ostensibly to study medicine, his father wishing him to follow in the paternal profession, but he so disliked the course that he paid it scarcely any attention, instead pursuing the passion for natural history that had been his primary avocation throughout boyhood at home in Shropshire.

Understandably, Edinburgh in particular and Scotland in general are eager to demonstrate their contribution to the development of Darwin's world-changing ideas. Edinburgh was then the 'Athens of the North', the capital of the Scottish Enlightenment, home to a roll-call of genius that included David Hume, Adam Smith and Walter Scott. The grip of dour Calvinism had been sufficiently loosened for the fruits of intellectual liberty to appear, so that when in his second year Darwin met the anatomist Robert Grant, sixteen years older than himself and equally passionate about natural history, it was to encounter a freethinker who had been convinced by reading Erasmus Darwin, Lamarck and Étienne Geoffroy Saint-Hilaire, and by discussion with his geologist colleague Robert Jameson, of the truth of biological evolution by descent from common ancestors.

By Darwin's own account Grant's radical convictions on this subject had no more effect on him than those of his grandfather Erasmus, whose *Zoonomia* he had already read. 'I listened [to Grant on evolution] in silent astonishment,' Darwin later wrote, 'and as far as I can judge, without any effect on my mind. I had previously read the Zoonomia of my grandfather in which similar views are maintained, but without producing any effect on me.' Obviously, though, the convictions of both Erasmus Darwin and Robert Grant – and others such as Robert Jameson and the radical espousers of the 'materialism' which was said to be 'too common among medical students' – indeed had an effect on Darwin; those ideas had merely to wait upon the accumulated evidence of his *Beagle* voyage and his reflection upon it, to convince him in their turn.

Darwin's brilliant powers of observation were already evident in the collecting, exploring and bird-watching of his childhood at The Mount in Shrewsbury. But they were fostered by his friendship with Grant, which was only occasionally clouded by Grant's habit of claiming credit for some of the discoveries Darwin made in their explorations along the shores of the Firth of Forth, studying marine invertebrates. In addition to Grant's tutoring, Darwin benefited from Jameson's geological lectures, lessons in taxidermy with the freed slave John Edmonstone, meetings of the Wernerian and Plinian natural history societies, and the specimens provided by his favourite recreations of shooting and fishing; all this fertilised the soil from which his later work was to flower. When he went to Cambridge immediately afterwards he began collecting beetles with his natural-history-mad cousin William Darwin Fox, more influenced by this than the fact that his rooms at Christ's College were those that had formerly belonged to William Paley.

Darwin's Edinburgh years gave not just his interest in the study of nature, but his skill in carrying it out, a tremendous boost. The attitudes and beliefs of those he encountered there likewise had an effect, though not immediately. Had he gone straight to Cambridge he would still have been a naturalist; a clergy career for younger sons, or generally for youths with no inclination for medicine or law, was the most amenable for anyone in love with natural history – Gilbert White of Selborne is the type of the clergyman more in love with insects and birds than preaching. But Darwin learned more, and more quickly, at Edinburgh by his exposure to like-minded people, and to the wonderful opportunity of exploring the shores of the Firth with Grant, than he would have done at Cambridge. And it has to be said, despite the hopelessness of proposing historical counterfactuals, that it is likely that modern evolutionary biology would be citing the name of Alfred Russel Wallace far more than that of Charles Darwin if Edinburgh had not been on his life's itinerary.

There is a general lesson in this. It is that climates of opinion, generally tendencies in the drift of ideas, opportunities for encounter between like-minded people, independence, the unfettered fostering of blue-sky interests, and the match of all or some of these things with a budding passion, make a powerful mixture. Of course original genius sometimes breaks through the antipathetic membrane of opposition and imposed orthodoxies. But Darwin's progress is like that of a ship given a good following wind and favourable tides; and Edinburgh is very much part of what wafted him on over the bar and out into the ocean of discovery.

Tocqueville on America

Books attain classic status by illuminating the universal in the particular, and by remaining perennially relevant. Tocqueville's *Democracy in America* is a classic in just this way. Tocqueville himself naturally hoped his book would be such a thing, but did not fully expect it; he was surprised by how quickly and widely successful it became. His aim had been to learn constitutional lessons from the American example, and to apply them to France and the rest of the Old World where, with equivocal feelings, he saw the spread of democracy as inevitable. When the book was published he found that he had done far more: he had added to the central literature of political science.

The book was the offspring of a fruitful marriage of differences, between on the one hand the perceptive and prescient mind of an aristocratic young European, le Comte Alexis-Charles-Henri Clérel de Tocqueville, and on the other hand the bustling, vigorous, expanding energies of Jacksonian America. Tocqueville travelled in America for a surprisingly short time, just nine months, but in that interval he covered a lot of miles, and an even larger territory of American mind and life. Apart from the brilliance of his intellectual and observational powers he had the great advantage of an intelligent friend at his side, Gustave de Beaumont, with whom he shared every step of the journey. Between them they took copious notes and wrote dozens of perspicacious letters home. Their journey is the subject of Leo Damrosch's *Tocqueville's Discovery of America*.

It is a long time since anyone has written in detail about Tocqueville's journey. Biographies naturally have to proportion the space they give those nine months in the fifty-four years of Tocqueville's life, and in any case their interest tends to focus on the period, several years later, encompassing the publication of Tocqueville's book and its reception. Damrosch has a different target. Making use of much material not available in English, which he presents here for the first time in his own translation, he is able to retrace Tocqueville's geographical and intellectual footsteps in detail, and by so doing casts much fresh light on the formation of Tocqueville's ideas.

But it is not only Tocqueville's ideas that come illuminatingly into view, but the young and uncertain United States of 1831 itself, for Damrosch takes us with Tocqueville and Beaumont to New York, the Great Lakes, the frontier woods and newly cleared farms, Boston, Philadelphia, the steamboats of the Mississippi, New Orleans and Washington, and on the way we meet every kind of American from the Bostonian Brahmin to the backwoodsman, the ambitious merchant, the welcoming log-cabin hermit, the cheerful steamboat captain, the slave, the leisured slave-owner, the dispossessed native American, and even President Jackson himself – in a White House that stood with a few other grand buildings dotted about in the otherwise scarcely tenanted wilderness of Washington as it then was.

It is essential to recognise that both Tocqueville and the democracy he was inspecting were young: he was twenty-six years of age when he explored America, and the democracy itself was not twice that. He was still young when his account of it was written and published. He had an old head, but as the rest of him caught up during the remaining half of his life, he was to become still less sure about democracy (he was half-unsure about it to begin with) and less convinced that liberty was its inevitable concomitant. To read of Tocqueville the elected representative, constitutionalist and government minister in his later years, or indeed to read other works he penned after visiting England, Ireland and Algeria, is to encounter a somewhat different person. But that does not diminish *Democracy in America*, as one sees all the more clearly because of Damrosch's account of the generous, open-minded but judicious and sometimes sceptical reactions of Tocqueville while he was actually on American soil.

The genius of Tocqueville is manifest in the way he unconsciously reprises Aristotle and anticipates both Marx and Mill in different ways. There could be no better description of Aristotle's 'megalopsychos' (the man of practical wisdom, following the middle path through situations of moral dilemma) than Tocqueville's picture of a certain American type: 'His features, which are lined by the cares of life, display practical intelligence and cold, persevering energy that is immediately striking. His gait is slow and formal, his words measured, and his appearance austere.' He anticipates Marx in writing of factory labourers under the Adam Smith pin-production principle, 'Nothing tends so much to materialize man and to eliminate every trace of soul from his work than the great division of labour.' Mill in *On Liberty* seems almost to paraphrase Tocqueville's observation that one of the principles underlying American democracy is that 'Each individual person … is the sole lawful judge of [his] own interest, and so long as it doesn't harm the interest of others, no one has the right to interfere.'

One could cull others of Tocqueville's many astute insights to illustrate the power of his mind, but the point of doing so would only be to reinforce the originality of his task: to explore – as he puts it – 'The future of democracy: the sole poetic idea of our time. An immense, indefinite idea. An era of renewal, of change in the social system of humanity.' That is what America represented to Tocqueville, and he was determined to examine its nature and implications. As Damrosch shows, Tocqueville had travelled thousands of miles across the rapidly expanding United States to feel the actuality, the lived reality of its people under their democracy, and by doing so he came to recognise its virtues and its dangers with special clarity.

Once home again in France, as he contemplated the wealth of material he had gathered, he had an epiphany: he saw that equality and despotism were not opposites, that there can arise a kind of 'soft despotism' accepted by the people who, welcoming its benevolent rule, still describe themselves as free. This was one of the deepest of the insights he brought home from the journey Damrosch describes. 'Above them,' Tocqueville writes of the citizens of a democracy which has mutated into a soft despotism, 'rises an immense tutelary power that alone takes charge of ensuring their pleasures and watching over their fate … it is absolute, detailed, regular, far-sighted, and mild. It would resemble paternal power if its object was to prepare men for adult life, but it seeks on the contrary to keep them in permanent childhood. It likes citizens to enjoy themselves, so long as all they think about is enjoyment. It labours willingly for their happiness, but it wants to be the sole agent of their happiness … The sovereign power doesn't break their wills, but it softens, bends, and directs them. It rarely compels action, but it constantly opposes action …'

This is pure genius. It describes quite a few contemporary Western liberal democracies, and the constitutional struggles of the Jacksonian populists over the Senate resonate with analogous constitutional tensions in a number of contemporary democracies. Today's United States is the achievement of a post-Civil War settlement and a continuing constitutional evolution that has addressed some of the doubts Tocqueville felt about democracy as always implying the risk of majoritarian tyranny; but the point is that Tocqueville saw those possibilities with clarity, and it is implausible not to think that his insight sometimes helped America take a more suitable path.

As the foregoing shows, although Damrosch's aim is to describe Tocqueville's and Beaumont's journey, inevitably that means describing the ideas they garnered as they went. This is lucidly and succinctly done. Damrosch does not sentimentalise Tocqueville's views of America and Americans, which were sometimes uncomplimentary to a degree, nor does he over-emphasise the many positives that Tocqueville found. But in general the portrait he gives of Tocqueville is an affectionate one, consistent with the satisfaction America has always taken in Tocqueville's account of it.

Damrosch's closing pages give only the briefest outline of the post-journey life of Tocqueville and his book, and do not reveal how different a man Tocqueville became from the one who saw America, and the implications of its constitutional arrangements, so clearly. But the interested reader should look to the biographies for that. Here Damrosch's central task – to give a kind of Tocquevillian *Anabasis*, and with it an account of the America he saw – is well and instructively done, and a highly useful addition to political literature.

Quantum Dirac

In the pantheon of heroic thinkers who effected the scientific revolution of the first half of the twentieth century, some are household names, at least in households with bookshelves: Einstein with his hair on end and his tongue sticking out, Heisenberg and Bohr at odds in Michael Frayn's play *Copenhagen*, and Schrödinger with his dead-and-alive cat. The other names of that revolution are less often on the general public's lips, among them Max Planck, Enrico Fermi, Wolfgang Pauli, Max Born and Paul Dirac.

Of these the last named is perhaps the most obscure in the public eye, but he was far from the least important. The main reason for his anonymity to all but scientists is that his work is so abstract and technical, so mathematical, that its Nobel

Prize-winning contribution to the formation of quantum mechanics in the 1920s and 1930s is not easily explicable apart from a detailed telling of that discovery's story.

But it is also in part the result of Dirac's diffidence and taciturnity, his shunning of publicity, his introversion, which is itself explainable by the fact that Dirac was probably to some degree autistic. Dirac himself attributed his marked social dysfunctionality to bullying by his Swiss-born father, who forced the young Dirac to dine alone with him and converse only in French (though they lived in the very English port city of Bristol where Dirac was born in 1902). The father's angry responses to linguistic mistakes were so terrifying that Dirac lapsed into a frozen silence that only thawed later with a few special friends, or when he was enthusiastic about something, or when he lectured on quantum mechanics.

Illustrative examples of his manner occur in the many stories told about Dirac in physics circles. One relates how a visitor to his Cambridge college, sitting next to him at High Table, attempted to engage him in conversation by asking whether he had seen any films recently. After considering this question for some time in his customary silence, Dirac replied, 'Why do you want to know?'

Absence of small talk, intense focus on his work, an obsession with precision, and a remarkable degree of abstract mathematical genius, made the thin, other-worldly figure of Dirac stand apart even in the small and highly rarefied world of early twentieth-century physics. Yet his story could be universally emblematic of creative genius in mathematics and science. It is a story of stunning achievements made when young, followed by long decades of fading powers and influence, increasing conservatism, dislike for the direction taken by the work of younger colleagues – Dirac's story is Einstein's story too, and the story of many lesser figures. Close to the end of his life Dirac said, in a sudden impassioned outburst to a visiting physicist whom he had not met before and who wished to discuss some ideas with him, 'No! I have nothing to talk about! My life has been a failure!'

The idea of the quantum was first proposed by Max Planck in the year 1900 as a merely heuristic device to solve the problem of why the glow emitted by a heating-up object changes from red through orange to blue. He suggested that we can give a systematic account of this phenomenon if we think of radiated energy as coming in discrete packages, to which he gave the name 'quanta' (Latin for 'amounts'). In the third of his three amazingly seminal papers of 1905, Einstein used Planck's idea to solve the puzzle of why metals produce electricity when light is shone on them, a phenomenon known as the photoelectric effect. This involved treating light as consisting of particles – photons – thus appearing to controvert the then prevailing and experimentally well-grounded view that light is a wave.

In 1912 Prince Louis de Broglie extended the idea of wave-particle duality from photons to other particles, a suggestion that was greeted with much scepticism until Niels Bohr showed that the quantum idea that implies it is indeed correct, for it explains why atoms are stable while yet being able to absorb and emit energy. If energy comes in lumps at discrete intervals on the energy gradient, so that the wavelength of an electron always has to have a whole-number value, then if it absorbs or emits energy it can only do so by jumping to another whole-number wavelength. When the mathematical basis of this picture was worked out, mainly by Heisenberg and Schrödinger, what resulted was an interpretation of electrons as in effect probability smears around the nuclei of atoms (these consisting of protons and neutrons), thus explaining why they seem to be both wave-like and particle-like. When electrons gain or lose energy they move instantaneously from one 'position' or orbit around the nucleus to another, with no staging posts between.

It was for this reason that Heisenberg formulated the 'Uncertainty Principle' stating that one cannot simultaneously measure both the position and the momentum (the mass multiplied by velocity) of a subatomic particle. This has profound consequences for the notion of causality and the idea in classical physics that if you knew everything about a physical system at a given moment, including the laws governing it, you would be able to deduce its past and future states. Quantum mechanics showed that this cannot be done; the neat world of classical physics had been overturned.

And since a quantum state consists not in a definite set of values but in a range of probabilities – for example: a particle does not have a definite path until it is calculated – it further seems to imply that reality only has a determinate character when it is measured (thus making physicists indispensable to reality). This is the idea behind the 'Schrödinger's Cat' example: the cat in the physics box in which a quantum event will settle whether a noxious gas is released or is not released, will be both dead and alive (both states will be in 'superposition') until the box is opened and someone looks in, at which point it will become definitely either dead or alive: the observation 'collapses the wave function'.

The philosophical weirdness of this way of thinking about reality was happily accepted by Bohr and his colleagues at his institute in Copenhagen – hence it is known as the

'Copenhagen Interpretation' – but Einstein and not a few others found it impossible to accept, and thought that it meant there is something fundamentally wrong with quantum mechanics. Dirac's response to the weirdness of the quantum world as revealed by the powerful mathematics in which it was expressed was to say, 'Shut up and calculate!' – that is, forget the philosophical angst, if the mathematics is beautiful, that is enough.

Indeed, mathematical beauty was Dirac's guiding principle, and it was what led him to the discoveries that earned him the Nobel Prize in 1933 and the placement of his portrait next to Einstein's on a wall in Princeton's Institute of Advanced Studies. His chief discovery was the equation – the Dirac Equation – that describes the behaviour of matter particles, but he also both made and anticipated a number of further discoveries, showing what a remarkable scientific imagination he had.

The Dirac Equation describes the wave function of electrons relativistically, and it led to his prediction of the existence of positrons (the antiparticle of the electron) and by extension the concept of anti-matter. He is the founder of quantum electrodynamics (and the coiner of this name), the part of quantum theory that deals with the interaction of photons with electrons and positrons. Satisfyingly for Dirac's love of precision and mathematical beauty, the theory (described by Richard Feynman as 'the jewel of physics') makes extremely accurate predictions of certain atomic quantities.

No account of Dirac's work – and his work was his life – is complete without mentioning that in it he joined Einstein's special theory of relativity to quantum mechanics, predicted the existence of magnetic monopoles, founded operator theory, and devised the notation (known as 'bra-ket' notation) standardly used in the field. In addition he anticipated, in sketch form, certain ideas in cosmology, and he even anticipated today's dominant theory of the fundamental structure of matter, string theory. One of his enduring services to science was his brilliant book, *The Principles of Quantum Mechanics*, whose clarity, logic, lucidity and innovations of formalism made it the standard text. His remark that his life had been a failure could therefore not be further from the truth.

His personal life was dogged by a sense of tragedy – he hated his father, suffered lifelong grief over his elder brother's suicide, and had a complicated relationship with his demanding mother. But Dirac bloomed in the all-male atmosphere of Cambridge, which was perfect for someone with his degree of autism: he was fed, looked after, closeted, allowed to spend six days a week doing nothing but mathematics undisturbed, on the seventh taking solitary walks in the surrounding fenlands.

But then Dirac married an ebullient and warm-hearted Hungarian divorcee, Manci, his 'anti-particle', so different were they, who by him had two children. This was perhaps the most astonishing thing Dirac ever did outside physics, but evidently it was a wise decision – and not lightly taken, as several years' worth of Dirac's dry and unemotional letters shows. When Manci wrote, 'Do you have any feelings for me?' Dirac replied, 'Yes, some.' The letters briefly ceased to be reticent after the honeymoon, during which Dirac seems to have fallen in love with his wife: sex unleashed passion for a while. He was very lucky to have married a divorcee; the idea of his marrying a virgin does not bear thinking about – or perhaps Ian McEwan has done that thinking for us in *On Chesil Beach*.

Despite being a Cambridge don in the years before 1939, and despite having much sympathy with communism and a great friend in the Russian physicist Peter Kapitza whom he frequently visited in the Soviet Union, Dirac was not one of the Cambridge spies. Although he contributed to the war work of developing an atom bomb, he did so on the margins of the work, refusing to become more deeply engaged. He was in most ways apolitical, a disengaged theoretician, whose single political act was to join the campaign to persuade Stalin to let Kapitza leave the Soviet Union.

At one point Dirac and Einstein had offices in the same corridor of the Institute for Advanced Studies at Princeton, but they scarcely interacted. Yet when news of Einstein's death reached Dirac years later, he wept; the only time his wife ever saw him cry.

The long years of unproductivity and marginalisation that Dirac experienced when his creative period was over – its prime years occurred between the mid-1920s and the early 1930s, when he was in his twenties – might have made Dirac feel a failure at last, not least because he never succeeded in solving his great puzzle concerning the interaction of electrons and photons; but if he could read biographical accounts of his life he would see that it had magic in it, and triumph: the magic of revelations about the deep nature of reality, and the triumph of having moved human understanding several steps further towards the light.

Thucydides

If there is a single must-read for students of history, politics, warfare and international relations, it is Thucydides' *History of the Peloponnesian War*, recounting the struggle between the empires of Athens and Sparta in the last three decades of the fifth century BCE. Its modern influence reached a peak – and has remained there ever since – in the second half of the twentieth century, as exemplified by Admiral Stansfield Turner's placing it at the head of the reading list for officers at the US Naval War College when he became its president in 1972. It has remained on all relevant reading lists since.

Turner was prompted to make his officer-students read Thucydides by the parallels that the latter's classic text offered. Thucydides wrote of the conflict between two great rivals who had shortly beforehand been allied against a dangerous third party – he meant Athens and Sparta against Persia; for Turner, the parallel was the US and USSR against Nazi Germany. But Turner also saw a parallel between Athens' failure in the Sicilian Expedition, launched in 415 BCE, and the bitter experience of Vietnam then still fresh in American minds. In the tensions of the Cold War it seemed to many more than Turner alone that Thucydides' overarching view – that war is the basic condition of mankind, and that the chief motives of international action are fear and self-interest – was unimpeachably right.

It is not only the matter but the manner of Thucydides' great work that is inspirational. He regarded the war between Athens and Sparta as the greatest and most significant that the world had seen to that date, and considered that the lessons it taught would therefore be of perpetual importance to mankind. (We might now attach a different weighting to the importance of the Graeco-Persian war half a century earlier, in which the Battle of Salamis, 480 BCE, saved the cradle of Western civilisation from Oriental invasion.) Moreover Thucydides claimed that he wrote his history in a thoroughly scientific spirit, with neutrality and dispassion, seeking the objective truth by sifting and examining evidence and weighing the inconsistencies between different accounts of what happened. His claim to be the first-ever rigorous historian is backed by the fact that he was actually there, at the outset as a senior participant and then as an avid spectator of all that happened.

Few historians are in a better position than Donald Kagan to evaluate Thucydides' merits and achievement, which is the task he set himself in a major study. Kagan's four-volume history of the Peloponnesian War, followed by a brilliant one-volume epitome of it, are the standard contemporary texts in the field, and he has parlayed the wisdom gleaned from his close study both of that war and of Thucydides' account of it into discussions of the origins of war, the possibilities of peace, and contemporary geopolitics. When therefore he argues that Thucydides' account of the Peloponnesian War is tendentious and revisionary, and in important respects misleading, one does well to sit up and take notice. For this indeed is the burden of Kagan's striking account, which in forensic and exacting style places Thucydides in the historiographical dock.

This does not mean that Kagan is hostile to Thucydides; not a bit of it. He is an admirer – who could not be – but an objective one. He reveals Thucydides as a thoroughly revisionary historian, bent on opposing the view widely held in his own day that Athens' disaster in the Peloponnesian War was the fault of Pericles, whose mistakes in foreign policy were its cause, and whose early management of it planted the seeds of defeat. Instead Thucydides wished to establish an alternative thesis: that the war was inevitable because of Sparta's fear of Athens' growing power, and that it was the decayed quality of Athenian democracy after Pericles, exemplified by the crudity of Cleon and other lesser men, that betrayed Athens to defeat. In the process Thucydides sought to defend the reputation not only of Pericles but also of Nicias, leader of both the peace party and the disastrous Sicilian campaign.

Kagan notes that Thucydides, in order to shape his readers' interpretation of events, is very selective in reporting speeches in the Athenian assembly, and very economical with the facts of what happened in various battles and campaigns, such for example as the loss of Amphipolis (where Thucydides himself had been in command, and whose loss resulted in his exile by his fellow-Athenians). Thucydides quotes only those speeches in the assembly that bear out his version of events; because he is on the whole careful and accurate in conveying the burden of what was said (apart from his own scruples, his contemporaries would have caught him out otherwise), he chose not to give the anti-Pericleans any ammunition by presenting the case made by those whose view of events he was determined to contradict.

By contrast Kagan tells us, among other correctives to Thucydides' picture, that though Cleon might have been a vulgarian and a hawk, he was a notable warrior, and that though Nicias might have been a dove stamped in the same mould as Pericles, his incompetence in Sicily turned a defeat into a catastrophe.

Thucydides was not trying to mislead; as he saw it from his own partisan viewpoint, he was trying to correct. In doing so he was revising the standard view of the war held by his contemporaries. Kagan likewise is revising our view – not of the war but of Thucydides himself; not to impugn him, but to set the record straight by revealing the great historian's bias and aim, and rescuing those he unfairly attacked. The case Kagan makes seems hard to fault, so carefully does he argue it and so copiously does he substantiate it; though doubtless among the scholars – whose ingenuity one should never underestimate – occasion will be found for nits to be picked.

Getting the record straight in Kagan's terms makes very little difference to the value of Thucydides' work as a textbook for politics and diplomacy. In these domains the intricacies of calculation explored by Thucydides, the dangers of weak allies drawing their stronger partners into conflict, the inevitability that suspicion and self-interest will exacerbate bad situations, and the ultimate fact that it is economics that wins wars, all remain starkly true. In an earlier book Kagan argued that the chief parallel between Thucydides' war and the recent past is with the First World War, and indeed in 1914 it was entanglements of alliances, looped round spinning axes of suspicion and self-interest, that drew each other and thereby an entire civilisation into the abyss. In the darkening days of 431 BCE it was the peripheral colonies of the major cities which began to skirmish, petitioning for their parent cities' help, and the parent cities, watchful of revolt and secession in their empires, became drawn in against their wills. The warning in that tale remains clarion clear today.

Montaigne

Michel de Montaigne's greatest successor in the tradition of the essay, William Hazlitt, said 'Montaigne was the first to have the courage to say as an author what he felt as a man.' This hits the nail on the head. There is no neater encapsulation of what is special about Montaigne: the frankness and directness of his self-revelation, his lack of pretension and conceit, and his amused but generous view of all things human, make him a wonderfully refreshing personality – and it is his personality that comes direct from the page along with the fruits of his wide reading and his liberal attitudes. He was fascinated by the world of human experience, and writing about it was his way of meditating on it.

After inheriting his father's rich estate in the lush interior of Aquitaine, Montaigne decided to quit public life as a magistrate in the *parlement* of Bordeaux, and devote himself to leisurely study. Instead of leading to the Horatian idyll of self-cultivation that Montaigne expected, the inactivity and desultory reading gave him a nervous breakdown. It was to steady himself that he began to write.

When I lately retired to my own house, with a resolution, as much as possibly I could, to avoid all manner of concern in affairs, and to spend in privacy and repose the little remainder of time I have to live, I fancied I could not more oblige my mind than to suffer it at full leisure to entertain and divert itself, which I now hoped it might henceforth do, as being by time become more settled and mature; but I find that, quite contrary, it is like a horse that has broke from his rider, who voluntarily runs into a much more violent career than any horseman would put him to, and creates me so many chimaeras and fantastic monsters, one upon another, without order or design, that, the better at leisure to contemplate their strangeness and absurdity, I have begun to commit them to writing, hoping in time to make it ashamed of itself.

Since he was neither a military man nor a man of affairs, Montaigne's only subject matter was himself; so he resolved to try (*essayer*) to assay himself, his nature, his opinions, his attitudes and reactions, pretending nothing and confessing all. 'I am myself the matter of my book,' he wrote; and he knew that he was engaged in something wholly original by being so. The result is a classic that has been admired, imitated and enjoyed ever since.

> Others form Man; I give an account of Man and sketch a picture of a particular one of them who is very badly formed and who, if I could, I would truly make very different from what he is; but that's past recalling ... I propose a life ordinary and without lustre: 'tis all one; all moral philosophy may as well be applied to a common and private life, as to one of richer composition: every man carries the entire form of human condition. Authors communicate themselves to the people by some especial and extrinsic mark; I, the first of any, by my universal being; as Michel de Montaigne, not as a grammarian, a poet, or a lawyer.

A major reason for the enduring attraction of Montaigne's *Essays* is that they do what all classics do: they illuminate the universal in the particular. In one way this should be a surprise, because Montaigne was a highly individual man, and by his own account a rather unsuccessful one. He frankly confessed his inabilities and shortcomings, his dislike of business, his yearning for solitude, his regret at being forgetful and not very clever, his physical lacks (he was short and had, he tells us, a small penis). Yet his frankness is refreshing and full of human truth.

Now I am something lower than the middle stature, a defect that not only borders upon deformity, but carries withal a great deal of inconvenience along with it ... Little men, says Aristotle, are pretty, but not handsome ...

Is it reasonable that, being so particular in my way of living, I should pretend to recommend myself to the public knowledge? And is it also reason that I should produce to the world, where art and handling have so much credit and authority, crude and simple effects of nature, and of a weak nature to boot?

Nevertheless Montaigne found a method of writing suited to the character of his mind – an aleatory, divagatory, exploratory method which meanders along with his thoughts, making his essays unsystematic and random, full of unexpected and invariably entertaining detours.

His great question was Socrates' question: 'how should one live?' and this makes him a contemporary for all times. Scholars like to emphasise the respects in which he was of his epoch, rooting him in the turbulent mixture of Renaissance and Reformation that made it possible for him to write as a pagan while in the midst of the sixteenth century's bitter Wars of Religion. His own family was divided between the Protestant and Catholic causes, but, following the example of Justus Lipsius, Montaigne himself remained scrupulously orthodox to outward view as a Catholic, though every indication in his writings tells us that he was a sceptic in religion as in everything else, and had – as Pascal critically noted – a pagan attitude to death as the end of one's existence. But when we allow him his universality we see why he speaks with equal clarity to his contemporaries at the end of the sixteenth century, to Voltaire in the eighteenth century, to William Hazlitt in the nineteenth, and to us today.

The two keys to Montaigne are his sympathetic imagination, and his scepticism. Like Hazlitt after him, Montaigne recognised that understanding human nature and the human condition is crucially a matter of entering sympathetically into the experience of others.

> I am one of those who are most sensible of the power of imagination: every one is jostled by it, but some are overthrown by it. It has a very piercing impression upon me ... I could live by the sole help of healthful and jolly company: the very sight of another's pain materially pains me, and I often usurp the sensations of another person. A perpetual cough in another tickles my lungs and throat. I more unwillingly visit the sick in whom by love and duty I am interested, than those I care not for, to whom I less look. I take possession of the disease I am concerned at, and take it to myself.

The other key to Montaigne is scepticism, the scepticism of the ancient Greek philosopher Pyrrho of Elis, as recorded by Sextus Empiricus. Pyrrho argued that because the arguments for and against any proposition are equally good or bad, one must suspend judgement (a state known as *acatalepsia*). This open-minded, non-committal, often ambiguous stance suited Montaigne. He accordingly chose as his motto *Que sais-je?* What do I know? said with a shrug of the shoulders. But there's a nuance here that was well spotted by the great late-nineteenth-century Montaigne scholar Pierre Villey: that Montaigne was a true Pyrrhonian only in his middle period – the period of Book

Two of the *Essays*. In Book One he was a Stoic, that is, one who believes that we must resign ourselves with courage to face life's inevitabilities, but must master ourselves with respect to what lies under our own control: namely our appetites and fears and desires. By the time of Book Three, written a decade after the publication of the first two books, Montaigne had come to accept what the Chinese philosopher Mencius before him, and Jean-Jacques Rousseau after him, independently believed: that man is naturally good.

This development in his attitude (it was not strictly speaking a change of view) is interesting. Montaigne retired from public life in 1568, the year that he inherited his estate. His nervous breakdown occurred around 1570. He wrote the essays comprising Book One in the first half of the 1570s, and the essays of Book Two in the second half of the 1570s. They were published together in 1580, and became an immediate best-seller. Montaigne then travelled for his health to the spas of Germany and Italy, keeping a journal; and in the late 1580s he wrote the essays comprising Book Three. These are far longer than the earlier essays, and to me they suggest a return to Stoicism – a revised, modified, sceptical Stoicism to be sure, but a form of Stoicism nonetheless, filtered through an even more intensely personal and modest self-examination. Remember his words, quoted earlier: 'Others form Man; I give an account of Man and sketch a picture of a particular one of them who is very badly formed and who, if I could, I'd truly make very different from what he is.' The journey to this mature reconciliation with himself came courtesy of his profound belief that anything viewed from the long perspective of history, or from vantage points quite different from one's own habitual attitudes, would put everything into perspective, making both enthusiasm and anxiety impossible. And he therefore arrived at the conclusion that, although 'badly formed', he did not need to remake himself differently even if he could.

> Were I to live my life over again, I should live it just as I have lived it; I neither complain of the past, nor do I fear the future; and if I am not much deceived, I am the same within that I am without.

That is the voice of someone who has come to terms with himself, showing that the process of writing the essays had achieved its intended effect after all.

But it was not only self-understanding and the desire to cure a nervous breakdown that motivated Montaigne. He found that the whole human spectacle demanded contemplation too, and he applied his ideal of Olympian neutrality, formed from his Stoic and Sceptic inclinations, to make sense of it. A controversial example is his reaction to the St Bartholomew's Day Massacre and the violent sectarian hatreds that both unleashed and followed it. The Massacre was that awful event in France in 1572 in which Roman Catholics murdered thousands of Huguenots, an assault that began on St Bartholomew's Day, 23 August, and continued in different French cities over several months.

These events occurred even as Montaigne was writing the first book of his essays, and his reaction to them was Stoic detachment, an attitude that made some of his later readers temper their admiration – especially the Romantics of the nineteenth century, who found him too dispassionate, too cool, in contrast to their style of enthusiasm. But those who had learned enough from life to understand the saying 'in youth I loved Ovid, in age I love Horace' well understood his point. Take for example Stefan Zweig as just such a reader; before his suicide in 1942 Zweig listed the general propositions that Montaigne, despite his sceptic *acatalepsia*, came to assert as convictions, all on the theme of being free: free from vanity, from partisanship, from ambition, from the fear of death.

Montaigne assumed the role of detached spectator of the human comedy, and advised having an intimately private 'room behind the shop' as he put it – rather like Virginia Woolf's 'Room of One's Own' – where one could commune with oneself in peace and solitude. This, he said, was a necessary condition for his plan of exploring humanity by exploring himself.

> For this design of mine, 'tis convenient for me to write at home, in a wild country, where I have nobody to assist or relieve me; where I hardly see a man who understands the Latin of the Paternoster, and of French little less. I might have done it better elsewhere, but then the work would have been less my own; and its principal end and perfection is to be exactly mine.

But although Montaigne extolled the virtues of solitude, he also advised conviviality and friendship, and the profound lifelong love he felt for the friend he lost early in life, the poet Étienne de la Boétie, demonstrates that he understood this on his pulses. That is an attractive feature of the man, and goes a long way to explaining the ingenuousness, modesty and sanity of his account of himself, offered as a self-portrait of humanity; for it is not possible to know oneself without knowing others, any more than one can know one's own country properly without having travelled abroad.

An important aspect of knowing others is the generosity and sympathy with which one views them. I've mentioned both characteristics already as defining features of Montaigne's attitude. They meant that he could, with a tinge of mischief sometimes, illuminate one idea by a very different idea. Thus, talking about how our desires and ambitions are augmented by the difficulties we encounter in pursuing them, he uses the example of how the lawgiver of ancient Sparta, Lycurgus, made it a rule that married couples should behave towards each other like secret adulterous lovers:

> To keep love in breath, Lycurgus made a decree that the married people of Lacedaemon should never enjoy one another but by stealth; and that it should be as great a shame to take them in bed together as committing with others. The difficulty of assignations, the danger of surprise, the shame of the morning, these are what give the piquancy to the sauce … Pleasure itself seeks to be heightened with pain: it is much sweeter when it smarts and the skin is rippled. The courtesan Flora said she never lay with Pompey but that she made him wear the prints of her teeth. And so it is in everything: difficulty gives all things their estimation.

That is a prime example of Montaigne's entertaining, insightful, rambling way with the subjects he wrote about. He sought to instruct by amusing, and invariably succeeds. He is a conversationalist in print, and it makes him a very good companion. He died in 1592 at the age of 61, not a bad age for that era, and bequeathed to us a literary and philosophical gem which, four centuries later, gleams as brilliantly as ever.

Socrates

Bertrand Russell was of opinion that Jesus was not as clever as Socrates or as compassionate as the Buddha. Although this view has its merits, by focusing on the differences among the three it misses an important similarity: that they all gained large followings because (and emphatically not in spite) of the fact that they wrote nothing. All their teachings are attributed by others, their lives are the stuff of followers' legends, their place in history secure because, inadvertently or otherwise, they anticipated the significance of the proverbial remark, 'Oh that my enemy had written a book!'

What little we know about Socrates comes to us, with a few exceptions, from his friends and their followers. The resulting portrait is on the whole an affectionate one, and testifies to his charisma as an individual. The same is true of the other large civilisational figures whom we know only through report; to those already mentioned we can add Confucius, Islam's Mohammed and Sikhism's Guru Nanak as examples.

The trouble with such figures is that they lend themselves to endless interpretation and reinterpretation, to reading-in and reinvention, to different and often competing depictions. As far as I know, however, in the case of Socrates there has never been such a jaw-dropping hagiography as the one provided by Paul Johnson, whose admiring – perhaps the better word is besotted – account of the ancient thinker has joined Iman Wilkens's *Where Troy Once Stood* (the book that places the Trojan war in England's East Anglia and, with perfect seriousness, claims that Achilles was a Dutchman) among my all-time favourite Amazing Books.

Is anyone able to extract the 'real, actual historic Socrates' from Plato's habit of interpolating his, Plato's, own take on things into accounts of Socrates' character and teachings? Paul Johnson claims that he can, and attempts to do so in his *Socrates: A Man for our Times* (2012). His 'real actual' Socrates is not just 'the noblest, the gentlest, the bravest man' but veritably a kind of religious prophet, a divinely inspired preacher of surprisingly Christian-like views, or perhaps (the portrait blurs in and out as the pages turn) a proto-quasi-John the Baptist making straight the way for St Paul – this by preparing the Greek world to be more receptive to the Christian message that Paul brought it.

Johnson gets progressively more carried away by this theme as his book proceeds, these encroachments on the *avant la lettre* Christianity-likeness of the Socratic 'ministry', as Johnson calls it, becoming dithyrhambic. 'It was the combination of Jesus's inspired Hebrew message of charity, selflessness, acceptance of suffering, and willing sacrifice with the clear Socratic vision of the soul's triumph and the eternal life awaiting it,' Johnson claims, 'that gave the Christianity which sprang from Paul's teaching of the Gospels its astonishing power and ubiquity and enabled it to flourish in persecution and martyrdom.' (A few lines later, with a sudden but all-too-brief awareness that nonsense hovers, Johnson contradictorily recants: 'Socrates was not a Christian precursor ...') The fact that Christianity adopted the neo-Platonists' version of the immortal immaterial soul several centuries into the Christian era, having until then been good Jews on the question of death by expecting actual bodily resurrection at the Second Coming, does not trouble Johnson because, obviously, he does not know it.

Ignorance is remediable; logic-blindness takes longer to correct. Johnson pounces on the fact that Socrates talked about his 'inner voice', the apotreptic ('warning-off') prompting that alerted him against making mistakes. He described it as the voice of a god, which was in keeping with the Greek way of speaking about everything from artistic inspiration to conscience. But Johnson inflates Socrates' inner voice to a full-blown Judaeo-Christian-like deity (the Voice of God), and its message to a full-blown ministry. From giving an occasional warning it becomes the determinant of the whole of Socrates' career: philosophy was, Johnson avers, 'the mission God had given him in life', and 'his inner voice from God ... ordained him to conduct philosophy as he understood it'. Note the language: 'mission', 'ordination', 'ministry'.

This magnification of the inner voice is merely over-excitement on Johnson's part; the failure of logic enters when he says that Socrates' philosophical 'mission' was to encourage people to think for themselves. So according to Johnson, Socrates is commanded by God to tell people to think for themselves, and he obeys. No paradox there? – hmm.

This is not the only contradiction. On page 92 of his book Johnson's Socrates is a postmodernist and relativist: Socrates is 'hostile not just to the "right answer" but to the very idea of there being a right answer'. By page 114 he is the direct opposite; he 'opts firmly for moral absolutism'. By page 119 Socrates is even more emphatically anti-relativist; he there espouses 'moral absolutism at its most stringent'.

Johnson asserts that Socrates' interests were strictly practical, in that he was not interested in 'justice in the abstract' but in actual workaday justice. This claim breathtakingly ignores Socrates' relentless quest for the essence – the abstract defining

211

quiddity – of justice, continence, truth, courage, virtue, knowledge, the good, and so on, which in the early dialogues typically terminates for the participants in 'aporia', the state of no longer knowing what one does or should think about the matter. Since Socrates' claim was that he only knew that he knew nothing (which is why the Delphic oracle pronounced him the wisest of men), he was officially excluded from himself offering a definition; his role in the elenchus – the method of enquiry by question and answer, conjecture and refutation – was to get people to see that they were as ignorant as himself. We are a far cry here, in knowing no answers, from knowing any absolutely right answers.

In the middle and later dialogues of Plato, where Socrates is even more obviously a mouthpiece than he is in the early dialogues, answers most certainly appear – Plato's answers of course – in the doctrines of the Forms and anamnesis (this latter literally means 'unforgetting', that is, recalling the total knowledge one's immortal soul enjoyed in its pre-embodied direct contact with the Forms, which are the eternal, immutable and perfect exemplars of things).

Johnson's misunderstanding of Socrates' aims as they appear in Plato's early dialogues, as well as in the tangential reports of others – admiringly in Xenophon, satirically in Aristophanes – and his insistent eagerness to make Socrates look like a Christ-like figure of perfect virtue and self-sacrifice, result in great distortion. Oddly, Johnson's desire in the latter respect chimes with Plato's own effort to portray Socrates as saint and martyr, though Johnson dismisses Plato's portrait with lofty (but as we see hubristic) contempt.

Johnson's beatification of Socrates leads him to claim that 'In terms of his influence, he was the most important of all

212 of all

philosophers.' Were Johnson acquainted with philosophy beyond the Teach Yourself level he would know that Plato and Aristotle between them have an influence which is as Everest to Socrates' molehill. A. N. Whitehead's description of philosophy as 'footnotes to Plato' does not exaggerate by much.

But what is the influence that Johnson thinks Socrates exerts? 'What he did,' Johnson claims, 'was to concentrate on making more substantial the presence of an overriding divine force, a God who permeated all things and ordained the universe. This dramatic simplification made it possible for him to construct a system of ethics that was direct, plausible, workable and satisfying.' Not one word of this even remotely applies to anything known of Socrates. Socrates was a religious prophet? Socrates was a pantheist? Socrates constructed an ethical system?

If you wish to know how Johnson gets to miss the point of Socrates so comprehensively you only have to note two things. First, he ignores the possibility that Aristophanes' depiction of Socrates in *The Clouds* probably contained enough truth to make a knowledgeable Athenian audience laugh.

And second, and at his greater peril, Johnson disdains Plato: '[the Republic] is not a text where, in general, the real Socrates speaks, though I think he does in this particular passage' – meaning that he (perhaps the Voice of God) knows better than Plato (or any Plato scholar of the last two and a half thousand years) when the 'real Socrates' speaks. When Plato's depiction fails to chime with Johnson's made-up version, it is dismissed as 'illustrating his [Plato's] irritating habit of foisting his personal views on others'. Pot and kettle here! so Johnson cherry-picks words and passages that suit his purposes, and discards the rest.

Yet only consider the views that Johnson foists on Socrates. He has Socrates teach that 'The most important occupation of a human being was to subdue his bodily instincts and train himself to respond to the teachings of the soul.' On another page, remember, his ordained mission was 'to teach people to think for themselves', as – purportedly – God told him to say: which is nevertheless a bit closer to the Socrates we see through the dark Platonic glass.

One of the biggest twists Johnson gives to the tale concerns the politics of Socrates' trial and death. Socrates and Plato had been associated with the aristocratic party that led Athens into ruin and subjected it to tyranny, and he was put to death by the democracy which supplanted it, a few years after the democracy had granted amnesties to various members of the tyrant party in the hope of soothing the troubled character of state affairs. That Socrates was brought to trial about four years after the amnesty suggests that he, alone or with others, was still regarded as a problem.

Subsequent history has blamed the democrats for executing Socrates, and Johnson tries to twist things round to distance the sage from the tyrant party and thus have him wrongly maligned and condemned. Here, at least and at last, he is with Plato and Xenophon in painting Socrates in victim's colours. But there is enough reason to think (the aristocratic fascism of Plato might alone make you think) that the smoke curling about Socrates' head had a bit of fire under it.

In fact, Johnson offers a portrait not of Socrates but of a fictional character, a portrait that says more about his own wish-fulfilment urges than any Greek who lived within five hundred years of Socrates. His account reads like the muddled conflation of sketchy bits of theology and misunderstandings of what you might guess were whisky-flavoured evenings spent riffling through some pages of Plato, idly turning some pages of Xenophon, and sleepily scanning a few secondary sources. It is a farrago. The good news is that it is one less book to burden your shelves.

But its existence is a severe warning against the tendentious use that some try to make of the past and its denizens, to bolster their own current prejudices. The corrective is to read primary texts for oneself – the dialogues of Plato in this case – to see how far the distortions and plain silliness of an account such as Johnson gives can go. For they go many miles beyond anything sensible and proportionate: and it is sense and proportion that the world always needs.

Edmund Burke

Even though two of Edmund Burke's works, *A Letter to William Elliot* (1795) and *Letters on a Regicide Peace* (1795–7), deal with the French Revolution in a more thorough and (as one would expect from their dates) more informed way, his most famous work remains *Reflections on the Revolution in France*. One reason is its immediacy and urgency; it was written within eighteen months of the fall of the Bastille in 1789, and is an expression of Burke's deepest convictions about what makes for good government and public order. The fact that this impassioned and highly polemical essay counts among the founding documents of political conservatism immediately indicates its general tenor: Burke's convictions were indeed profoundly conservative, and as the course of French history unfolded in the years after 1789 its argument came to be that of those who strove for the return of 'legitimacy' (which, by the end of the long wars that the kings of Europe fought against France, meant the restoration of the Bourbon monarchy to Versailles).

And this in turn alerts one to something that the title of the work does not by itself lead one to expect: that Burke's central concern is not so much France and its revolution, as a defence of the monarchical principle in the British context. Burke felt that such a defence was necessary because proponents of radical reform in Britain were excitedly invoking the spirit of the French Revolution to argue for change at home.

The immediate prompt for Burke's essay was the publication of a sermon delivered at the Old Jewry meeting house in London on 4 November 1789 by Dr Richard Price, the eminent Dissenting minister and educator. The sermon was entitled *A Discourse on the Love of our Country*, and in it Price profited from the fact that a revolution was in full swing across the Channel to remind his audience of Britain's own revolution in 1688, the 'Glorious Revolution' that had ousted the Catholic King James II, placed William of Orange and Queen Mary on the throne, and established a new constitutional settlement. Price spoke of what 1688 meant for the people of Britain, as he and his fellow reformers saw it, thus: that the monarch was the people's servant and occupied his throne by their consent, and correlatively that the people could frame their own governments for themselves by choosing them and if necessary cashiering them for misconduct.

Although Price bemoaned the fact that efforts to reform the system of parliamentary representation had stalled (first steps towards this had to wait another generation, until the Reform

Bill of 1832), even so he could rejoice at 'the favourableness of the present times to all exertions in the cause of public liberty'. Alluding explicitly to France he added,

> I have lived to see the rights of men better understood than ever, and nations panting for liberty, which seemed to have lost the idea of it. I have lived to see thirty millions of people, indignant and resolute, spurning at slavery, and demanding liberty with an irresistible voice, their king led in triumph, and an arbitrary monarch surrendering himself to his subjects … now, methinks, I see the ardour for liberty catching and spreading, a general amendment beginning in human affairs, the dominion of kings changed for the dominion of laws, and the dominion of priests giving way to the dominion of reason and conscience.

These sentiments sparked Burke's indignation and anxiety. 'This doctrine,' he fulminated, 'as applied to the prince now on the British throne, either is nonsense and therefore neither true nor false, or it affirms a most unfounded, dangerous, illegal and unconstitutional position. According to this spiritual doctor of politics, if his Majesty does not owe his crown to the choice of his people, he is no lawful king.' And Burke proceeded to challenge each of the claims Price made regarding the British subjects' right to 'frame a government' for themselves by choosing and dismissing their governors. 'This new and hitherto unheard of bill of rights,' Burke wrote, 'though made in the name of the whole people, belongs to those gentlemen and their faction only. The body of the people of England have no share in it. They utterly disclaim it. They will resist the practical assertion of it with their lives and fortunes.' By denouncing the reformist view of the 1688 Revolution Burke assumed responsibility for interpreting it in a way that would make it seem different from what was happening in France. It was a tall order. It was after all a seminal event, in which the British deposed a king, and their parliament installed another, and thereby – as representatives of the people – made themselves effectively supreme. He had to find arguments showing, despite all appearances, that William of Orange's accession did not consist in a grant of the crown by popular election, but was in fact the very opposite: a reaffirmation of the principle of the crown's heritability. And he argued that, anyway, if the people had ever had a pre-existing right to choose their kings, the parliament of 1688 had abjured that right for itself and all its successors for ever.

That these are implausible and, frankly, spurious arguments might be shown in any number of ways. Parliament, notionally (if the electoral system had been better) the representatives of the people, had in truth chosen a king, and in doing so had become greatly more powerful than before. It had thereby won its long struggle with monarchy in the seventeenth century. What Burke called 'this seditious, unconstitutional doctrine' was fact, though at that stage in the transition from monarchy to parliamentary democracy the reins of power had gone from throne to establishment and not yet to the people as such. But Price was right; what had happened in 1688 was a version of what was happening less circumstantially and disguisedly in France.

Burke in fact gets into a tangle in trying to refute the inferences drawn by Price from the 1688 settlement. He acknowledges that 'they who led the Revolution [of 1688]' charged James II with 'having broken the original contract between king and people' – so, there was such a contract, even if implicit, and breaking it gave the people a right to cashier the monarch. Again, Burke inadvertently strengthens Price's case by acknowledging that the statutes enacted by the 1688 parliament established that 'the whole government would be under the constant inspection and active control of the popular representative and of the magnates of the kingdom' and that 'the next great constitutional act, that of the 12th and 13th of King William [established] the further limitation of the crown and better securing the rights and liberties of the subject'. Here again, Price's inferences are supported rather than refuted, though the subjection of the crown to the popular will was then, as in Price's own day, still indirect – and the implication of Price's praise for the French Revolution, as his hearers would have understood (and certainly Burke did), is that it shows how the process could be more comprehensively realised.

In short, you might characterise Burke's famous *Reflections on the Revolution in France* as an act of political special pleading. He summed up his own conservatism by extolling what he saw as a characteristic and guiding British attitude: 'A politic caution, a guarded circumspection, a moral rather than a complexional timidity were among the ruling principles of our forefathers in their most decided conduct.' It was to defend this approach that he undertook his constitutional reinterpretation of Britain's own revolution, by rewriting the history of 1688 to turn it from a revolution into a shining example of politic caution and guarded circumspection.

Given that Burke's chief aim was to dampen the French-inspired ardour of reformers in Britain, he could not restrict himself to refuting Price's inferences from what happened in 1688; he had to put his case into the context of contemporary events in France, and compare them with an idealised British way of doing things, either directly or by implication. In the bulk of the *Reflections* Burke therefore describes and attacks what was happening in France, praises the ancient practices of the English, waxes poetic over the charms of Marie Antoinette, criticises the fecklessness of the Assembly in Paris not least over financial affairs, surveys historical examples from Roman times to the recent past, glances at the shortcomings of French agriculture and commerce, bemoans the degeneracy of France's nobility, and in general ranges to and fro over everything his expansive mind saw as relevant to decrying the example then being set by the revolution. But his chief target throughout is the set of principles and hopes enunciated by the Old Jewry sermon.

Burke's hostility to the ideas expounded by Price had a mixed set of roots, ranging from a deep dislike of democracy, then widely perceived by ruling elites as no better than mob rule ('ochlocracy') with all the ignorance, depravity and anarchy that this implied, to a shocked sentiment of chivalry at the incivilities to which Queen Marie Antoinette had been subjected by French crowds. Price alluded to both points in the Preface to the Fourth Edition of his sermon, where he had an opportunity to respond to Burke's attack: 'But what candour or what moderation,' asked Price, 'can be expected in a person so frantic with zeal for hereditary claims and aristocratical distinctions as to be capable of decrying popular rights and the aid of philosophy in forming governments, of lamenting that the age of chivalry is gone, and of believing that the insults offered by a mob to the Queen of France have extinguished for ever the glory of Europe?' This conflict of views between Burke and Price is the pivot on which the *Reflections* turn. Price was not the only one to answer Burke's answer to Price; even more famously, Thomas Paine did likewise, in his *The Rights of Man*.

It should not be forgotten that in the 1790s, fearful of what events in France portended, the British government enacted a number of highly illiberal laws, suspending habeas corpus, outlawing political reform organisations, prosecuting radicals for sedition and treason, and going to war partly out of fear that the contagion of revolution would spread. (The other reason was to grab French overseas possessions while France itself was distracted by internal turmoil.) The efforts and hopes of reformers were quashed for a generation; illiberal and reactionary government persisted (with only a brief break in the form of the Ministry of All Talents with Charles James Fox among its leaders in 1806) until 1832. Burke was on the winning side of this period of reaction and oppression, and indeed might be considered its chief intellectual architect.

For all its diversity of content, the *Reflections* is nevertheless a political classic – and also a literary one. The great essayist William Hazlitt was emphatically opposed to Burke's political outlook, but greatly admired both the excellence of his writing and the power of his mind; he described Burke's style – the style both of his prose and his thought – as 'forked and playful as the lightening, crested like the serpent'. In an age of strongly partisan politics such generosity in recognising the qualities of an opponent was most unusual, for party sentiment coloured every judgement. No two thinkers could hold views so utterly different; Hazlitt was a lifelong supporter of the French Revolution's founding principles. But Hazlitt's recognition of Burke's literary and intellectual talents even across the bitter political divide of the time is a striking testimony to Burke's powers, and reminds one why he is still worth reading today.

The Unity of the Good

It was an assumption of the ancients, and a desire of the early moderns, that there should be a deep connection between what is of value in the world and the well-lived life. That connection is simple but can be variously expressed: that a life is well lived if lived in conformity with what matters; that the pursuit of what matters is constitutive of the worthwhile life; that lives shaped and guided by value-based goals are the best kinds of lives. The trick was to establish what matters; living in conformity with it might not always be easy (weakness of will and insufficient luck, as Aristotle noted, are among the greatest barriers to doing so), but this seemed the lesser problem.

Behind this assumption was another: that values – the things that matter – form an interconnected, mutually supportive and therefore integrated whole. If this were not so then the connection between values and the worthwhile life would at least be complicated, if not compromised. Suppose there to be an unresolvable tension between two great values – say, individual liberty and social justice – such that the pursuit of one is a stumbling-block to the other. At the very least, an individual who cares about both will be condemned to live with the strain of the conflict. Isaiah Berlin famously saw this as the tragedy of the liberal condition.

There are of course always resolutions on the further reaches of the spectrum of views about political morality: for the libertarian on one wing and the totalitarian on the other, it is easy to see which value is subordinate, or not even a value. But for those who think that the moral realm is in some sense a kingdom of ends, these are not options; for them the hope is that one person's liberty does not have to be bought at the expense of injustice to others, that fairness for all does not have to limit or obviate the legitimate choices of each.

The view that such hope is vain has been embraced with enthusiasm by some, infected by the postmodernist relish for contrarian and relativistic options. But it has also been accepted more rationally by others, or has posed itself as a peculiarly difficult obstruction to systematic accounts of values and virtues, and most particularly to the achievement of consistency in depictions of personal ethics and political morality. There is a distinguished roll-call of recent and contemporary philosophers who have taken this view, even if they sought also to argue that it is not wholly destructive of the idea of moral life: chief among them Thomas Nagel, Bernard Williams, Michael Stocker, David Wiggins, John Kekes, and of course Isaiah Berlin himself.

Ronald Dworkin took up cudgels against this trend in order to make the case for the unity of value in his last great book, *Justice for Hedgehogs* (2013). 'The truth about living well and being good and what is wonderful is not only coherent but mutually supporting,' he writes in it; 'what we think about any one of these must stand up, eventually, to any argument we find compelling about the rest.'

Making this case required Dworkin to bring together ethics, morals, politics and law in a complex tapestry of argument that contests some of the most widely accepted contemporary views in philosophy. The cases he makes about truth and interpretation, free will, the status of moral claims, justice, law, liberty, democracy, and the mutually supportive relations that hold among them, are therefore controversial and often radical. This is all the more so because Dworkin is an applied philosopher; these topics are matters of practical importance, making a difference in legislatures and courts of law, and through them touching hundreds of millions of individual lives.

That is what gives the overall argument its urgency, for one notes that Dworkin's principal applied aim in establishing the unity of value is the familiar and central one for him: the question of justice and political morality.

Dworkin says that the two fundamental conditions of legitimacy for any government are that it should display equal concern for each individual under its sway, while at the same time recognising the right and responsibility of all individuals to choose how to make good lives for themselves. These principles constrain acceptable theories about how governments should distribute opportunities and resources among the governed. In particular they rule out theories that promote the virtues of unbridled markets as well as those, at the other extreme, that urge equalisation of resources independently of individual efforts and talents. So the demand is for a way to effect just distributions that respect both principles. This is what Dworkin seeks to do in the book's closing sections. But the journey to that goal involves confronting many currently entrenched views entailing the disunity of value; the meat of the book is a mighty battle against these.

One such entrenched view is that there will inevitably be a conflict between the justice thus sought, and liberty. Dworkin offers a view that rules such conflict out. He starts by distinguishing freedom from liberty, the former being what one can do without restraint from government, the latter being that part of freedom which a government would do wrong to forbid. He does not think that there is a general right to freedom, but instead a set of rights – to ethical autonomy, free expression, ownership of property and due legal process – which together flow from the right to equal concern owed to them by government (hence due process and ownership) and from the right and responsibility to find their own way to a good life (hence free expression and autonomy). This means that the concepts of liberty and equality are fully integrated; there is no way to decide what liberty requires without having a view about which way of distributing resources and opportunities will display equal concern for each person.

The alleged threat of conflict remains, however, between these two values, just reconciled, and democracy. Here the idea is that a majority might vote to pass laws diminishing or abrogating liberty and the just distribution it requires. Having a right to participate in making such decisions therefore offers the prospect of conflict. Dworkin says that the answer is to discriminate more finely among senses of 'democracy'. If instead of resting content with a majoritarian or statistical definition of democracy one argues for a partnership conception of it – that is, one having it that each individual is an equal partner in the process, thus having an equal stake in the outcome of decisions, not just an equal vote in arriving at them – then one sees that democracy in fact requires liberty and justice in just the senses given.

A standard line in discussions about political theory is that we face a perennial threat of conflict between justice and law. The idea is that there are no guarantees that laws will be just, and when they are not, those who apply the laws will accordingly be required by them to perpetrate injustices. Dworkin's response is to argue for a shift in perspective on the nature of law to see it as a branch of morality, and hence incapable of conflicting with it. This requires a twofold adjustment of viewpoint: there has to be an emphasis on ideas of fair governance as well as just outcomes, what Dworkin calls 'procedural justice', and one has to see the claim that law is part of morality as locating it on a flow-chart of conceptions in which the most general one, ethics (the living of a good life), embraces morality (how one treats others), which in turn embraces politics; and law, in its turn again, is embraced by political morality.

Dworkin acknowledged that this approach might seem to gain him his victory too easily – arriving at the unity of values by mere redefinition of terms, thus conjuring conflict away. But each step of the argument is vigorously and fully argued in successive chapters of the book; the test he set himself – that 'what we think about any one of these must stand up, eventually, to any argument we find compelling about the rest' – is applied throughout. Indeed his insistence on a coherence criterion for the sustainability of these claims – the requirement that they are fully interlocking and mutually supportive – is fundamental to his case. How else, he asks, could our conceptions of political values be conclusively persuasive unless they form an integrated whole? En route there are therefore arguments about the notions (truth, free will, the nature of moral claims) which are vital components of the structure that brings them together and holds them there.

Obviously enough, a crucial one is truth. If an argument is to be successfully made that such-and-such a way of thinking about a given key concept – liberty, say, or equality – is the right one, then there has to be a test of rightness, and before that a community of understanding of the concept itself. Agreements and disagreements over concepts are genuine when the parties all share the same understanding of them. Lots of cases are easy to settle, for example a dispute over how many apples are in the basket, because we agree on what counts as an appropriate test. But we also share some concepts in a different way, on the basis of what Dworkin calls 'interpretation'. Here he makes a move reminiscent of Wittgenstein. There can be a community of understanding about such concepts because of the way they figure in our shared experience and form of life, allowing us to recognise them as concepts describing values even if we disagree about the values themselves. Such a disagreement would not merely be a verbal one of the sort that a dictionary could settle, or one concerning matters of fact. It would be a disagreement that requires us to invoke other values as justifying our view about the value in question – which itself shows that values are inseparably interconnected.

Because of the significance of the concept of interpretation for Dworkin's account, he devotes two chapters to it, one on its general use across a wide range of subject matters including literature, history, law, sociology and more, and one more specifically on conceptual interpretation, bearing directly on moral reasoning. In the first Dworkin offers a general theory of interpretation which is value-based, arguing that any interpreter, whether of a law or a literary text, an historical occurrence or a political act, has 'critical responsibilities' which, when best lived up to, constitute the best interpretation of the law or text in question. Despite all the puzzles that the idea of interpretation invites, not least that in offering one we sometimes 'feel' that our own is right (or true) even when we cannot explain why in opposition to someone else's contrary interpretation, nevertheless 'the distinctive truth-seeking and argumentative phenomenology of interpretation survives. Interpretation would be a radically different intellectual activity if interpreters did not characteristically claim truth and assume disagreement rather than only difference.'

This invites the 'daunting' task of explaining what makes interpretative judgements true, if they are true. Here is where Dworkin's 'value theory' bites. We interpret as we do because there is a practice or tradition of interpretation that we can join, and this practice aims at truth. In offering interpretations we both intend, and are understood as intending, to say something true. We do not regard our interpretative activities as pointless endeavours; we seek to achieve something by them, often important things. We assume that something of value is served by interpreting, and we accept our responsibility to promote that value. 'Interpretation is therefore interpretative, just as morality is moral, all the way down.'

It is a corollary of this that Dworkin was an objectivist about value: there really are wrong acts and unjust institutions, and cases can be made for saying so. In this he goes against the majority trend of thinking about value in contemporary debate, and not just as part of the academic game: 'We cannot defend a theory of justice without also defending, as part of the same enterprise, a theory of moral objectivity. It is irresponsible to try to do without such a theory.'

One of several key moments in furtherance of this argument is reached in Dworkin's chapter on conceptual interpretation. Having distinguished interpretative concepts from others in a taxonomy of concepts, and insisting again that moral concepts are interpretative concepts, he adds, 'That claim has great significance for moral and political philosophy. It offers to explain, for example, why the popular idea is mistaken that philosophers can provide an "analysis" of justice or liberty or morality or courage or law that is neutral about the substantive value or importance of those ideals.' There can be no such neutral analyses, for anything said about any of these ideals is itself in the end an endorsement or rejection of them. In particular application to morality, the claim is that there are no meta-ethical statements, where 'meta-ethics' is second-order philosophical reflection on the nature and status of moral claims. Rather, there are only normative first-order ones; a putative meta-ethical statement such as 'there are no objective moral truths' is, Dworkin argues, itself a normative ethical statement.

One big thing this means is that debates about where value comes from, and whether we should be realist or anti-realist, constructivist or minimalist about them (to employ the terms of vigorous recent debates about their metaphysical status), are, says Dworkin, beside the point, for value is independent. There is no question of having to match value judgements to moral entities of some kind existing 'out there' as the truth-makers or breakers of what we say. Such judgements are true, when true, because of the case that can be made on behalf of them. All talk of values is value-talk; there is no extra level of talk about values – their status, their analysis – which is not itself value-laden, and therefore in fact just value-talk.

Another way of putting the point is to say that any theory of such values as justice or liberty is moral 'all the way down'. And that means that moral responsibility is a crucial matter. We might not be able to demand agreement from our fellows in society, but we can demand that they be responsible in their reasoning and acting, taking seriously their interpretations of fundamental moral concepts and placing them in the overall scheme of values which accommodates and supports them. But the idea of responsibility as a virtue, to which Dworkin devotes a chapter, in turn requires that we conceive of ourselves as beings possessed of free will; and here Dworkin offers important arguments for a 'compatibilist' view to the effect that the idea of ourselves as genuinely responsible agents is consistent with any plausible assumption we can make about what causes our decisions and what follows from them. His starting point for the case is ethical, set in the phenomenology of agency – the fact that no one can literally believe 'pessimistic incompatibilism', the view that because 'all behaviour is determined by past events [it is] never appropriate to attribute judgemental responsibility to anyone'. By itself, of course, this phenomenological point is not an argument for what matters to Dworkin, namely 'judgemental responsibility', but it reminds us of the capacities that are relevant to its expression – being able to form true beliefs and to make decisions consistent with one's normative personality. The immediate importance of these capacities is that no one can live well – the ethical goal – unless they often enough make the right decisions based on true beliefs. And the question, 'How should one live?' is the central and fundamental question.

Dworkin also presents a sustained argument for the view that we all have an overriding responsibility to create something of value in our lives, and further argues that our responsibilities to others follow from this responsibility to ourselves. The value we seek to promote in both cases is 'adverbial value' – it arises from how we live, from the manner of our living. Dignity and self-respect, taking one's own life seriously, asserting the right and accepting the responsibility to make ethical decisions for ourselves: this is the stuff of the good life, and it implies an attitude of respect for others – hence, the ethical promotes the moral – because in the fulfilment of our own humanity we recognise and respond to the humanity of others. There are many familiar but important questions in the offing here which, in a succession of chapters, Dworkin considers, variously regarding whom we should aid and when, why we should not harm them, what our obligations to them are and whether obligations are graduated by degrees of membership in various communities. This in turn raises the question of justice, which is where the book ends, completing the demonstration that politics is part of ethics, and that the values which constitute the overarching network of ethics form ipso facto a unitary and integrated system.

Dworkin's rejection of meta-ethics is tied to a particular reading of Hume's insistence that value cannot be derived from fact, a reading which denies that this insistence amounts to scepticism about morality. In saying that all moral judgements and claims are both normative and truth-valued, and that their truth, when true, is established by the case that can be made for them, Dworkin is, as we see, firmly repudiating views about the nature of moral judgements premised on their not being literally true or false. Such views analyse moral judgements as exhortations to behave in certain ways, or as expressions of attitudes or preferences; on such views assertions like 'that is good' really mean 'behave like that!' or 'I like that!' Now, it would be a feeble attempt at a counter to Dworkin to say that rejecting meta-ethics is itself a meta-ethical position, given that he has a better theory about first-order moral claims, namely, that they are true or false and that their truth-values are established by argument. But it is worth pointing out that one can agree with him on this while rejecting the Humean fact-value distinction. There is an attractive alternative to it which says that there are certain facts about sentient creatures, and most obviously human beings, that are value-soaked right through, and whose truth is what makes certain moral assertions true. For example, the capacity of sentient beings for suffering and pleasure, and their preference in general for the latter over the former, places an immediate constraint on the choices of an agent aware of this fact and conscious of the conformity of his own preferences with it. To charge someone with insensitivity, cruelty, malice, sadism and the like, if he harms other sentient creatures despite knowing that, like himself, they would prefer not to be harmed, rests squarely on appeal to these very facts. This has seemed so obvious to many moralists from Epicurus onwards that it is rather Hume and G. E. Moore who seem to hold the queer view, in opposing the objectivity of morality and describing, in Moore's case, the natural view as a fallacy (indeed, 'the naturalistic fallacy'). Dworkin's argument that morality is objective and its judgements evaluable for truth does not depend on prior acceptance of the Hume argument, and might indeed be strengthened by the opposite view. His acceptance of the fact–value divide might in part be motivated by the desire to treat the making of value judgements as a self-consistent and independent exercise not vulnerable to 'meta' debates about their status and whether or not they assume something other than the practice itself of making them, as if appeal to naturalistic facts amounted to a concession that for value-judgements to make sense and do any work they require a realm of truth-makers and breakers. But if, as suggested, the facts are value-soaked, then the independence of the value realm is assured: that is why there is nothing else, outside them, that a meta-theory can insist must be invoked.

But the fact–value distinction plays another role in Dworkin's account. If there is one discussion in a book so internally connected and systematic that can be lifted out for separate inspection, it is the case he makes for a compatibilist view of judgemental responsibility. The free will–determinism debate is so trodden over and riddled with efforts at escape-clause distinctions that, for the most part, it has become impossible to explore without having to heave a mountain of surrounding discussion around first. Its sheer difficulty is well illustrated by Thomas Nagel's confession that the idea of an uncaused cause, which is what a human will would be if agent causation existed, is both unintelligible and irresistible.

Dworkin takes a fresh tack into the problem from his starting point in the ethical demand for judgemental responsibility and the everyday experience – the 'ordinary economy' – of exercising it. 'Deliberate behaviour has an internal life,' he reminds us; 'there is a way it feels deliberately to act. We intend to do something, and we do it. There is a moment of final decision, the moment when the die is cast, the moment when the decision to act merges with the action decided on. That internal sense of deliberate action marks the distinction, essential to our ethical and moral experience, between acting and being acted upon: between pushing and being pushed.' This is right. The phenomenology of freedom, even granting the pressures, expectations and obligations that constrain us when we choose and act, is sharply different from the phenomenology of coercion, of 'being made to act against our will'. There is an entire palette of cases where we straightforwardly recognise the difference: hypnosis, mind control by drugs and mental illness are examples.

The question becomes one of control, understanding different concepts of which illuminates the principles connecting the causes of an agent's decisions to his responsibility for them. One, which Dworkin calls the 'causal' sense of control, makes judgemental responsibility turn on the originating causes of a decision, while the other, 'capacity' control, is what an agent feels when he exercises a capacity to face a decision and make it without someone or something else doing it through or for him. The first embodies a third-party perspective, the second a first-person perspective. They each imply different principles as underwriters of responsibility, and they contradict each other. Dworkin's way of choosing between them is to argue that the capacity control principle makes better sense of the rest of ethical experience and opinion, whereas the causal principle is an 'interpretative orphan: we can find or construct no good reason why it should be part of our ethics'.

Capacity control, on the other hand, fits into an integrated picture of the value our lives have to ourselves and in themselves, and relates better to the fact that the character of our decisions is part of their value, which is not just a matter of their origins. But the 'unfolding drama of self-conscious life' requires what might be described as ownership of its essential elements, those constitutive and life-directing decisions which a proper account of character and biography would not be able to ignore if it were well given. This last is not quite how Dworkin puts it, but in line with his idea of interpretation as a process which, responsibly done, gives right answers or best outcomes or truth, the interpretation of a life would most responsibly focus on the sober self-attribution of responsibility for those decisions which made the life what it was.

This argument is a very important one. Proponents of versions of compatibilism closer to the causal control model, and certainly proponents of the hardest determinism, will have to ask again about the plausibility of any view that relegates to a massive and systematic error theory the salience of capacity control in our ethical autobiographies, and what it entails and is required by in our interpretation of human life – even more, of well-lived life, if the notion retains a purchase without the integrated view of values in which genuine responsibility plays a central part.

Dworkin offers a one-system picture that requires us to see that political morality flows from personal morality and that personal morality in turn flows from ethics. The view is controversial, and seems to imply that 'a community's law is always what it should be'. But that is not what Dworkin meant; what he meant is the family of differences that would be made by having law studied in philosophy and politics departments as well as in law schools, making a difference to each of the disciplines in question – and to the nature of their application in the real world.

H. G. Wells and Mr Lewisham

Most first novels tend to be largely autobiographical. Although by the time he wrote *Love and Mr Lewisham* H. G. Wells had published ten books – seven science fiction novels, which he called 'fantasy romances', three science textbooks and a number of short stories – this was what he thought of as his first 'proper' novel, and it indeed draws heavily on his own life. With the exception of the timing of young Mr Lewisham's meeting with Ethel Henderson and their subsequent re-encounter and marriage, the events of the novel closely follow Wells' own experience. Both in literary and in biographical terms, therefore, *Love and Mr Lewisham* is a fully paid-up example of literary realism.

But in being so it is, for all its wit, readability and surface clarity, a darker and more complex work than it appears. It cost Wells a great effort to write it; he told friends that he had thrown away much more than he kept, and that more time and care had gone into it than into (as he put it) a work of scientific research for the Royal Society. What reads easily is often the result of assiduous polishing and editing, and this is the case here. It follows that Wells left much between the lines that he would later (in *Tono-Bungay* and *Ann Veronica*) be more frank about, especially regarding sex. The competition between aspiring mind and youthful body is, familiarly, all too often a one-sided one, but what in the Arcadia of Longus would have been a simple matter is, in *Love and Mr Lewisham*, the source of a tragic diversion of talent and opportunity. This, with its setting of associated themes, makes one look at *Love and Mr Lewisham* with a more interested and more instructed eye.

The novel tells of the effect of love on an aspiring youth, the eponymous Mr Lewisham, who at the novel's opening is a teenaged teaching assistant in a provincial town, without connections or money. He there meets the engaging but otherwise very ordinary Ethel Henderson, a young woman trapped in a net of unappetising dependencies. Some of the live themes of the day – education as the doorway to opportunity for the lower classes, socialism, science, spiritualist charlatanism and a still-stifling sexual and social morality – drive the tale, which follows a course whose predictability is a main part of its point.

Lewisham and Ethel are attracted; one day they go for a long walk which involves Lewisham neglecting his teaching duties and Ethel neglecting the possible harm to her reputation. As a result he is dismissed from his post and she is sent back to her useless and venal mother in London to seek work as a typist. They lose contact.

Lewisham gets a place at the Normal School of Science in London, and at first shows great promise. He there establishes a friendship with the dowdy and earnest Miss Heydinger, who believes in his potential to become a Great Man and a husband for herself. But then at a spiritualist séance where Lewisham is a sceptical observer he meets Ethel again; she is secretary to a wealthy dabbler in the occult, and she abets the fraudulent spiritualist displays of her uncle, Chaffery. Lewisham is appalled by Ethel's involvement in deceit, but his attraction to her is rekindled in urgency, with the inevitable result that she comes to displace his commitment to education, his friendship for Miss Heydinger, and indeed his common sense.

The most poignant moment in a novel which begins with wit and light and grows increasingly dark as the coils of consequence wind around Lewisham and Ethel, occurs at the end of the simple register office wedding which unites their destinies. 'The little old gentleman made no long speeches. "You are young people," he said slowly, "and life together is a difficult thing … Be kind to each other." He smiled a little sadly, and held out a friendly hand.'

That is the fulcrum of the story, summarised by Wells himself as being about the diversion of a young man's hopes by youthful infatuation and the resulting heavy commitment of an unsuitable, too young and ill-provided marriage. In our own day infatuations and the strong sexual imperatives of youth only rarely lead to such mistakes, and in any case the mistakes are more easily remediable now. But for Lewisham and Ethel the finalities of a restrictive code meant that all sorts of possibilities were blighted by the all-too-human needs whose denial was the price that a chance to make progress exacted.

Wells did everything Lewisham did in the way of teenage teaching and then the Normal School for Science (founded shortly before Wells went there by T. H. Huxley – and Huxley was one of Wells' teachers), but he did not make his first marriage until later than Lewisham did, and it was not the reason for his taking longer to finish his science education. Wells was self-confessedly a man of powerful sexual urges, and his first marriage, to his cousin Isabel, was a failure because she was unresponsive. But the lineaments of Lewisham's story are strongly those of Wells' own; whence its almost-documentary character arises.

The realism point is a significant one for appreciating *Love and Mr Lewisham*, because it bears on the fact that he was intent on iterating in his own way and from his own experience a truth, however ordinary and familiar, about aspiration and its competition with other imperatives. In an earlier period of literary history he would have had to do this by indirection, perhaps in allegory or something close to it. But by the closing decades of the nineteenth century it had became possible for fiction to address the lives and experiences of a broader and more realistically identified social range than hitherto, and to do it without undue drama – for the drama is in the ordinariness, the familiarity of the pattern.

Consider: Dickens paraded a colourful troupe of the urban poor, criminals, orphans, slum dwellers, the lower middle classes and the aspiring middle classes, but his characters are closer to types or caricatures than those in the works of Wells' contemporaries Thomas Hardy, George Gissing and Arnold Bennett. George Eliot is cited as an innovator in English realism, though the major influence for late-century novelists might more plausibly be Balzac and Zola across the Channel. Yet however one traces the genealogy of literary realism, it is clear that by the end of the century it was not merely permissible but interesting for novels to be about individuals like Lewisham and Ethel, and about themes – socialism, spiritualism, science – that were current matters of discussion.

No doubt the widened literacy of the age had created a readership as interested in recognisable individuals with some of the same experiences and problems as other or earlier readers were interested in Clarissa and Lovelace, Elizabeth Bennet and Darcy. Wells had a keen sense of the actual, a trait that explains the success not only of his straight fiction but also of both his 'fantasy romances' and his polemical writings. You might say that he was to his contemporary readers what television is to its majority audience today, and in that way he anticipates the kitchen-sink realists writing novels and plays in the 1950s, perhaps even helping to prepare the way for them.

It would, though, be a mistake to relegate Wells to a place in the history of the novel as though that were the chief thing to be said. His writerly skills are sometimes under-appreciated because of the popularity and breadth of his output; for he was able to convey place, mood and situation with precision even when – as sometimes happened – he descended into archness and facetiousness. In the earlier chapters of *Love and Mr Lewisham* an affectionate but accurate gaze is bent on the young Lewisham's grand designs for progress towards success in the form of his 'schema' and highly intellectual reading list. This is not only straight out of Wells' own past, but the pasts of many hopeful young folk. Most who read this novel will therefore experience a pang of recognition and a stab of regret, knowing that even though we do not now have anything like the same barriers that faced Lewisham, schemas and grand designs have a general tendency to collapse at their first encounter with the real world and its testing of our commitments. Wells explores this with the deftness and facility that reveals his gift as a writer, and the fact that by the time he came to write *Love and Mr Lewisham* he was an accomplished practitioner.

Writerly skill is only part of the story. The theme of the novel is a significant one for an age in which opportunities for intellectual ambition were greater than ever before because of wider schooling and increased literacy, yet the enemies of promise, as Cyril Connolly was to call them half a century later, had not been defeated – largely because some of them, as Wells sought to show, are undefeatable. That is the observation, the commentary, that Wells felt it worth offering; and it was not then the cliché that it might seem to some now.

At the end of the novel Wells has Lewisham ponder the implications of the fact that Ethel is pregnant, and then base an insight upon them. At this point, remember, Lewisham has a wife, a forthcoming child, a mother-in-law, a dismal tenement home in a grim suburb of London, no qualifications, missed opportunities to regret, and limited prospects – and yet he proceeds to welcome the thought that the child is the future and the future must be served. The idea that the present must subordinate itself to the future is not, in all frankness, any more appealing in Wells' pages than it was in the Soviet injunction to suffer today in order to build tomorrow's glorious society.

This is the chief respect in which form (the need for an up-tick at the close) and sentiment overcome Wells sufficiently for a false note to sound; but there is a way of looking at it which excuses him. It is that anyone placed as Lewisham then was might well reach for the nearest justification for enduring or accepting, of making the best of the situation by having (what is natural for a would-have-been intellectual) a fine-sounding principle. 'The Future!'

Yet on the other hand the Wells who is true to himself might say that the real message of the novel lies in Miss Heydinger's wordless departure from her last discussion with Lewisham; at that sad moment she is the embodiment of the failure of hope, which is Lewisham's own experience too. This is a bleak result, to be sure, and itself not invariably true to life; but the logic of Wells' tale points in that direction, though while reading the early pages of the novel with their charm, wit and freshness you wish you could expect otherwise.

Fishing with a Golden Hook

In his life of Augustus Caesar, the Roman writer Suetonius reports the emperor as saying that wars should only be undertaken in the confident expectation of large rewards. To go to war for small or uncertain returns is, Augustus said, like 'fishing with a golden hook': nothing one could catch is worth the risk of the hook's loss.

In this age of asymmetric conflicts, in which tribal insurgents can bleed mighty military empires for years on end, many a golden hook has been lost in sterile waters. Among the many thoughts this prompts, one is that to reduce conflict in the world, the world should deglobalise. Less developed regions should be left to themselves, which in any case is exactly what their inhabitants wish. If they export trouble, they should be put into quarantine, in the not-too-sanguine hope, at least in the medium term, of maturation.

And deglobalising does not have a price, but a prize: not just the saving of lives, but the saving of the planet. For globalisation is principally about profit and economic growth; it is driven by the quest for raw materials, cheap labour and new markets – not always a consistent triad. And it is the restless quest for more profits, more growth, more wealth, which is increasing conflict while reducing the health of the planet.

Alas, deglobalisation is unlikely to be feasible; its opposite has too long a history. Rome conquered much of the world it knew about, at great expense; Julius Caesar's Gaul campaigns cost more than a million Gallic lives and the extermination of whole tribes, among them the Nervii. While Rome was the sole superpower it easily dealt with the recalcitrants along its borders, save for the Germans, who after many centuries of frequent violent stand-off eventually conquered the Western empire and sacked Rome itself.

From then until the mercantilists began preying on other people's spices and silver in the sixteenth century, globalisation reversed; conflicts again took place mainly along the margins between tribes and peoples and the few emerging nation states.

But it was with the beginning of modern globalisation at the hands of Portuguese adventurers, and then the Dutch and English, that the real trouble started.

Globalisation as the quest for raw materials, cheap labour and new markets often involved and still involves forcing others to accept the incursion if they will not accept it willingly. It is driven by the old economic imperative of getting wealth or protecting it when got, and it is initiated by businessmen who then drag their governments and militaries along to protect their investments.

Conflicts arise when different perceptions collide. By its nature, globalisation brings deeply different perceptions into contact with one another. For a familiar example: the West and its bikinis, bars and secularism meets the Islamic world with its closeted women and simple, unshakeable religious certainties. There is less immediate fraternal recognition there than would be helpful.

Sometimes one side of the equation adopts with fervour some of the other side's perceptions. When a numerous people embraces an alternative perception, as China has embraced the essentially nineteenth-century idea of an industrially rich base for military prowess, there is just as much potential trouble, because the embracing tends to be selective. China goes for the money and guns without the democracy and civil liberties, which sends a chill down one's spine in contemplating the world's future.

But in all cases the trouble arises from the attempted mixing of cultural and ideological oil and water. Developed and major developing nations are trampling around the planet in search of profit, and many of the trampled resent it, and become pugnacious. The pugnacity of the tribesman with a

Kalashnikov is enough to nail down the feet of the mightiest military power, as we have seen repeatedly in the stony valleys of Afghanistan to this day.

Deglobalising would mean leaving those regions, fencing them off if necessary, letting them get on with their own business their own way; and accepting the diminution of cash profits that result from losing access to raw materials, cheap labour and potential markets. The real profit, to repeat, would be saving the lives of our soldiers, and slowing the despoliation of the planet from unrestrained 'growth', as the economists, in unconscious Orwellian Newspeak, like to call it.

It means that we all take a drop in living standards to sustainable levels. It cannot be a cheering thought that the amount of stuff we buy and energy we consume is paid for by the lives of men killing each other along with the women and children who get caught in the crossfire.

No doubt some will be horrified at the thought of leaving residents of undeveloped lands without internet access and modern medicine, and it is true that it would be good if they could have them peacefully. But the point is that they and the whole of the rest of mankind are being asked to pay a very high price for those things, even if they want them (and do the Pashtuns, for one vivid example, really want them?).

An alternative use for the money spent on those military golden hooks currently being dangled and lost in murky waters would be to invest in women all over the developing world. Female literacy in the Middle East is only 46 per cent. In Africa elementary education for women results in their having fewer and healthier children and taking a greater part in public affairs. Almost everywhere in religiously devout parts of the world women (and gays, and minorities of other religious persuasions) suffer oppression; there is a healthily inverse relationship between education and religious fervour. The globalising of female literacy is the only kind that promises rich returns for the world as a whole.

Speeches

L egend has it that Demosthenes, the greatest orator in ancient Athens, attended lectures by Plato when he was a young man. One day while doing so he saw a great crowd of people hurrying to another part of the city, and on enquiring was told that the people were eager to hear a notable orator there. He immediately followed them, saying that if oratory could command such a following, he was going to give up philosophy for rhetoric.

The story does Demosthenes little credit, but it illustrates a truth that until recently had become obscured by the television age: that oratory is a powerful thing, able to sway masses, change minds, influence events and thus alter the course of history. I say 'until recently' because the example of US President Barack Obama in his first election campaign reminded us that a skilled orator can work magic even on the distancing medium of television. Think of his acceptance speech in Bryant Park, Chicago, and then imagine what it was like to be in that park as those persuasive cadences flowed. The combination of a consummate speaker's words and the strange mass psychology of crowds is electric in its effect. This fact is exploited by good and bad people both, by Hitler and other demagogues as well as by Winston Churchill and Martin Luther King.

The French statesman Charles Talleyrand once said that 'speech is given to man to disguise his thoughts', and his remark can be adapted to say something even more true, that 'speeches are made by politicians to disguise their intentions'. To say this is not merely to repeat the old and not wholly accurate cliché that politicians are dishonest by profession, but to acknowledge that politics is a difficult art, akin to herding cats, and every political utterance has a multiplicity of competing audiences, demanding of the speaker that he pick his words with vast care and as little explicitness as possible. In wartime, and when one is on a moral crusade, an absolute line can be followed, and one's oratory can soar; in the dog days of ordinary political life every syllable has to be weighed, lest the press pounce and twist and make the difficult business of government even harder.

Everyone yearns for plain, honest, solid leaders who will say what they mean and mean what they say. Everyone comes to despise the tricksy politician whose words twist their way round the minds of the populace, only to be found out later as mere speechifying, full of empty promises and false sincerity. Herein, perhaps, lies the key difference between statesmen and politicians: the former speaks, the latter makes speeches.

Sleep

If ever there were a puzzle and a blessing wrapped together in the same blanket, it is sleep. A third of life is given over to it; without it we go mad; it is the best healer, soother, painkiller and friend if it comes, but the worst tormentor if it stays away. Poets and philosophers praise it; Ovid likened it to the fallow year of arable land, which produces its best crop afterwards, and Schopenhauer believed that the more you sleep the longer you live.

This last point is controversial. There is some evidence that afternoon naps shorten life. As always, there is also some evidence that it does the opposite. The best evidence is what one's own body says; and if it says a snooze after lunch feels right, then it is.

The sleep patterns of famous people are intriguing. Churchill slept in two short bursts, the first in the pre-dawn and the second in the afternoon. Lady Thatcher is said to have scarcely slept at all, and some would say it showed. As we age we sleep less, subconsciously aware that we are soon to sleep for ever.

Studies of sleep indicate that one of its purposes is bodily self-repair and, in childhood, growth. But its chief reason seems to be mental organisation; sorting memories, securing what has been learned, resting the brain from the barrage of external data it receives while awake.

The big puzzle is dreaming. Scientific study of dreaming is known as oneirology, and one of its chief findings is that electrical activity in the brain during most dreams resembles waking activity, and is accompanied by rapid eye movements – we dreaming humans do with our eyeballs what sleeping dogs do with their paws and whiskers. Oneirologists suggest that dreaming is for 'synaptic refreshment' in the brain – synapses are the connections between nerve cells – and that bizarre dreams are therefore indicators of 'accumulated synaptic efficacy errors'.

That might be right, but it misses the romance. One does not have to believe, nor should one, that dreams are prophetic (though in Freudian fashion they might reveal deep dark aspects of ourselves) to appreciate the amusement they offer, even if sometimes the terror too. Nightmares are commonest in childhood and in stressful times; that suggests dreams have psychological and not only neurological uses. They amaze us sometimes; and sometimes we find that during them we can fly; with drunkenness and madness they are the origin of religion.

Scientists and laymen alike agree that none of us sleeps enough. Without a good eight hours asleep, our sixteen awake will never be as good as they could and should be – which any good night's sleep proves.

Success

To each walk of life there is a concept of success peculiar to it. Success as an Olympic high-jumper is not the same as success in business or academia. It is accordingly hard to give a general definition of the concept, the more so because one person's view of it might not be shared by others endeavouring in the same arena. For example: one high-jumper might see getting into the Olympic team as success in his sport, while another regards getting only a silver medal, and never the gold, as a failure.

As this suggests, there is an element of subjectivity in the concept because it is so allied to one's hopes. This can raise a problem: if hopes are allowed to metamorphose into expectations, the resulting view of what counts as success is easily distorted. If one's expectations are sufficiently low, one can be a perpetual success; if too high, a perpetual failure.

But success is not wholly a matter of subjectivity. There are objective criteria in any field where outcomes can be measured to show advance over an earlier stage. Interestingly, 'success' once literally meant 'outcome' and only came to mean 'favourable outcome' in modern times. It now implies outcomes which are positive, and usually highly positive: it suggests the gain of wealth, status or both, and with them the acclaim of others.

This is what most people think they want, although there are better kinds of success which do not bring the burdens that can accompany status and money. People who achieve quieter forms of success in their chosen doings tend to be more secure in their enjoyment of them. Only consider: the person who becomes very rich might have to employ bodyguards for fear that his children will be kidnapped, while the person who becomes famous is sure to become a literal prisoner of her fame, unable to do so simple a thing as visit shops in the high street, at least without being stared at and followed by photographers.

These inconveniences are no deterrent to aspirants. For them the great question is, 'What is the secret of success?' There is no shortage of sage answers. Keep on trying; regard every failure as a stepping stone; ignore the jeers and catcalls that greet your efforts; remain loyal to your dreams; make your own luck; never forget that the greatest failure is not to have tried at all.

All these familiar pieces of advice are true. The more cynical among us claim that it is equally true that many lives have been wasted in futile and misguided attempts to 'try, try and try again', or to relish failure and regard it as a guarantor of future achievement. But this cynicism is misplaced. Nothing we do in life is wasted, even the failures that are not stepping stones to success. This is not a paradox. He was wise indeed who first noted that endeavour counts just as much as outcomes.

For it is not what we get but what we become by our efforts that really counts in life, and becoming something happens whether or not we win the prize which, or so we believed, lay at the end of our strivings.

Mark Twain, an accomplished cynic, once offered a recipe for success: just combine ignorance with confidence. The mixture often works well. Not knowing the likely difficulties beforehand, and full of assurance about overcoming them anyway, a breezy entrepreneur can succeed where better informed and more level-headed folk would not dream of venturing. The nice thing is that when such a person succeeds, he instantly changes from being an idiot to a genius; which encourages any others still hesitating on the brink of adventure.

Somerset Maugham remarked that it is wrong to think that success spoils people by making them arrogant and egotistical. His own experience, he said, was that most successful people are kind, tolerant and humble. This is a striking observation, and one that is often proved true. Partly it results from the fact that most success is built out of the bricks of failure – or the bricks that other people threw, as someone once drily observed – and this makes successful people sympathetic to the trials and difficulties of others.

'Success is not final,' Churchill said, 'and failure is not fatal; what counts is the courage to continue.' None of the many pieces of advice about trying to succeed is as good as this. One reason is that it contains a warning: that success is never quite the end point one expects it to be. The glow of success invariably fades; a higher peak becomes visible from where one now stands, and new ambition dawns; the feeling of achievement is temporary. 'Nothing recedes like success,' some joker rightly said.

If there is one sure lesson about success it is that its main point is not success itself but the effort to achieve it, for what one gains by the effort is the really lasting success. It is long after we have experienced what we thought was failure that we recognise this lovely and heartening fact.

Retirement

Is it an irony, a hint or an encouragement that the traditional gift to a retiring employee is a watch? It is an irony if retirement is the state in which time no longer matters, and the days drift into each other, all resembling Sunday. It is a hint of mortality if retirement is seen as the last chapter in life's story, for then it will measure the counting down of one's days.

But it is an encouragement if it suggests that the time has at last come to have freedom, fun, opportunities, variety, classes, travel, projects, hobbies, new beginnings.

All this is obvious. So too is the fact that all but one of the things just mentioned – namely, travel – need not cost much, a consideration when the reward for a lifetime of work is straitened circumstances. Which of these three meanings the gold watch acquires will depend on the determination of its possessor; the third requires most of that tough substance.

What is less well known is that the one thing better than retirement is not retiring. The following explains why. I had a friend who played so much rugby while reading medicine at Cambridge that he was astonished when his name appeared on the final pass list. Knowing scarcely any medicine he decided not to inflict himself on live patients, and therefore became a pathologist. His first job was at a large London hospital, and began shortly before Christmas. The chief mortuary technician told him that he would not be much needed until January; 'Not many people die at Christmas,' said the technician, 'but we will be swamped after New Year.' My friend asked why, surmising flu and pneumonia, but the technician said, 'People see family and friends over the holidays. But for the old and ill, early January is the start of a long, cold, dark time, with nothing to look forward to. They switch off in droves.'

So struck was my friend by this that he always thereafter examined the history of his autopsy subjects. He found that people with vivid interests in life or work lived longer, and defied illnesses better, than people who had become muted and unfocused in their post-retirement years. He was amazed at how some folk, who by textbook standards should have died long before, outlived people with relatively minor complaints: the classic case of the latter, he said, was the recently retired man, feeling useless and purposeless, giving in to an otherwise survivable heart attack.

If governments require us to work longer before retiring, they could be doing us a favour. Otherwise it is the third use of the retirement watch we must choose: the one that requires determination.

Happiness

Is happiness the point? If so, why not put Prozac in the public water supply? Many people achieve the same effect with drink, drugs and either the brainwashed or the cherry-picked-for-convenience versions of religion. A better answer might lie in the choice made by some when asked, 'Which would you rather be: a happy pig, or an unhappy Socrates?'

To start thinking about happiness properly, read Sissela Bok's illuminating discussion of it, *Exploring Happiness* (2011). She surveys many views and definitions from classical antiquity to current 'happiness studies' using brain-scanning techniques. Among the chief conclusions she draws is that happiness is such a various and layered thing that all approaches to it, from autobiography and ancient philosophy to neuropsychology, are relevant and mutually informative, and have to be adopted together. Her book is an exemplar of this interdisciplinary approach, which is alone capable of doing justice to the differences and the intersections of both the subjective stance – the phenomenology of happiness as felt experience – and the objective stance of scientific measurement and test.

It also confirms for me what I have always thought about the big concepts – *happiness, beauty, truth, knowledge, goodness* – which is that in investigating them we should not use those words themselves, but paraphrases that are richer, more specific and therefore more informative. They are big baggy words because they denote big baggy concepts; and Bok shows just how over-capacious and therefore internally heterogeneous the concept of *happiness* is.

This emerges from what she describes as the 'daunting multitude of reflections, analyses and flights of the imagination, of experience of happiness and of happiness only longed for' that one encounters when examining the literature. All these perspectives and views deserve a place in the discussion because they all have something to offer. But if the need for a synoptic approach is one of Bok's main themes, another equally important one is that there are limits to the meaning of happiness imposed by 'perennial moral issues about how we should lead our lives and how we should treat one another'.

For example: if one accepted Willa Cather's definition of happiness as the state of 'being dissolved into something complete and great', then the 9/11 mass murderers were happy. But not only is there serious reason to doubt that true happiness is consistent with doing harm, but one also has to remember Jonathan Swift's scathing remark that happiness is nothing other than 'being well deceived; the serene peaceful state of being a fool among knaves'. In the case of those imagining rewards in an afterlife for crimes in this life, one is tempted to give Swift's view one's vote.

There is certainly a Babel of voices on the subject of happiness, and a wide range of approaches, some from diametrically opposite sides of the field. Look at how Aristotle and the Stoics clashed over both ends and means: Aristotle thought that happiness is achieved by increasing the satisfaction of appropriate desires, while the later Stoics recommended limiting desires. More than two millennia later Bertrand Russell and Sigmund Freud adopted very similar respective positions, the former thinking that a more expansive approach to life is the route to happiness, the latter doubting whether happiness of anything more than a transitory kind is possible. Schopenhauer thought only brutes are capable of happiness, because they live in the moment, whereas humans are condemned to suffering by living in time, plagued by regrets about the past and anxieties about the future.

There are those who think self-forgetfulness is the mark of happiness (thus Iris Murdoch), and a variety of others who think that creativity, or unthinking religious faith, or the exhilarations of love, are its source. Empirical research in more recent times indicates that a degree of wealth and material comfort promotes happiness, but only up to a point; after surplus has been achieved the returns are diminishing ones. But similar studies cited by Bok show that successful relationships are a consistent correlative of happiness – which is hardly surprising, but the social sciences are good at confirming what we already know.

What the psychologists call 'resilience' is cited as one essential ingredient; those haunted by memories of traumatic events are being insufficiently resilient in coping with them. But then one asks: is this a hidden request for indifference or obtuseness? Bok quotes William James: 'Happiness, like every other emotional state, has blindness and insensibility to opposing facts given it as its instinctive weapon for self-protection against disturbance.' Obviously enough, too much resilience is morally undesirable.

Is it acceptable to be happy on the basis of illusions – say, religious beliefs, or false information about one's situation? It is indeed not only possible for people to be blissful because of belief in falsehoods, but this is a surer route to bliss than knowledge of the truth. Is truth so valuable that it should trump comforting illusion? The question is all too pressing, and Bok discusses it, quoting Horace's story of Lycas who applauded and laughed in an empty theatre because he imagined scenes being played there. Throughout history the example of Lycas has been invoked on both sides of the question, pitted against Socrates' dictum that 'the unconsidered life is not worth living'. Alexander Pope was on Lycas' side, but Bok cites Confucius, the Buddha, Montaigne, Voltaire, Diderot, Kant and others as firmly of the view that because self-knowledge is crucial to maturity, it was right that the doctors 'purged and cupped' him (Pope's words). Were they right? I am with Bok and Kant in thinking that they were.

Bok is right to caution against the move now under way to give too little weight to subjectivity in 'happiness studies'. Objective measurement and observation is the norm in scientific investigation, quite rightly, and the fantastic window into the mind afforded by functional magnetic resonance imaging (fMRI) of the brain is a cornucopia of new insights.

But in the investigation of psychological states by objective and testable techniques of measurement, there is a stubborn reality: the existence of 'unquantifiables', which by definition are not amenable to the measuring ambitions of empirical enquiry. 'Few of the experiences of happiness that are conveyed in autobiographical writings and literature can be fully measured by psychological or neuroscientific research,' Bok points out. 'Nor can most of the philosophical and religious claims about the nature of happiness or about the role it plays in human lives. Must such issues, then, be thought of as lying beyond the purview of what has come to be called "the science of happiness"?' Her answer is No: once again, both kinds of perspective are necessary, because only then will we begin to answer questions about whether temperament determines happiness, genius must be melancholy, solitude or its opposite are necessary for it, and much besides.

We need, as ever, a clear overview of the subject. Bok's book is not only a helpful starting point for further study, but provides a salutary reminder that looking at happiness from only one viewpoint is going to miss a great deal. Every white coat in the scanner lab, in short, should have Aristotle and Seneca in its pockets.

Teachers

There is not much middle ground when it comes to teachers. They are either good, in which case they are among the most important people in the world, or they are not good, in which case at best they represent a missed opportunity – which is a serious matter – and at worst they are positively harmful. Teachers are harmful when they put students off a subject of study, thus depriving them of a chance at the fullness of what it could offer. To put the matter harshly, the crime involved is not far removed from poking out someone's eyes with a sharp stick. Perhaps indeed intellectual blindness is worse than physical blindness, which makes one wonder what should be the fate of the teacher who turns students against any area of knowledge or enquiry.

Another and even worse kind of harmful teacher are those who undermine their students' confidence, making them lose self-belief, humiliating and ridiculing them, picking one out and turning other students against him or her, poisoning their students' outlook either in a general or a particular respect. What should be the fate of someone who uses the role of teacher to do such injuries?

Good teachers do exactly the opposite of these things, and as a result inspire, guide and give their students a broader sense of life's possibilities. Aristotle thought that teachers are more important than parents, because whereas parents (merely, he said) give their children life, teachers give them the art of living. This is partly right, and the part in question is larger if a child is thereby given a chance to escape prejudices and idiosyncracies of outlook that might happen to form the conceptual framework of his or her origins.

There is of course much in the way of knowledge and skill that has to be taught, and good teachers ensure that the majority of students under their care – more precisely, all capable of doing so – acquire both. But there is even more in the educational process that cannot be *taught*, only *caught*; and the chief of what a good teacher can achieve in this respect is to give students the desire to know more, understand more, achieve greater insight. In short: the good teacher inspires.

If one were to analyse what goes into being an inspiring teacher in this sense, the list would include enthusiasm, charisma, a capacity to clarify and make sense, humour, kindness and a genuine interest in students' progress. Much of this is a matter of natural capacity; which implies that teachers are born, not made; and this in turn explains why teaching is so often described as a vocation.

Consider each characteristic. Enthusiasm is important because it is attractive and catching. Enthusiastic teachers want their students to be enthusiastic about their subjects, and will succeed with some of them. Charisma does not invariably accompany enthusiasm, but can be a by-product of it. A charismatic teacher is a Pied Piper for the subject taught, and can draw students to it even if solely from the desire of emulation. Teachers who know their subject thoroughly, and have a knack for making it clear and putting it well into context, are invaluable: they are illuminators. Put all three characteristics together and you have a teacher who can completely change students' lives for the better.

Humour, kindness and genuine interest need no explanation. Some new teachers worry about manifesting these qualities too overtly, not wishing to appear weak to students, who are merciless with anyone unable to keep discipline. One result can eventually be the substitution of bullying for authority – the worst kind of bullying being the undermining of confidence mentioned above – but there is no inconsistency in being both kind and firm, humorous although not prepared to tolerate messing about, and interested without being partial. It is a matter of operational tact and good timing.

Almost everyone can point to a teacher (if they are lucky, to more than one) who was inspirational and helpful. I had several at school and university who made me interested in their interests, who were encouraging and enabling, who were on my side. It is an amazingly potentiating thing to have someone believe in you; whether they are right to do so because they recognise a genuine capacity in you to succeed, or whether their attitude is itself the prompt to acquire such a capacity, is neither here nor there. It has the right outcome either way.

It is a pleasure to name names. Jim Marshall and Tony Nuttall taught me English literature, Peter Williams taught me Latin, Timothy Sprigge, Bernard Harrison, A. J. Ayer and Peter Strawson taught me philosophy. They were each of them good teachers because they combined the above-listed characteristics in individually various proportions, the net effect being to make it possible for me to teach myself. And that, paradoxical as it may seem, is the best outcome of good teaching. Independence of endeavour, and soon therefore of mind, should be one of the fundamental aims of education.

Teachers know that the best way to learn is to teach: *docendo disco* as the tag has it. And obviously enough: the better one's students, the more one learns. The chief of several reasons for this is that the effort to help others understand requires a good grip of the topic on the teacher's part. Students' questions and doubts compel one to think and rethink, often prompting one to see things that had not been noticed before. For this reason it is never boring to teach the same subject repeatedly. Like re-reading the classics, or revisiting familiar places, new insights always offer themselves, and better ways of doing things with them.

Good teachers are those who remember being a student. They hear themselves as their students hear them. They know which aspects of their subject might present a difficulty, which require to be grasped before which, what else and next their best students will be keen to know, and why. A sense of how the constituents of a subject hang together, so that one knows the best order of their presentation, is something that being on the receiving end of both good and bad teaching helps one to acquire.

It is a significant fact that after the First World War a number of the twentieth century's leading philosophers turned to education, either in theory or practice, in the belief that the future security of humankind depended on an intelligent understanding of its accumulating knowledge (especially science) together with cultivation of the ability to think. Bertrand Russell, Ludwig Wittgenstein and Karl Popper all taught in schools; Russell founded one. It is easy to think that education fails to deliver its eutopian (sic) promise – namely, a world of reflective and considerate people living co-operatively – but the real point to consider is what the world would be like without it. It is well said that ignorance is far more expensive than education. This is an observation about the general effect of education in society, but there is also the unquantifiable good that education offers individuals – for people are far more than the jobs they do, but are also (and perhaps more importantly) voters, neighbours, lovers, parents, friends, travellers and more, and for all the different parts they play they require to be informed, to think, to choose and to act. Education is for all aspects of life, not just one such.

If education is this important, and if education starts with teachers, then teachers are this important too. True, we can learn from others, from nature, from books – all these things might teach us more, and more deeply. But at crucial junctures education needs teachers; the better they are, the more fruitful will be all the other forms of education that life affords.

Education and Rationality

Michel Foucault said that 'anyone who thinks rationally is suspect'. It is quite possible that he first had this thought (for, despite everything, that is what it is) in a Parisian café lit by electricity, while drinking a cup of hot coffee and nibbling on a baguette, unconscious or (worse) dismissive of the contrast between these outcomes of human rationality – light, coffee, bread – and this bit of poseur philosophy. He was a supporter of the Ayatollah Khomeini and the Iranian revolution, almost exclusively because it was a revolution (what fun) and certainly because he had no conception of what the Ayatollah's revolution was intended to effect: the medievalisation of Iran under the reactionary and oppressive thumb of clerics. (And the wrong medievalism: there was a quite different medieval Persia with irreverent poets and atheist *philosophes*, with science and music, with beautiful figurative art and exquisite porcelains.)

Would the foregoing entitle someone to conclude that I think the Shah's regime was just dandy, and that Foucault had nothing interesting to say about the control of truth by power? If the dispiriting figures on literacy annually published by the US Department of Education are a guide, and if they more rather than less reflect the situation in the Western world at large, the answer would be affirmative though wrong. The US surveys consistently show that 'reading proficiency' as exemplified, for instance, by the ability to 'compare viewpoints in two editorials' is possessed by only 13 per cent of the US adult population. By extension one might think that the ability to take things on their individual merits, which means being able, for example, to agree with some things and criticise other things in Foucault, is a minority skill.

The same applies to valuing the intellectual skills associated with literacy while also being able to value, as one should, the different and in many ways saner, more down to earth, more rational, intellects of illiterate people, as exemplified by the Central Asian peasants to whom Aleksandr Luria talked in the 1930s. He showed them the kind of pictures used in IQ tests, of groups of objects, one of which is an odd-one-out: in one, a hammer, saw, axe and log of wood; in another, three adults and a boy. The peasants refused to see the log or the boy as odd ones out in the pictures. Anyone who rejected the log of wood, said one peasant, was either a fool or had plenty of firewood already. The boy was necessary because the three adults would require him to run and fetch things as they worked. Theirs, in short, was a more inclusive rationality. It reminds one that the word 'sophisticated' started life as a pejorative.

But the fact is that illiteracy is a luxury that the contemporary world can no longer afford. The world is too complex and various for its residents to be ill-informed, and therefore more likely to be prejudiced, incapable of distinguishing differences and connecting comparables, and unable to concentrate long enough to grasp a point or acquire all the data needed for a sound judgement. Almost everyone is capable of all this if given the opportunity and the right encouragement; if the quoted statistics are right, it must be that most are not given enough of either. After the horrendous debacle of the First World War some of the best minds of the era concluded that education of the young was vital to save the future: as we saw earlier, all three of Bertrand Russell, Ludwig Wittgenstein and Karl Popper became school teachers for a time in the 1920s in an effort to make that difference. Of course they soon realised that they could make better contributions by working to the grain of their real aptitudes, which turned out not to be (and, so to say, by a long chalk) primary school teaching. But the idea was right: education is the key: not only of children, but of everyone at all ages all through life.

Education is the key, but not the panacea; Foucault was an educated man, if not indeed over-educated; and like most of the over-educated (no exceptions implied) capable of sometimes being a fool as a result. So there are no guarantees that education, and the literacy that lies at its core, will people the earth with angels. But it would make things better, because knowledge reduces fear, and the fear born of ignorance is one of the chief causes of hostility between people and peoples.

What is the Point of the Arts?

Imagine a world in which people rise to labour in the fields or factories all day, and go home in the evening to sit over their plates of food, after which they sleep until the next day's labour. Imagine that they do not read, or watch comedy or drama on television, or go to the theatre, or visit an exhibition of painting or sculpture, or listen to music.

Imagine that in their world there are no pictures – not even the advertisements are illustrated, but are all words, and very plain ones at that, with no playfulness or humour in them, no miniature narratives.

Imagine that the buildings are completely austere, without a single decorative feature anywhere. The towns consist entirely of plain buildings, of two kinds; places to eat and sleep, and places to work. None of the dwellings have pictures on the walls, of course, but neither do they have ornaments on the mantelpieces, and even the bedclothes are a plain functional colour.

Such a world is a world without art in any form. Imagining it immediately tells us of some of the purposes of art: to brighten and enliven our world, to decorate it, to provide it with grace notes, elegance, fun, colour, variety, to tell us stories and amuse and enlighten us, to bring us images and ideas of other places, other times, to make us see the familiar afresh, to educate our eyes with colourful shapes and our ears with varied sounds, and to expand our vision of the world as a whole, so that our lives are not confined to what is merely local and transient – to the here and now of any moment – but can range over great varieties of possibility in time, space and meaning.

Some of these things are important far beyond what they represent in the way of entertainment. Art can be challenging and disturbing too, and can jolt us out of preconceptions and prejudices. We can be made – 'made' is a word of enforcement – to see things in different and unexpected ways. We might not always like what art shows us or makes us think; it might be very far from being beautiful or enjoyable; but in stretching us, and introducing us to new perspectives, it can do us a profound service.

The arts – the plastic arts of painting, sculpture, ceramics, tapestry and the like; the performing arts of theatre, dance, music, and their combinations; and the literary arts – exist because human beings are essentially intelligent and social creatures. Many of the arts are forms of communication, in which responses to the world and commentary on the human condition are shared by makers and performers with their fellows, who constitute an audience, observing and responding in their turn and thus taking part in the conversation. Some of the arts are abstract and attract by their formal properties alone, or by the sheer inventiveness they display, these being attractive to the intelligence and interest in novelty that almost all people share.

Literature and theatre are good examples of how art answers very fundamental human needs. In this case the needs are – to put the matter at its most basic – gossip. Gossip is a human essential because it provides information about the nuances, difficulties and dimensions of human life. We all like a bit of gossip, and literature is (so to speak) organised gossip in its highest form: it consists in stories about people, what they get up to, what they feel, what happens to them – the very stuff, therefore, not just of gossip itself, but of soap operas, and of course even of the grandest literary works of the classical canon.

Another success story in art is painting. Most people love to look at pictures because we are visual animals, and pictures variously tell stories, or are beautiful, or at least interesting –

and as abstract paintings show, pure shapes, or arrangements of materials, fascinate the eye too, and draw us to them. The activity of looking, observing, appreciating, is a refreshment in itself, and this is the most basic thing that happens when we wander round an exhibition or gallery.

What the arts do for us, in short, is to enhance and deepen our experience of our world, each other, and ourselves. If our interest is roused by something, if we become absorbed in a story, if we are shaken by a new and disturbing idea, if we are entertained, soothed, made to laugh, feel moved by beauty, feel an upsurge of sadness or wonder or poignancy in response to a piece of music, an image or a tale, then our own experience of living is enriched, and the world itself has more texture and meaning for us.

Without art, we would scarcely be ourselves: we would be living empty lives, unadorned by the works of our own intelligence and creativity, and desperately the poorer for it.

To ask what art is good for is not exactly the same as asking what its purpose is. Art does not have to have a purpose – it does not exist *in order* to do the things described above; it does not exist specifically and on purpose to teach, to urge a moral point, to entertain, to distract, to amuse, to promote beauty, to support a revolution, to disgust, to challenge, to stimulate or to cheer. These are the effects it can have, and typically does have; but even if these things are the intention of some – even many – of its makers, it cannot be a requirement of its existence that it exists in order to do these things. Principally, it exists for its own sake. It is the artist, not art as such, that might have an aim in mind, and his or her aim might be to do any of the things just listed. But equally, artists might just make art because they feel compelled to. Because the work is its own justification, no further aim or goal is necessarily required to explain or, still less, to justify its existence.

But to say that art does not have to serve an aim beyond itself, even though it might sometimes do so, is not to say that it is good for nothing. On the contrary, as one of the greatest goods of human experience, it is good for many things. The distinction here lies between things that are instrumental, and things that are ends in themselves. An instrument exists for something beyond itself, namely, for what it can be used to do. An end in itself is its own justification for existing. Even though art can sometimes be instrumental, that fact is not essential to its nature. What art is 'good for' arises from its being an end in itself, or more accurately: the embodiment of many different things that are valuable for their own sakes.

The word 'art' does duty here, as noted, for painting, sculpture, music, literature, dance and theatre performance, and whatever else (to quote Andy Warhol) anyone can get away with in calling it 'art'. But the generalisation that art, whatever else it is, is always an end in itself, applies to them all. This can be shown as follows.

Art is one major form of response to the world. It is often an attempt to capture an aspect of the world, to draw attention to something about it, to comment on it, to present a surprising or fresh angle on it, to represent it for the sake of exploring something about it, or enjoying or celebrating it – for example, the colours or shapes of an object, its eccentricity or typicality, the interest or repugnance it provokes.

For a loose comparison, think of laughing at a joke. We do not laugh so that we can achieve a further goal – in order to be healthy or relaxed, say, even if we thereby succeed in being healthier or more relaxed – but simply because the joke has elicited that reaction. But though it is merely a reaction, laughing is in fact good for something nevertheless; it does make people feel better. Art is a reaction in the same way. Cézanne painted Mont Sainte-Victoire repeatedly because he was fascinated by it, not because he thought that painting it would say something about politics or society or human hopes. Being fascinated by something, attracted to it, repelled by it, keen to reveal an unusual aspect of it, are all responses to that thing; the making of art is one outstanding way of expressing such responses.

But art is a response not only to things in the world, but to experience of the world, which lies inside the artist himself or herself. And it is also often an expression of what presses from within the artist without being elicited by externals. Music is a prime example. A symphony, unless it has a programme and is devised to represent bird song, rain, battle and the like, is an abstract expression of a composer's conception. The impulse to make art, as with poetry, can result in the artist imparting a message, but the art lies not in the message but the way it is conveyed. An interest in materials and techniques without any explicit content, as in abstract painting or contemporary dance, leads to a form of distinctively modern art that switches the focus of attention, as when people look at a frame rather than the picture within. It is still art, still an expression of a response to something within or without.

When artists get to work responding and expressing, whether or not also to urge a point, entertain, distract, support a revolution and the rest, they are producing something that someone else will react to in some way; and that is what art is chiefly good for: namely, that by its relationship with its audience it can make something move in the realm of thought and emotion, where such movement is life.

Darkness

In his chronicle of the Gothic peoples, the historian Jordanes (6th century CE) tells of a place called Scandza – today's Scandinavia – where the sun does not shine for forty days in midwinter, to the grief (he says) of the people there. As this shows, even then people knew about Seasonal Affective Disorder (SAD), which doctors attribute to problems with either the neurotransmitter serotonin or the hormone melatonin, caused by too little exposure to daylight.

For SAD sufferers the time change in late October is bad news, for immediately it happens the approach of winter darkness quickens. Each day is suddenly shorter and gloomier, and the horizons of the world seem increasingly to crowd around one in murky confusion.

It was in opposition to the dying of the light that our ancestors devised feasts and jollifications, with fires and bright lights, gifts, games and parties to keep the dark at bay. We still celebrate versions of them, adding more recent traditions from the bonfires and fireworks of Guy Fawkes to Christmas lights and New Year partying. The descendants of Jordanes' Scandza Goths created the festival of the yule log, a giant tree trunk that burned constantly for twelve days from the winter solstice onwards, by which time daylight was already perceptibly increasing again. The Druids decorated their temples and homes with holly and ivy, the Romans celebrated the Saturnalia between the 18th and 25th of December. That latecomer Christianity took over these traditions and bent them to its own purposes. Northern Europeans have a candles and gift-giving feast-day for Saint Nicholas (Santa Claus) on 6 December; he has mutated into Father Christmas and his coming is postponed until after the time of the longest nights.

All these were ways of alleviating the dark and cheering everyone up. And paradoxical as it might seem, winter darkness was traditionally a time of plenty – the harvest had long been gathered and stored, the pigs slaughtered and their flesh salted – and the austerities of spring, when supplies were used up and the year's hard work had to begin, were far off. The dark part of the year was therefore a welcome season of holiday.

For such timid and defenceless creatures as mice, darkness is a friend. But for such timid and defenceless creatures as children, darkness can be a theatre of terrors, when the ordinary objects of day change shape and loom, and new and peculiar noises are heard. Both fear of the dark and SAD might be a hangover from our deep evolutionary past, in the form of a hibernating ancestor for whom the dark was a hostile terrain. Making light of the dark with fireworks and feast-days is a sensible response.

These words are written in New Delhi on the night of Diwali, Festival of Lights. The firecrackers have been going all evening, ever since the populace finished making *puja* (worship) to Lakshmi, goddess of wealth, and Ganesh, elephant-headed god of luck. A lot of people gamble on Diwali, hoping to make a fortune after propitiating these deities. Do they do better on Diwali than other nights?

I am here on a return journey from the lovely kingdom of Bhutan, which hides among the Himalayas between India and Tibet. Flying from Kathmandu to Paro in Bhutan one sees Everest and then, after a short while, K2 glittering in the sun, a mighty sight. Everest rises from behind the bastion of a long ridge. K2 is the centremost peak of several on a giant stone and snow massif. Both are unquestionably pillars of the sky, saving the world from being crushed by the frozen weight of blue crystals above.

You can see on YouTube what it is like to fly into Paro. The plane skims some peaks, then banks sharply to the left round one of them, then sharply right around another, sharply left again around a third, and sharp right round yet a fourth, to swoop suddenly onto a short runway beside a river, braking hard. All the passengers clap with relief and genuine admiration. Our pilot was a relaxed Australian, which prompted confidence.

It is a few decades only since the country opened its borders. Traditionally known as 'Land of the Thunder Dragon' it maintained the reputation of its name against all comers for centuries. But it is in fact a peaceful and welcoming place, Buddhist in inspiration and practice. The men wear comfortable robes that look like dressing gowns, and the few roads are bumpily narrow. Between Paro and the capital Thimphu the highway winds dizzily along river valleys, littered by regular and substantial rockfalls. Every mountain has another and higher mountain behind it, so that as one gasps for breath in that altitude, reflecting that one is only a third of the way up, one wonders what it would be like to go higher. Still, if one ran out of breath altogether in that clarity of air and distance, it would be a nice way to end.

The Hinges of History

There are plenty of candidates for moments when the course of history changed dramatically – the assassination of Archduke Franz Ferdinand of Austria on 28 June 1914, precipitating the First World War, is an example. But sometimes historical moments are not as precise as that; it might be something that emerged during the course of a century that, from the long perspective of hindsight, emerges as a great divide between what went before and after. And sometimes there is a record of this more diffuse kind of event which captures it and its significance – not necessarily a direct record, as in a diary entry or minute book, but in a literary work. As a prime example I have in mind Aeschylus' *Eumenides*, the third play in the *Oresteia* trilogy. He there portrays the swinging of history's hinges in that what went before was archaic, what came after was the beginning of the history of Western civilisation.

The *Oresteia* tells of Agamemnon's return from the Trojan war, his murder by his wife Clytemnestra and her lover Aegisthus, and what even more horribly followed, namely the avenging of his death by his son Orestes, who was duty bound to the task. But that meant Orestes had to kill his own mother, Clytemnestra; and the murder of a parent was so hideous a crime that it had to be avenged by the Furies (in Greek the Erinnyes), three underworld goddesses themselves born from the murder of a parent, having sprung from the blood of Ouranos when he was castrated by his son Kronos.

The Furies accordingly pursued Orestes with torments and agonies, driving him to near-suicide. The *Eumenides* tells how Orestes finally got to Delphi where he begged Apollo's help, explaining how it had been his duty to avenge his father but alas the person upon whom vengeance had to be taken was his mother, *et cetera*; and now he was in great trouble with the Furies. Apollo, minded to be helpful, told Orestes to go to Athens to ask for Athena's help, because she was so clever and would know what to do; meanwhile he, Apollo, temporarily put the Erinnyes to sleep so that Orestes could escape.

Athena agreed to help Orestes. Her scheme was to summon a jury of Athenian citizens to hear his case. Apollo volunteered to serve as Orestes' defence attorney, and argued that Orestes had not murdered a parent because a mother is not a parent but merely a receptacle. This is an unpersuasive argument today, but it satisfied half the jury, who voted to acquit Orestes. Athena used her casting vote in his favour too, so after many painful bounds he was at last free.

At just that moment the Furies arrived in Athens, angrier even than usual because of having been tricked into sleep; and they saw what had happened. They were, as was their wont, furious. 'You young gods,' they say to Athena (in effect: this is not a translation of the text), 'have usurped our role; it was our task to punish Orestes, but you have summoned a jury, talk talk talk, and have let him off.' To which Athena replied (in effect: this is still not a translation), 'Yes; for we live in a new world now; we do not follow the old way of revenge, an eye for an eye, but we gather together and discuss and decide what to do on the basis of that discussion.' She then offered to host them in Athens in perpetuity if they would give up their vengeful ways and be renamed the 'Eumenides' or Kindly Ones. They agreed.

The moment thus captured is the shift from the old way of seeking justice to the new; a shift from vengeance to law, from the *warrior virtues* of endurance, courage, ferocity in battle, preparedness to die for the tribe or settlement, the use of force to settle disputes and right wrongs, to the *civic virtues* required by urban life, community, co-operation, government by agreement and laws, negotiation, institutions that regulate the relationships and interactions of society.

Of course, revenge and the warrior characteristics remain as both vices and virtues even in our day, useful as the latter in such circumstances as war; but the civic virtues are dominant, and have grown in significance since the classical period – grown unevenly, to be sure; and with setbacks; but now they are the distinctive and central feature of civilised life wherever civilised life flourishes.

It is interesting to reflect on Aeschylus' portrayal of the moment when the Furies, as agencies of the old justice, yielded to the new. Note that it is the goddess of wisdom who subdues them into civility; that it is triumphant Periclean Athens which hosts these and so many other hinges of history in that brilliant period; that it is a particularly chilling and ghastly series of events that brings matters to a crisis, where reason trumps emotion at last in resolving them. The significances studding the story repay contemplation, but the central theme – that a new world had dawned: that 'the young gods had usurped the old' – is the key to it, and to our own world.

The Whole Life: The Point of the Humanities

You hear the following question being asked with increasing frequency these days: 'Why would anyone go to university to study the Humanities – philosophy, literature, history, languages, the classics – now that life is so competitive, making it essential that an investment in education should be an investment in a career?'

The answer might come as a surprise even to those for whom life is nothing but a career – a banausic view, but a practical one after all; so it is good to be able to report that studying the Humanities is an excellent investment in this respect. And this is a bonus to something even more important: which is that studying the Humanities is an excellent investment – here almost all who know what they are talking about say: the best investment – in life itself.

They say this because although a successful and flourishing career provides the resources and much of the satisfaction on which the rest of life depends, it remains true that people are more than their jobs. They are also neighbours, voters, citizens, parents, lovers, travellers – there are many things that constitute an individual existence in addition to a career, however defining and essential that career might be. If an education equipped people both for careers and for the larger life around it, would that not be an education mightily worth investing in?

Of course there will always be a need for doctors and engineers, physicists and computer scientists, experts and researchers in technical fields of various kinds. These vocational subjects will always flourish, because the world requires them. But it also and emphatically needs the Humanities.

It is easy to see how study of the Humanities can widen the horizons and deepen the insights of anyone who studies them attentively. They introduce fresh perspectives, a wide variety of experiences, distillations of wisdom and observation, challenges and thought-provoking questions, new opinions, assumptions and outlooks, that must healthily influence any mind that contemplates them. I say 'healthily' because all these enquiries broaden the sympathies of educated minds, and make them more perceptive, so that they 'see things steadily and see them whole', as Matthew Arnold famously said. And this provides a powerful countervailing force to the narrowness, prejudice, limitation and bad mental habits that are the offsprings of ignorance.

It is narrowness, prejudice and the rest that motivate divisions and conflicts in the world, and make people reactionary, stuck in traditional attitudes and ways. The cultivation of mind provided by a Humanities education, by contrast, promotes creativity, open-mindedness and flexibility. And it does this while remembering that the past has many lessons to teach, and that there are some things from the past that are not broken and do not need to be fixed.

Attentive study of the Humanities thus provides the materials for individual lives to be well-lived. This is no small matter. Fulfilled people with alert, outward-looking interests and understanding are always going to be a civilising influence in the world. But study of the Humanities also provides the basis for successful work-place careers because they equip their students with two invaluable possessions: an overview of human affairs whose lessons and examples can be applied in response to new challenges; and a capacity to think – really, properly, genuinely *think* – which among many other things means an ability to handle and evaluate ideas and information, to solve problems, to apply the lessons of experience, to see new opportunities, to innovate and to lead.

The Humanities have always provided thought-leaders and people-leaders in society. To study the Humanities is to study the example and insights of our forebears in the great human story. Only think of the lessons taught by history and literature, and the analyses offered by philosophy and psychology: the study of these subjects yields knowledge of human affairs, and it demands the acquisition and honing of a repertoire of intellectual skills of great value, applicable in the work-place, the boardroom, the courtroom, the editorial office, the art studio, the debating chambers of governments, civil service offices, lecture halls and classrooms, the City of London and Wall Street, the surgeries of doctors and the meetings of diplomats.

It has become a commonplace, but no less true for being one, to say that in a rapidly changing world one of the fundamental purposes of education must be to render people fit to deal with unpredictable changes and challenges. This includes having to compete in a global economy, evolving fast and in often unexpected ways. In all the identities people have, as individuals, as citizens of the world as well as of a particular state, and as workers in whatever field, they more than ever need flexible, alert and well-informed minds. Otherwise they will fall behind and end by playing a passive rather than active part in the tumultuous and noisy affairs of our contemporary world.

Being left behind is the opposite of what people would wish for themselves, for their children or their fellow-citizens; so, given that education is the great resource for enabling people to be actors in their own lives rather than the acted-upon by life in general, we have to ensure that education – the expansive, sharpening, informative education of the Humanities – continues to be available and encouraged.

As all this shows, there is a deep connection between a study of the Humanities and the question of the flourishing life. There is an obvious connection between the idea of a life that feels good to live, and the idea of a life that is successful and productive. This is not to say that a quietly withdrawn life cannot feel good to live; for a certain sort of person, that is indeed the ideal existence. But for most people satisfaction comes from activity.

The first big question is: what kind of activity? It goes without saying that we are talking of legal, decent and life-enhancing activities, for however satisfying a malefactor might find evil-doing, no rational person will concede that his satisfaction justifies his actions. All the Humanities and all human experience teach us this. Pleasure and happiness can only be regarded as worthwhile aims when they are not enjoyed at the expense of others' misery. So whatever we mean by 'good' in talking of good activity, we have to mean something that stands up to searching moral scrutiny. And to undertake such scrutiny, we need to be educated and informed – by the Humanities, which prompt us to think about values, and to act on our thoughts.

In the nineteenth century John Stuart Mill made the controversial claim that intellectual activities – reading, learning, enquiring, thinking – are of higher value than such physical activities as eating and drinking or playing sport. He did not say that these latter are not good, and he accepted that they are pleasurable; his point was that they are of less value than things of the mind, so that if there had to be a choice between the two kinds of pleasure, the pleasure of mental activity should always win. It is as if he were saying that study of the Humanities should trump any other kind of activity.

Critics point out that this is exactly what you would expect a philosopher to say, and that it is a snobbishly elitist view. Where does he get the right to place the pleasures of kicking a football or drinking a beer lower down the scale, when these might in fact be as great or greater to one who enjoys them, as the pleasure an intellectual gets from reading Aeschylus?

There is no need to get lost in this quarrel, for it is clear that someone capable of both intellectual and physical pleasures is much better off than someone who has access to one of them only. The more important point is that all worthwhile activities can be pleasures, or greater pleasures, when approached in an intelligent and well-informed way.

Someone who has a knowledge of the Humanities comes off the football field with more left in the day to enjoy – conversation, reading, the theatre or cinema, the pleasures of reflection on the game itself and its place in life. To be nothing but a footballer is to be not much more than the football itself – and that is not an idle point, for Socrates said that the life most worth living is the considered life, the informed and chosen life. The unconsidered life is the opposite of this – it is one lived by people who are other people's footballs. They do not choose their own goal, but go where chance and others kick them.

The Humanities are the resource for considering life in all its variety and complexity. Because they prepare one for all aspects of life – including work – they are described as providing an all-round education. So they do: because human beings are all-round creatures, and to live full lives they need the nourishment that the great conversation of humankind provides. And that is exactly what the Humanities add up to: participation in the great conversation of humankind.

Optimism

There are two surprises in store for anyone who delves into the concepts of optimism and pessimism. One is that the words themselves are of very recent origin; they were given currency in eighteenth-century France.

The second surprise is that the words come from the writings of the philosopher Gottfried Wilhelm Leibniz, author of the idea that we live in the best of all possible worlds – an idea made famous not by Leibniz himself but by Voltaire's satirical attack on it in his novella *Candide*.

This second surprise is no surprise to philosophers, however, who know how many words come straight from their professional lexicon: for example, such words as 'concept', 'idea' and 'consciousness' entered English in the seventeenth century straight from the writings of John Locke and his contemporaries.

Leibniz wrote a book called *Theodicy* in which, starting from the orthodox theistic premise that the world was created by God, he argued that since God is entirely good, this world must be the best possible world there can be – even with all its imperfections of disease, tsunamis, war and evil. For, he said, all of these things must have been foreseen and planned by God, for whom a *perfect* world – one in which such things do not exist – would not be the *best* world, presumably because it would not give the right opportunities to his human creatures to have faith, endurance, helpfulness and the other virtues necessary for admission to heaven.

'Theodicy' is the task of justifying the ways of God to man, as Milton put it, and Leibniz was trying to solve what philosophers call 'the problem of evil', summed up in the question: how can the perfect goodness of a deity be consistent with such horrors as, say, childhood cancer?

Leibniz's clever answer has persuaded few; no ordinary father would subject his children to the sufferings and terrors that this world is capable of imposing, even for a few seconds, with the aim (the optimistic aim?) of making them 'better' in some way. But in the process he gave us the words 'optimist' and 'optimism', derived from his use of the Latin *optimum*, 'best', and his claim that this world is *optimal* even though imperfect. From 'optimist' it is easy to coin 'pessimist': and that is what the French did, under Voltaire's influence.

But though the words are new, the attitudes are of course as old as humanity, for there were undoubtedly optimists and pessimists among our caveman ancestors. And that raises an interesting question: since we are here today to discuss the matter, which of those attitudes most prevailed among our caveman ancestors? One cliché (and clichés tend to be true) says that pessimists are realists. Is that how they survived among the sabre-toothed tigers and woolly mammoths?

But another cliché says that optimism is essential to achievement and progress, because, as the psychologist William James pointed out, pessimism leads to weakness whereas optimism gives power. Were our cave-dwelling ancestors mainly optimists therefore?

This dilemma is reflected in the rich tradition of opinions, jokes and philosophical reflections relating to optimism and its opposite. 'The optimist says this is the best of all possible worlds, the pessimist worries that he is right' is a standard example of the joke variety.

Bar-room opinion tends to the view that pessimism is the right attitude to take, because experience teaches that if things can go wrong they will, that human life is full of disappointments and anyway leads only to age, illness and death, that the individual is confronted by such massive forces of nature and society that it is ludicrous to suppose he can prevail against them – and so gloomily on. This is described as realism, and Mark Twain said that if anyone was still an optimist after the age of fifty, therefore, there must be something wrong with his head.

But although it is only rational to be realistic, it is arguably rational – and not inconsistent – to be optimistic at the same time. The Italian philosopher Antonio Gramsci put it neatly by saying, 'I am a realist because of intelligence, an optimist because of will.' A realist sees the difficulties ahead, the optimist looks for the opportunities they offer. If one were defeated by the prospect of difficulties, one would assuredly be a pessimist; the belief that difficulties in their own way present opportunities is the characteristic optimist's response. One is reminded of the tremendous remark by the French poet Paul Valéry, that 'a difficulty is a light; but an impossibility is the sun'; for the optimist, problems and hitches teach valuable lessons, and offer stepping stones to rise higher or detours to a better road.

From the philosophical point of view there are two good responses to pessimism. If one views pessimism as the habitual expectation that things will go wrong, that effort will more likely fail than succeed, and that therefore there is never much use in trying, one sees it as nihilism, a negative and defeated view of life which makes living less valuable than not living.

This is what Albert Camus had in mind when he said that the great philosophical question is whether or not one should commit suicide; for if one's answer is 'no', this will be because one believes that there is something worth living for – which means: something worth doing and being – which is the optimist's view. So by implication, the true pessimist has no reason to live. When Winston Churchill said, 'I'm an optimist; there doesn't seem to be much use in being anything else,' he was summing up just this point.

The second response is to see pessimism not as nihilism but, as it typically indeed claims to be, genuine realism, and to accept the resigned attitude of stoicism that this implies. Stoicism is the noble philosophy of classical antiquity which said that we must achieve self-mastery over things we can control, namely our appetites and fears, and that we must face the things we cannot control – the vicissitudes of life – with courage and endurance; because by doing so, said the Stoics, we will have made life not merely bearable but worthwhile, despite everything.

Those who are sceptical about optimism see it as idealistic, naïve, bound for a fall, and therefore more than somewhat ludicrous. 'There is no sight so sad as a young optimist,' quipped Twain. And yet when one considers the characteristic optimist's response as described above – the one that finds opportunity in difficulty – one sees that it explains why most achievements, most progress, most new companies, most buildings, most great careers, all began with optimism, that 'journey to somewhere that started from nowhere with little or nothing'.

For even if it were true that most lives and their ambitions end in failure, that would not be a reason for not trying. It would be a reason for being more thoughtful and careful, better prepared, equipped with plans B and C, fortified by courage, determined to hold one's nerve, to keep trying, to learn from mistakes and defeats: all of which is the very stuff of life itself, and is what makes life worth living. Which is in short to say: that what makes life worth living is optimism.

Making the World a Better Place

One way to make the world a considerably better place would be to get really serious at last about the place of women in almost all societies. A quarter of a century ago the United Nations calculated that women do nearly 70 per cent of the world's work in exchange for 10 per cent of its income. Has anything changed? In 1999 UN figures showed that 70 per cent of the world's women live in 'abject poverty'; its 2002 figures show that only 1 per cent of all land is owned by women; its 2001 figures show that in Africa women produce 80 per cent of foodstuffs, and in Asia contribute up to 90 per cent of the labour for rice production (figures from the UN Food and Agriculture Organisation). The UN's 'Women's World' survey of 1995 showed that on average world-wide, women work two hours longer every day than men. (That looks like a considerable underestimate; it was a commonplace of my childhood in Africa to see women hoeing in the maize fields, babies tied to their backs, while the men fanned themselves lazily in the shade, discoursing of this and that – most of the day, most days.)

The cumulative picture of profound injustice that these raw data give is exacerbated by the associated conditions in which women's lack of education and exclusion from decision-making processes in economic and political respects is endemic in the great majority of societies. In today's Middle East a shocking

53 per cent of women are illiterate and almost all of them are wholly excluded from the public sphere. In Africa it has been found that just two years of elementary education for girls, giving them basic literacy and numeracy, reduces birth-rates and improves child mortality, and enables women to get access to medical care, contraception and other benefits. In South Asia micro-loan schemes for women have dramatically improved the conditions of life for women and their children in areas where they are available, as shown by the success of the Grameen Bank in Bangladesh.

The twin keys are education and participation in the public sphere made possible by fully applied sex equality laws. There is hardly anywhere in the world, including the US and Europe, where there is genuine equality between men and women, yet it is obvious that the most developed countries have the highest female participation in public and economic life. Historically this has been a result of development rather than its cause, but arguably such development would not have been sustainable without it, because having the skill potential of one half of the population unavailable would eventually have constituted a brake – despite in the earlier phases having been part of the slave or virtual-slave labour on which all major economies have depended at their outset (and today's China, in violation of human rights, still does).

I write of developed countries as having 'the highest participation in public and economic life' by women, and yet despite the fact that in the US more women gain university degrees than men (57 per cent), they are still in a minority in the higher reaches of science, education and public life, have a tougher time getting there, and earn less when they arrive: this is a familiar picture, and all the less acceptable for being so.

There are many reasons for all this, most of them by now well known: in advanced economies the refusal of organisations to restructure working patterns and hours to accommodate family life, in backward countries the repressive presence of religion, in all dispensations the persistence of attitudes and practices that structurally weigh against women, making it very difficult for them to combine domestic commitments and access to what a male-orientated world regards as economically rewardable while at the same time grossly undervaluing women's vital contributions in child-bearing, home-making, and work as educators and carers.

Ours is a fabulously unjust world – to the criminally unfair position of women we could add labour exploitation of most of the world's male workers too, and exploitation of children; massive disproportions in wealth and power between countries; and inequalities of opportunity and access to the goods of the human condition (e.g. education, medical provision, books, information, jobs) in almost every sphere both within and between societies. And again this leaves aside the fact that women are subjects of abuse, violence and exploitation, much of it sexual, and too often without redress or the hope of protection, which deepens their disenfranchisement. But the injustice suffered by the world's women in particular in economic and political respects creates and perpetuates a myriad problems entailed by the skewing of public interests in the direction of such less desirable male propensities as aggression and war. It takes quite a propaganda success to convince women that they bear and raise children so that those children can end as battlefield corpses; left to decide for themselves on such issues, women would very probably see to it that there were far fewer such corpses lying around.

There is no ground for deriving a great part of the explanation for the difference in the experience of men and women from reproductive biology alone. The difference is a datum, sure enough, but a just and considerate society would value the difference properly, and accommodate itself to its exigencies. We have equality laws in more advanced countries, but we do not yet have equality; in less developed countries the situation of women screams out for attention, yet it occupies far too little of our thoughts. For the future's sake this absolutely and imperatively has to change.

Index

The text of this book is set in Adobe Garamond. It is one of several versions of Garamond based on the designs of Claude Garamond. It is thought that Garamond based his font on Bembo, cut in 1495 by Francesco Griffo in collaboration with the Italian printer Aldus Manutius. Garamond types were first used in books printed in Paris around 1532. Many of the present-day versions of this type are based on the Typi Academiae of Jean Jannon, cut in Sedan in 1615.

Claude Garamond was born in Paris in 1480. He learned how to cut type from his father and by the age of fifteen he was able to fashion steel punches the size of a pica with great precision. At the age of sixty he was commissioned by King Francis I to design a Greek alphabet; for this he was given the honourable title of royal type-founder. He died in 1561.